The String Quartet

The String Quartet

PAUL GRIFFITHS

with 82 music examples

THAMES AND HUDSON

for my son Rupert Edward
who makes us four

First published in the USA in 1983
by Thames and Hudson Inc.,
500 Fifth Avenue, New York,
New York 10110.
First paperback edition 1985

Library of Congress Catalog Card Number
83-70402

Printed and bound in Great Britain.

Contents

Acknowledgments

The publishers are grateful to the following for kind permission to quote extracts: Boosey & Hawkes Music Publishers Ltd (Britten, Shostakovich, Stravinsky and Xenakis), Editio Musica Budapest (Bartók no. 1), Oxford University Press (Gerhard), Peters Edition London (Cage and Ferneyhough), Theodore Presser Co. (Alfred A Kalmus Ltd) (Rochberg), G. Schirmer Limited, London (Carter and Ives), Schott & Co. Ltd (Ligeti and Tippett), Southern Music Publishing Co. Ltd, London, and Charles Ives (Ives), Chant du Monde/UMP (Milhaud), Universal Edition (London) Ltd (Bartók no. 5) and Universal Edition (Alfred A. Kalmus Ltd) (Berg, Schoenberg, Webern and Zemlinsky).

Part One

Introduction c. 1759-1771

To search for the origins of the string quartet is as vain as to search for the origins of man, and for similar reasons. More than any other sort of music in the western tradition, the string quartet has enjoyed the stability yet also the capacity for constant renewal of a living species. For though the history of the mass may be longer, the history of the symphony no less glorious, only the string quartet is at once a medium and a genre, even a form. And a form or a genre is not defined by a single work, any more than a species can be traced to a single parent. Rather it evolves, and once evolved it provides an image or an ideal for subsequent works. And though, naturally, the image of the string quartet has changed and developed during its history – this will be one underlying theme in what follows – the constant presence as executants of two violinists, a violist and a cellist, four persons to whom all quartets are in the first place addressed, has given the string quartet an identity unknown in any other repertory.

It is the gradual achievement of that identity that makes it hard to determine a particular starting point for the genre, and also the scantiness of the information available to us, again as in palaeoanthropology. One important element of the string quartet, the notion of composing for four voices, goes back at least to Pérotin at the end of the twelfth century and had become the norm by the time of Josquin at the end of the fifteenth. Since the instruments of the violin family were all fully in existence by the time of Monteverdi, one must expect that the occasional australopithecine of the string quartet will be unearthed from this period, and indeed one such, a sinfonia by Gregorio Allegri (1582-1652), has sometimes been hailed as originating the genre. However, Allegri's is an isolated use of the medium, and so too is the set of four *Sonate a quattro per due violini, violetta e violoncello senza cembalo* (c.1715-25) by Alessandro Scarlatti (1660-1725).

Indeed, the 'senza cembalo' of Scarlatti's title tells us why. The whole first half of the eighteenth century resounded to the tones of the harpsichord, and its presence in chamber music was practically universal, to the extent that its absence has to be specially signalled. The standard form of chamber music at this time, the time of Bach, Handel and Telemann as well as Scarlatti, was the trio sonata, most usually for two violins with a 'basso continuo' of harpsichord and a bass instrument, often the cello. Thus the development of the string quartet out of this ensemble entailed not only the addition of a viola but also, and more significantly in many respects, the exclusion of the harpsichord, a revolution so drastic that it took many years to be accomplished. If Scarlatti's sonatas embody a presentiment of the four-part conception that is the essence of the string quartet, then in a conservative centre like London the harpsichord or piano continuo was common in chamber and orchestral music until the end of the century.

However, the decline of the continuo was not a cause but a symptom of the great change in music around the middle of the eighteenth century, a period of more confusion in the art than any before the present. As in our own century, new ways of composing, performing and listening to music were giving rise to new forms: opera buffa, the symphony, and the string quartet. Moreover, these new forms arose in close connection. The symphony grew out of the operatic overture and gained an enormous amount from the quick wit of the new comic mode. It also seems unlikely that in the middle of the eighteenth century there was any clear distinction between orchestral and chamber music. Since the basic orchestral scoring was for two violins, viola and 'basso', it was perfectly possible for a work to be marketed in one publication as a symphony and in another as a quartet, to say nothing of less scrupulous arrangements; and there is no way of being sure with what grace composers accepted this situation.

Another characteristic of a transitional age, again making it difficult to sort out what was going on, is the lack of a standard terminology. In particular, there were no terms for the new kinds of chamber music that were being written; and so in the 1750s musicians invented various titles – divertimento, serenade, notturno, cassation – all suggesting light music to be played out of doors. And though it is perhaps too neat to assume, as some have assumed, that the conditions of outdoor performance dictated the removal of the keyboard continuo (else why did this not happen earlier?), certainly the ancestry of the string quartet, most intimate of musical genres, must include the muzak of the rococo.

Our understanding of the music of the mid-eighteenth century is further complicated by the fact that there were so many local traditions and specialities. Mannheim was the place for spectacular orchestral playing and bold symphonies, Naples for comic opera, London for music in taverns and pleasure gardens. And among composers one need only consider the different interests of the sons of Bach: Carl Philipp Emanuel (1714-88), in northern Germany, cultivated an excited expressiveness in his many keyboard sonatas, while Johann Christian (1732-95), the 'London Bach', pleased his public with elegant orchestral and chamber music, and Wilhelm Friedemann (1710-84), working in Dresden and Halle, probably pleased only himself in mixing his father's gravity with the lighter fashions of the time and with his own eccentricity.

Thus the abundant music that survives from the 1740s, 1750s and 1760s presents a bewildering diversity of styles and media, all at least potentially influencing each other, to the extent that it is quite impossible to trace a single line of descent for a genre as central as the string quartet, or indeed the symphony. Nor are the documents much help. Perhaps the earliest dated reference to string quartet playing comes from the autobiography of Carl Ditters von Dittersdorf (1739-99), where he mentions that in the winter of 1756-7: 'We went to work on six new quartets by Richter; Schweitzer played the cello, I and my older brother the first and second violins, and my younger brother the viola.' If this reminiscence is accurate, then Franz Xaver Richter (1709-89), one of the leading composers attached to the Mannheim court, must count as the author of the first works known to have been played as string quartets. And if Dittersdorf is alluding to the set of quartets by Richter published in London in 1768, or to another group of divertimentos not printed until two centuries later, then Richter was to some degree already looking forward to the future of the new medium. As can be seen in the following quotation from the 'development' section in the first movement of the Divertimento in B flat, the four parts share the melodic interest on almost equal terms, exhibiting an interplay that only became, and remained, a hallmark of quartet style in the 1770s, though hardly then in such an elaborately baroque style as this:

Allegretto

1 Franz Xaver Richter: Divertimento in Bb, first movement

However, Dittersdorf dictated his memoirs towards the end of his life, and one may reasonably doubt how reliable his dates are when he is looking back three or four decades.

Even if we were to accept Dittersdorf at his word, and accept too that he is talking about works from among those of Richter that survive, there would still be a lot of uncertainty in the early evolution of the string quartet. It is time, therefore, to introduce the creation myth, and with it a name not mentioned here so far, that of Joseph Haydn (1732-1809). Until the present century nobody doubted that Haydn was the father of the string quartet, and that single-handedly he invented the form out of his boundless imagination. Indeed, it is still possible that it was so, for though we now know that the circumstances were right for the emergence of the quartet, there is no definite evidence that any existed before Haydn's op.1. What is less acceptable is the charming notion that Haydn's first quartets came about because of a chance occurrence, as was suggested by Haydn's early biographer Georg August Griesinger at the beginning of the nineteenth century:

A Baron Fürnberg had an estate in Weinzierl, several stages from Vienna; and from time to time he invited his parish priest, his estates' manager, Haydn and Albrechtsberger (a brother of the well-known contrapuntist, who played the violoncello) in order to have a little music. Fürnberg asked Haydn to write something that could be played by these four friends of the Art. Haydn, who was then eighteen years old, accepted the proposal, and so originated his first Quartet, which, immediately upon its appearance, received such uncommon applause as to encourage him to continue in this *genre*.

The main problem with this story is that Haydn at eighteen was still barely competent as a composer, whereas his early quartets are decidedly more than correct. Also, there is other evidence to suggest that Haydn's association with Fürnberg, with whom there is every reason to connect the first quartets, took place later in the 1750s. Probably Haydn composed the ten early quartets between around 1757 and 1762. Almost at once they began to circulate in manuscript copies among the great houses and monasteries, then major centres of secular as well as sacred music: at this period there were no music presses in Vienna, and so music was commonly disseminated in manuscripts produced by professional copyists. Music publication in the middle of the eighteenth century was centred in Paris, the biggest city in the world and hectically commercial in the years before the Revolution, and it was there that in 1764 there appeared the first edition of any of Haydn's music, when Louis-Balthasar de la Chevardière brought out *Six simphonies ou quatuors dialogués pour deux violons, alto viola & basse obligés. composés par Mr. Hayden*, under which typically untrustworthy title he assembled the first four quartets of Haydn's op.1 and two flute quartets by another Mannheim musician, Carl Joseph Toeschi (1731-88). Chevardière's second edition of 1768-9 was no better. The Toeschi pieces were indeed dropped and replaced by genuine Haydn, but one of the new works was an orchestral symphony deprived of its oboes and horns and insinuated here into Haydn's quartet oeuvre, where it remained for nearly two centuries. For when, in 1801, Haydn's pupil Ignace Pleyel (1757-1831) came to set his master's quartets in order, it was unfortunately this much reprinted Chevardière collection that he regarded as authentic, and gave the dignity of 'op.1'.

Haydn op. 1

In the meantime, Johann Julius Hummel, no relation of the composer Johann Nepomuk Hummel, had published in Amsterdam in 1765 the first real sextet of Haydn quartets, including the five genuine quartets of op.1 (nos.1-4 and 6) and one more, omitted by Pleyel and now known as 'op.0'. Hummel, however, was no more conscientious than Chevardière or any other music publisher of the day, or perhaps no more careful. In 1765-6 he issued another batch of Haydn quartets, of which two, the third and fifth, were in fact composed as sextets with horns, and again this set was incorporated into the canon of Haydn's quartets by Pleyel, as op.2. There is, therefore, no authority for regarding opp.1 and 2 as sets, nor necessarily for assuming that op.2 is later than op.1, as a whole. Instrumental works in the eighteenth century were commonly expected to enter the world in groups, and often in sixes (cf J. S. Bach), but if Haydn intended any ordering of his ten early quartets – the five of op.1, the four of op.2 and 'op.0' – it has been lost.

What unites these ten works, and distinguishes them from all other Haydn quartets, is their five-movement form, which may also be an original invention of Haydn's. Eight of them are symmetrically shaped, with a slow movement surrounded by minuets with trios and on the outside by fast movements. The other two, op.1 no.3 and op.2 no.6, throw the weight to the front by starting with an adagio and then continuing with minuets and prestos in alternation. This idea of beginning with a slow movement, inherited from the slow–fast–slow–fast pattern of the old church sonata, was one to which Haydn returned in later quartets – op.9 no.5, op.17 no.3 and op.55 no.2 – each time making the initial slow movement a set of variations, as in op.2 no.6.

That sort of consistency makes one wonder whether Haydn decided each time that a set of variations was right, or whether he felt instinctively that an opening slow movement had to be in variation form. And the question is not an idle one, for it raises the whole issue of what choice in matters of form was available to the eighteenth-century composer. For instance, it is hard to imagine Haydn wondering whether an opening fast movement ought to be in sonata form: he had no alternative. Sonata form, another product of the period of musical ferment in the middle of the eighteenth century, arose simply because the Baroque had bequeathed no suitable way of making a fast movement in something other than dance pattern. It was not an arbitrary construction but an intuitive principle, and its naturalness may be gauged by the fact that it was not adequately described until the 1820s, by which time composers had been using it for almost a century and Beethoven had taken it to an unequalled level of complexity. Either one argues that nobody had noticed sonata form throughout this period, which would be absurd, or else one accepts that musicians found it so obvious as not to merit attention. As so often, only when it ceased to be obvious could it be noticed.

And indeed sonata form is an obvious way of extending music. The first part of such a form, or 'exposition' as it has come to be called, moves from the tonic or home key to the dominant, conventionally a fifth above in the case of a major key, or else in a minor key to the relative major, i.e. the major key with the same key signature: the general term 'secondary key' will sometimes be used here to indicate the dominant in a major key or the relative major in a minor key. The move from tonic to secondary key is a basic facet of the major–minor system: simple tunes very often modulate from tonic to dominant in their first halves and then back to the tonic in their second. In sonata-form movements this move is simply lengthened and emphasized, often by having a second theme or group of themes in the dominant. Then the symmetry of return is delayed by a period of waiting, or 'development', where the composer can explore conceivable avenues of escape from the inescapable: the return of the 'exposition' and the tonic key. And this 'recapitulation' is customarily made more decisive by cutting out the earlier move to the dominant, so that all the 'exposition' material is now heard in the home key.

Haydn's early quartets, dating from the springtime of sonata form, naturally include many movements where this natural process unfolds in perfect equilibrium, but they also include a couple where Haydn takes sonata expectations as a background on which he can play. A simple instance is the first movement of op.1 no.2, where the recapitulation starts surprisingly early, after only eight bars of development, then stops to make way for a much longer development section before resuming: this is the earliest of the 'false reprises' in which Haydn was to delight, and it must indicate that the conventions of sonata form had been thoroughly absorbed by the musical consciousness of the time, even if nobody had called attention to them.

If Haydn may have felt himself to be following nature in the sonata forms of his fast movements, simply extending his material as it needed to be extended, then in the slow movements he must have been aware that he was choosing models from elsewhere. For it is in their slow movements that these early quartets betray their recent emergence from the trio sonata, as in op.1 no.3, or their proximity to the violin concerto, as in op.1 no.1: even at this early stage, as later, the string quartet is a genre striving not to be a showpiece for the leader, or else succumbing to the temptation. By contrast, in the minuets and trios the four instruments are much more nearly equal, often because they enter in canon or are arranged in couples of couples. The twenty minuets also show the constant fresh stimulus that Haydn found in this form, and not only here but in the countless minuets of sonatas, quartets and symphonies he was to write during the next forty years.

The early quartets already show too that he was starting to differentiate between orchestral and quartet styles, the latter exploiting the transparency and intimacy to be achieved when soloists are involved. It is fairest to make the comparison in the case of one of the

13

several symphonic slow movements of the period that Haydn composed for strings alone, such as this from the Symphony no. 1 in D:

2 Haydn: Symphony no. 1 in D, second movement

This is music conceived in broad strokes for massed forces, quite different from the little serenade for solo violin with delicate accompaniment that comes at the centre of op. 1 no. 6, though the key is the same G major:

3 Haydn: Quartet in C op. 1 no. 6, third movement

There is, however, only one of these early quartets with a real quartet slow movement, as opposed to a display piece for one or two solo violins with accompaniment, and that is op. 2 no. 4 in F. The adagio here is also the only one of the fifty movements in the minor mode: it is in F minor, for Haydn a particularly personal key, the key also of the Symphony no. 49 'La passione', of a notable set of piano variations and of two later quartets, op. 20 no. 5 and op. 55 no. 2. No less significantly, this adagio is the only slow movement of opp. 1 and 2 in sonata form: a quite natural innovation in a movement that leaves behind the old patterns of song, concerto and trio sonata.

Other features, too, mark out op. 2 no. 4 as the most interesting of Haydn's early quartets. In the first movement, the return of the opening theme comes not in the home key of F but in the subdominant (a fifth below, therefore B flat), and then development continues before a more orthodox recapitulation of the secondary material only, with no further appearance of the first theme: as in the simpler case of op.1 no.2, the false reprise turns out to have been the right one, and here its unexpected key gives the impetus for a second stretch of development. The scheme is represented below, where the bold letters represent the kinds of material, the lightface letters the keys (lower case for minor) and the numbers the lengths of sections in bars:

> **abcbcdef** (F) 22
> **gfecc** (C) 12 :‖
> ‖: **abad** (C–d–g–D) 15
> **ac** (B♭–E♭–f–B♭) 7
> **hc** (G) 12
> **cf** (c) 6
> **gfecc** (F) 12 :‖

Here the conventional outlines of sonata form are quite clear: the exposition has an opening section in the tonic, F, and a second section in the dominant, C; the development ventures further afield; and the recapitulation returns to the tonic and to the substance of the exposition, as indicated by the brackets. The compression of the recapitulation and its emphasis on the secondary material (natural enough, since this is what has been heard earlier in the dominant) are typical of Haydn but not of the early quartets, which tend to be more straightforward in structure.

However, since each quartet contains two fast sonata movements, usually first and last, Haydn is obliged to distinguish between them, and he does so not only by choice of metre – the finales are all in the very quick 2/4, whereas the first movements may alternatively be in 3/8 or 6/8 – but by making the finales formally simpler. For instance, that of op.2 no.4 has none of the complication of its companion movement above:

> **aa** (F) 10
> **bcde** (C) 24 :‖
> ‖: **a/b** (G–F) 14
> **aabcde** (F) 28 :‖

This time, though the exposition has exactly the same number of bars, it is less diverse in content, the development keeps much nearer home, and the recapitulation is only marginally contracted. As is proper for a finale, the movement overcomes with ease all the hurdles of the first presto.

Haydn also establishes differences between the two minuets contained in each of these early quartets, for though both will nearly always be in some manner intriguing, the second will be more intriguing than the first. Again op.2 no.4 provides an exemplary instance. The first minuet and trio presume a rather stately tempo, and are linked by a motif of four semiquavers descending in a scale (in the minuet) or arpeggio (in the trio). By contrast, the second minuet and trio skip along, and the second part of the trio plays with 2/4 metre contained within the triple time of the form.

In recent years there has been a good deal of scholarly argument about whether such music would originally have been performed by a string quartet as we know it today, or whether Haydn's early quartets would have been played with a double bass on the bottom line (as the harmony occasionally suggests – though much later in his career Haydn was not above momentarily forgetting that the quartet, unlike the symphony, has no provision for octave doubling of the bass), or with several instruments to a part, or with a harpsichord continuo. And the vigour of the argument has not been unduly affected by the lack of documentary evidence or the different leanings of the musical text, how the more trio-sonata-like slow movements seem to expect a harpsichord, how some of the minuets could easily be transferred to the orchestra, exactly as one might expect of a genre in genesis. In any event, even if one could ascertain exactly how these works were performed in the 1760s, that would still be no sure guide to Haydn's intentions, for he may very well have intended something quite different from the norm, and in some areas he perhaps had no particular intention at all. Anything not represented in his scores must therefore remain unknowable, and certainly beyond the power of any 'authentic' performance style to come near. The only thing we can be sure of is that for two centuries Haydn's opp.1 and 2 have been played and enjoyed as string quartets.

?Haydn 'op. 3' They did not, however, immediately change the face of chamber music. It was long supposed that Haydn wrote his next set of quartets, 'op.3', around 1765, but it now seems clear that these works, though accepted as authentic by Pleyel and the aged composer, were not written by Haydn. They may have been the work of Romanus Hoffstetter (1742-1812), a Bavarian monk who certainly wrote other quartets attributed to Haydn, and who once confessed that 'everything that flows from Haydn's pen seems to me so beautiful and remains so deeply imprinted on my memory that I cannot prevent myself now and again from imitating something as well as I can'. If 'op.3' was indeed his, then he was the author of one of the hit tunes of classical music, the so-called 'serenade' that is the slow movement of no.5. Certainly there is nothing to link these works with the sophistication of Haydn's

op.2 no.4, nor do they make much sense as experimental forays between Haydn's early quartets and his next undisputed set, op.9: they are too various for that. Rather it seems that Haydn, unaware he had invented a new genre, went on during the 1760s composing chamber pieces for other combinations, and especially, after his appointment to the Esterházy household in 1761, for the trio of baryton, viola and 'basso', the baryton – a kind of bass viol with zither attachment – being a particular favourite of Prince Nikolaus Esterházy.

If the string quartet had not yet achieved a position of any dominance within chamber music, still Haydn's early quartets, or 'divertimentos' as he would have called them, were noticed by other composers. The influence is unmistakable in the divertimentos written in the early 1760s by Johann Georg Albrechtsberger (1736-1809), later a famed contrapuntalist and teacher of Beethoven, but at this stage in his career organist at Melk Abbey. Griesinger's suggestion that his brother played in the first performance of Haydn's op.1 no.1 is suggestive, but the evidence for a connection is plain in the music alone. A quartet in A is modelled exactly on Haydn's five-movement form, while others explore different possibilities: one in B flat (1760) is particularly interesting, since it anticipates the principal form of Haydn's next batch of quartets, opp.9 and 17, following an Allegro moderato with a minuet, a slow movement and a quick finale. Other composers influenced by Haydn at the same time included Hoffstetter, Johann Baptist Vanhal (1739-1813), Franz Asplmayr (1728-86) and František Xaver Dušek (1731-99), all of them, like Albrechtsberger and Haydn himself, working in or around Vienna.

This, however, was not the only style of quartet composition in the 1760s, even in Vienna. The Emperor Joseph II apparently liked to listen to quartets but disdained Haydn: he preferred a good fugue, and quartets making play with fugues were written for him by the court composer Florian Leopold Gassmann (1729-74). There was also Luigi Boccherini (1743-1805). He came from a quite different tradition, in many ways that of Giovanni Battista Sammartini (1700 or 1701-1775), but at this date both his own Lucca and Sammartini's Milan were within the Austrian Empire, so that their works were known in Vienna, and therefore probably known to Haydn. Even though Haydn late in his life vehemently denied that he had learned anything from Sammartini, the evidence, not least that of his vehemence, suggests otherwise: Sammartini was, after all, one of the founding fathers of the symphony and of classical sonata form.

According to his own catalogue, Boccherini's first set of quartets, his op. 2, was composed in 1761, though the works were not published until 1767, and so the correct date may be a little later. Even so, the scale of his ambitions is announced in the very first of the group, in C minor, perhaps the earliest quartet in a minor key. All six are in the common three-movement form, fast–slow–fast, the second ending with a fugue, and the same form, together with something of the same contrapuntal conscience, can be found in three quartets of the same period by Sammartini, though even here Sammartini's ideas are brief, busy and repetitive, his harmony polarized between tonic and dominant. It is instructive to compare the opening of one of these quartets, in E flat:

4 Sammartini: Concertino in Bb, first movement

with the opening of a Haydn quartet of similar date in the same key,

18

for in Sammartini the tonic triad fixes the music's field of operation, whereas in Haydn it is a subject for discussion within a wider context:

5 Haydn: Quartet in Eb op. 9 no. 2, first movement

This last example has introduced Haydn's next unquestionably genuine set of quartets, op.9, probably composed in 1769-70 and followed in 1771 by a companion set, op.17. Unlike opp.1 and 2, opp.9 and 17 were conceived by Haydn as sets, and, as he was to do in all his later collections of quartets and symphonies, he used a different key for each work: no other composer of the time seems to have felt this need for variety, just as no other composer could supply it. And the creation of integrated variety had become of paramount import- ance in the first movements of these quartets, eight of them unfolding an abundance of material at moderate tempo, by contrast with the quick presto dispatch of ideas to be found in the early quartets. The exceptions are op.9 no.5 and op.17 no.3, both starting with slow variations, and the last members of each set, both reverting to the presto beginning.

Haydn opp. 9, 17

Nor are these the only points of similarity between the two sets. Both make a show of brilliant writing for the first violin, with several opportunities for cadenzas – a feature perhaps owed to the presence in the Esterházy establishment of Luigi Tomasini (1741-1808), one of the great violinists of the day and himself a composer of quartets. Both sets also include, for the first time in Haydn's output, a quartet in the minor mode: op.9 no.4 is in D minor and op.17 no.4 is in C minor.

However, as these two works may indicate, there are also important differences between the two collections. The D minor quartet is the more overtly dramatic in its minor-ness. It ends with the four instruments in fortissimo octaves emphasizing D minor, and it includes a long minuet in the minor, whereas the major trio is short and slenderly scored for violins alone. Moreover, its first movement exemplifies well the essential tragic nature of sonata form in the minor, since an exposition which, in this case, is almost equally divided between the minor key and its relative major has to give way to a recapitulation entirely in the minor; and the prominent shading of A minor, a fifth above the tonic, also makes the minor feeling more acute. In op.17 no.4, on the other hand, it is F minor, a fifth below the tonic, that makes a similar appearance and relaxes the tension, and there is also much more of E flat in the exposition than of C minor: the music even begins as if it is in E flat, and though this might have made the recapitulation's C minor all the more telling, in fact this latter section moves through various keys, and no stability is achieved until the coda, in C major, preparing for a minuet in the major around a much inflected C minor trio. The finale, too, is tonally ambiguous, and ends more in the major than the minor. Where the D minor quartet carries the fierce expressive charge found in some of Haydn's symphonies of the period – and sometimes attributed to the stirrings of sensibility that were also giving rise to the literary movement known as *Sturm und Drang* ('storm and stress') – in the C minor quartet the conflicts have been internalized, and used to create a more subtle structure.

This increasing wholeness and subtlety is characteristic of op.17 throughout, for just as the movements of the C minor quartet are linked by harmonic ambiguity, so those of the E flat quartet op.17 no.3 are joined by motivic similarities at their openings (and here, of course, the first movement has prepared one to attend to variations). Even more striking is the greater inventiveness of the sonata structures of op.17. The basic techniques are assembled in three of the finales of op.9: the construction of an exposition so that it does not simply end but leads back to its beginning for the repeat (no.3), the drastic compression of the recapitulation (no.4), the false reprise (no.5) and the addition of a coda (no.5 also). As so often, Haydn's innovations here are not gratuitous conceits but are stimulated rather by the ways music works within the mind. A compressed recapitulation can balance an exposition better than a complete one, partly because memory itself shortens what has been heard some while ago, so that ten present bars may equal twenty remembered from the past, and partly because, as already mentioned, there is less felt need to recapitulate what has already been heard in the tonic (and Haydn's contractions commonly affect this material only, leaving the secondary, dominant material intact). Similarly, a coda will be needed to ground a particularly long and lively finale, like that of op.9 no.5.

In op.17 the same techniques are used more widely and to greater point, and in the finale of the first quartet of the series, astonishingly, they all appear together. The opening movement of this quartet, in E major, is an excellent example of the new moderato style, wandering easily through a great variety of material and including, for the first time in a first movement, a false reprise. But the finale is extraordinary. The development starts with exactly the same music that began the exposition, for eleven bars: in other words, there is a false reprise even before there has been any development. The effect of this is to unsettle expectations completely, so that for a moment one is unsure whether one is hearing the exposition for a third time, or going straight into the recapitulation, or experiencing, as is in fact the case, an unusually witty development. Curiously, this same technique is used again, though more briefly and to less deluding effect, in the first movement of op.17 no.2, tempting one to guess that here at least the published order reproduces the order of composition.

Quite apart from such ingenuities, there is in these quartets of 1769-71 a new spirit abroad, and it can be heard even in the first movement of op.9 no.1:

6 Haydn: Quartet in C op. 9 no. 1, first movement

For although op. 1 had been published as 'quatuor dialogués', this is the first instance in a Haydn quartet of true musical conversation, where an idea is not just imitated, as in canon and fugue, but turns and changes as it is passed from voice to voice. Curiously enough, this sort of dialogue, of decisive importance to the future of the string quartet, had been predicted before it had been achieved, for by the time Chevardière chose his title the idea of chamber music as dialogue was commonplace. As early as 1743 a set of works for flute, violin, bass viol and continuo by Louis-Gabriel Guillemain (1705-70) had been published as *Six sonates en quatuor ou conversations galantes et amusantes*, and in 1760 the Newcastle composer Charles Avison had written a preface to his Six Sonatas op. 7 for harpsichord, two violins and cello, stating that:

This Kind of Music is not, indeed, calculated as much for public Entertainment, as for private Amusements. It is rather like a Conversation among Friends, where Few are of one Mind, and propose their mutual Sentiments, only to give Variety, and enliven their select Company.

All the essentials of the classical string quartet are here: the idea of music as an amicable conversation of wit and sentiment (very much a late eighteenth-century concept), and the privacy.

Besides this tradition, as yet more philosophical than practical, Haydn had good reason at the end of the 1760s to be thinking of music as conversation: he had started writing operas for the Esterházys. Two quartet slow movements, those of op. 9 no. 2 and op. 17 no. 5, sound like transcriptions of scenes from opera seria, but it was comic opera that bequeathed to the quartet the much more ubiquitous gift of witty dialogue, just as it bequeathed to instrumental music generally the fast pace and short, regular phrases that made the classical style possible. Here, for example, in a quartet from Haydn's opera *Le pescatrici* (1769), to a Goldoni libretto, is a snatch of that musical dialogue which has as yet only been glimpsed in the quartet literature, but which will become one of the most characteristic resources of the medium:

7 Haydn: Le pescatrici, *second act finale*

Possibly it was the stimulus of writing music like this that caused Haydn to return to the string quartet after several years, or possibly he was able to do so because his prince was not exhausting all his creative energies: earlier in the 1760s, in addition to the operas, he had had to produce dozens of baryton trios, though the experience had not been wasted, for in this genre he had been able to try out ideas he later used in quartets, like the possibilities of an opening moderato. It may also be that Haydn took up the quartet again for sound financial reasons. Since the publication of his op.1 in 1764 there had been a boom in the demand for string quartets, and publishers had, as usual, been a mite unscrupulous in satisfying it: that established Haydn source

Chevardière had in 1768 brought out a set of six 'quartets' as 'op. 4' that consisted in fact of five symphonies and a non-quartet divertimento. There is, however, no evidence that Haydn wrote any quartets specifically for a publisher until opp. 54 and 55 two decades later.

Boccherini, on the other hand, was certainly composing with an eye to the Paris presses, which produced in quick succession after his op. 2 his opp. 8 (1769) and 9 (1770), and also two sets of light quartets each having two movements, opp. 15 (1772) and 22 (1775). Thus were founded two distinct genres, called by the composer the 'opera grande' and the 'opera piccola', that he was to continue to practise to the end of his life, though never again with the same energy and commercial success. Nor, perhaps, with the same imaginative vitality. Grace and freshness are all in these early Boccherini quartets, and if Haydn had never existed they might be more easily enjoyed (though if Haydn had never existed we probably would not be listening to string quartets of any kind). The comparison with Haydn, though, is devastating, and caused the contemporary violinist Giuseppe Puppo to refer to Boccherini as 'Haydn's wife' – a remark unfair only in its suggestion that wives are necessarily gentler and less adventurous. Here, for instance, is Boccherini developing, in the first movement of his C minor quartet op. 9 no. 1:

8 Boccherini: Quartet in C minor op. 9 no. 1, first movement

And here is Haydn at the equivalent point in his op. 17 no. 4, also in C minor and written only a year later:

9 Haydn: Quartet in C minor op. 17 no. 4, first movement

Boccherini starts with a wholesale repeat of his opening material in the relative major, E flat, and then, in the eighth bar of the quotation, transposes another section of the exposition from E flat to F minor.

Haydn begins by taking his opening material at once into A flat and then embarks on a process of real development, isolating and recombining motivic units, and as he does so he ventures much further from home, into the warm, strange territory of G flat, then A flat minor and so on.

But even though op.9 no.1 is Boccherini's first quartet in the Viennese four-movement form, to compare him with Haydn is to compare Italian sensuousness with Austrian intelligence. Seen in the light of contemporary Italian quartets – such as a G major work written at Lodi on 15 March 1770, the first string quartet of Wolfgang Amadeus Mozart (1756-91) – Boccherini's is a model of sensitivity and imagination, for in κ80 the thirteen-year-old Mozart could manage only a trio-sonata-like adagio, a sonata allegro of the rudest Sammartini belligerence and a monochrome minuet. Nevertheless, this otherwise insignificant piece is raised far above Boccherini by the fact that it is the first of a series of twenty-six quartets that will include some of the outstanding masterpieces in the genre, and also by the fact that its first movement contains a presage of *Le nozze di Figaro* (specifically of the Countess's aria 'Porgi amor'). This is not mere romanticism. Of course, κ80 can tell us nothing about its great successor in the same key, κ387, and nothing about *Figaro*, but it does embody shadows of melody, rhythm, texture and harmony that indicate how much of the mature composer's musical personality was already held by a boy, just as much of the nature of the string quartet had been sketched in the first dozen years of its history.

Exposition 1772-1799

Anyone who takes an interest in contemporary music in the late twentieth century can only contemplate with awe the prospect before his predecessor of two centuries. A person born in, say, 1747, could reasonably expect to live through the whole creative lives of Haydn and Mozart, and if he survived to the age of eighty, then he would also witness as they appeared the last works of Beethoven and Schubert. However, this is not to take account of the conditions of musical communication obtaining at the time. Quite apart from the fact that most of Schubert's music was not publicly available until long after his death, opportunities to hear orchestral and operatic masterpieces were rare, and of course limited to a small proportion of the population. Today recordings and broadcasts make it possible for almost anyone, at least in the developed world, to acquire a familiarity with Mozart's piano concertos or Haydn's symphonies that would have been unimaginable in the eighteenth century. And this raises another difference between our world and theirs: then one could hear very little but contemporary music, whereas now the balance is quite reversed. We need less density of greatness from our composers.

But if the great orchestral, choral and dramatic works of the eighteenth century were only marginally available to their contemporaries, there was one arena of relatively free musical intercourse: the string quartet. Boccherini had dedicated his first set of quartets to 'veri dilettanti e conoscitori di musica', and though this was a stock phrase of the time, it does draw attention to the nature of the public to whom string quartets were addressed around 1770. In the first place there were the 'dilettanti', the amateur performers, and it has become a truism to say that string quartets are written for those who play them. But, as Boccherini recognized, quartets can be appreciated also by observers, by connoisseurs. This was a new audience, and its arrival helps to explain the development at this time of the two important new musical media: the string quartet and the piano. For whereas the great princely families, like the Esterházys, could afford to maintain an orchestra and even an opera house, the new bourgeoisie needed music on a more modest scale. The harpsichord had never been a satisfactory instrument to listen to by itself – it is surely significant that the one work written for a listener rather than a player, Bach's Goldberg Variations, was designed as a soporific – and so the piano was invented as an instrument that could suitably function in the middle-class drawing room. And at the same time the string quartet came into being, together with, from the mid-1760s onwards, an increasing flood of publications for it. Anyone who had access to the salons of the well-to-do, or who could take a part in a quartet, was thus placed in contact with much of the greatest artistic thought of his time.

Haydn op. 20   Appropriately enough, the real dawning of the string quartet begins with the Haydn set nicknamed the 'Sun', and so known because the title-page of the second edition incorporated a sun motif. If his earlier collections had included individual works worth hearing more than once – op. 2 no. 4, the paired quartets of opp. 9 and 17 in minor keys, the astonishing op. 17 no. 1 – this new set, op. 20, is an entire volume of deeply fascinating works, and in modern times it has come to hold a place in the repertory unknown to Haydn's earlier quartets. Yet op. 20 was written only a year after op. 17, in 1772, and, what is even more extraordinary, strikes off in quite a different direction.

The development in Haydn's quartet writing from op. 9 to op. 17 would seem to suggest that his next set would be more integrated, more subtle, more teasing in form, less anxiously dramatic. But op. 20 is none of these things. It positively exults in contrast and variety. There is little of that proximity to the violin concerto which had been such a feature of the two preceding sets (the slow movement of no. 6 in A major brings the closest recall of the earlier manner), but otherwise all possibilities of texture are vigorously exploited. In formal terms, op. 20 marks a retrenchment in such matters of deception as the false reprise, and where this does occur, in the first movements of the E flat quartet no. 1 and the D major no. 4, its effect is not at all humorous but rather to urge on a development that has ended too quickly. And indeed continuity of development is very much a feature of the sonata movements, particularly the opening sonata movements, of this set. The one structural innovation from op. 17 (specifically no. 6) that Haydn does pursue here is the continuing of the development within the recapitulation, and he also moves much more freely into other keys, even in expositions. Most powerfully, there is an unusual preponderance of the minor mode in op. 20. Two of the quartets make their home in this domain, no.3 in G minor and no.5 in F minor, whereas all Haydn's later sets, like opp.9 and 17, have only one work in the minor. Two other op.20 quartets, those in C and in D, have slow movements in the tonic minor. This leaves only the A major quartet and the E flat, though the latter also makes a tonal withdrawal in its slow movement, this being in the subdominant, A flat: E flat was the key Haydn chose most often for quartets, ten times in all, and in every other case he wrote the slow movement in the dominant, B flat.

What remains to be mentioned is the new aspect of op.20 most frequently remarked: its counterpoint. This comes violently to the surface in the fugues that conclude the quartets in C, F minor and A, but it is present much more widely in the set, and in its strictness it all but excludes the conversational polyphony that had begun to appear in opp.9 and 17. In this respect, as in so many others, op.20 is an astounding achievement away from the main route of the string quartet's development, most spectacularly and mercilessly bizarre in its fugues, since fugue, in its ordained responses, its direct imitation and its lack of characterization in the voices, is the very antithesis of dialogue:

10 Haydn: Quartet in C op. 20 no. 2, fourth movement

Where had Haydn got this from? It used to be thought, in the days when fugue was imagined to have been the personal property of J. S. Bach, that he must have been browsing in the *Well-Tempered Clavier*, but it is much more likely that the influence came from within the string quartet literature, from the composers writing for the Emperor Joseph II. However, the agility and virtuosity of Haydn's contrapuntal imagination is instantly underlined if one compares his fugues with theirs – with this, for instance, which opens the finale to the last of the op. 1 quartets by Carlo d'Ordonez (1734-86), who was wholly a Viennese musician despite his exotic name:

11 Ordonez: Quartet in G op. 1 no. 6, fourth movement

To be fair, Ordonez's aims here were rather different from Haydn's in op. 20. The fugues in his op. 1 were devised as sober conclusions to works of a sober cast, each beginning with an andante rather than, as in Haydn, a quick or moderately paced movement. Haydn's fugues, by contrast, are final releases of contrapuntal energy, weighty enough to conclude works of unusual density and variety (unlike the 2/4 finales that had still served in most of Haydn's quartets up to op. 17), and offering, just as had the old form of prelude or fantasia followed by fugue, a highly unified structure to justify previous extraordinariness.

In the case of the C major quartet the fugue also balances a first movement based largely on a contrapuntal invention:

12 Haydn: Quartet in C op. 20 no. 2, first movement

And this illustrates another innovation of op. 20 in general: the melodic importance of the cello, which here takes the top line, and which throughout the set proves itself to have forgotten completely its origins in the basso continuo. The variety of texture available within the quartet is thus multiplied, and Haydn takes advantage of this throughout op.20, ranging within the C major quartet from the counterpoint of the outer movements to the extreme drone-bound homophony of the minuet and, in the slow movement, to an operatic recitative which now, by contrast with the situation in the parallel movements of opp.9 and 17, involves all four players as simultaneous protagonist, playing in octaves and affirming the new identity of the quartet.

If in the C major quartet the final fugue and the opening sonata serve to contain two much less contrapuntal movements, in the F minor quartet the weighting is quite different, not symmetrical but progressive. The first movement of this work is the most complex sonata structure so far imagined, with a recapitulation that diffuses twice into extra development and ends with a substantial coda. Not only that, but these additional sections of development learn from the past: the opening of the coda, for instance, is based on a figure that has not appeared in this form until the most recent phase of development. The whole movement, indeed, displays Haydn's drive at the time to make his music develop continuously, the accent to be understood on both verb and adverb, and it must have been obvious to him that the sonata principle would be his aid. Thus the initial Allegro moderato of the F minor quartet is followed by a minuet and trio each itself a miniature sonata, like the minuet of the C major quartet, and then the F major slow movement also has the main outline of a sonata form. Finally, after three movements in the most advanced contemporary structure, the fugue is based on a tag familiar from Handel, Bach and countless other fugalists (cf the chorus 'And with his stripes' in *Messiah*), although, as in the other two op.20 fugues, the old polyphony is at war with the new harmony, thematic definition and regular cadencing.

Together with the F minor quartet, that in D major holds a high place within the set. Its finale is not a fugue but a sonata marked 'Presto scherzando' – the first time one encounters the latter term in Haydn's quartets, unless 'op.3' is his (and this, of course, makes it all the more likely that 'op.3' was in fact written by someone else after op.20). The term is apt, for this finale is the funniest movement in op.20, with its comic dialogue not of instruments but of ideas, again including recitative in octaves:

13 Haydn: Quartet in D op.20 no.4, fourth movement

As in the C major quartet, too, the internal movements are violently opposed: a richly harmonized and emotionally laden set of variations in D minor is succeeded by a movement marked 'Menuet alla Zingarese', with a gipsy tang that Haydn probably acquired at first hand at the Esterházys' summer palace, and that had already appeared fleetingly in the last movement of op.17, also in D major. Both the middle movements of op.20 no.4, however, begin with the same four-note pattern in the first violin: A–D–E–F.

If Haydn learned from other composers of his time in op.20, then certainly his quartets were by now being noticed and imitated far beyond the circle that had been influenced by opp.1 and 2. In 1772 Charles Burney heard Haydn quartets played in Vienna by an ensemble including Ordonez and also Joseph Starzer (1726 or 1727-87), a composer who produced at least two mildly attractive quartets owing something to the manner of Haydn's op.9. The English historian also gives us information about reaction to Haydn's music further afield (and, as so often, it is the negative reaction that distinguishes what is important while decrying it): 'A friend at Hamburg wrote me word in 1772,' he notes, 'that "the genius, fine ideas and fancy of Haydn, Ditters, and Filz, were praised, but their mixture of serious and comic was disliked, particularly as there is more of the latter than the former in their works; and as for rules, they know but little of them."'

The rules, of course, were changing. The classical style was coming into being precisely on the basis of a 'mixture of serious and comic', exemplified at its most humorous and extraordinary in the finales of op.17 no.1 and op.20 no.4. What was also new about the classical style was that it was producing classics. Haydn's op.1 is the earliest music by a named composer (plainsong is thus excluded) to have been in continuous performance since the moment of its composition, and it was not by accident that the string quartet arose at the same time as this wholly new idea of music as a continuing tradition. Performance of a quartet presupposes the presence of at least four musicians, among whom, as in Burney's group, one might well expect to find composers, since in the eighteenth century most composers were also string players. Composers were thus placed in intimate contact with each other's music, and a genre that was beginning to foster musical conversation within a work became a natural outlet for conversation between works. Among Haydn, Boccherini, Sammartini, Ordonez and Starzer some of the links and divergences have been sketched, but Haydn's main partner in the discourse of the 1770s and 1780s, the discourse that established the classical string quartet and so much else, was to be Mozart.

Mozart K136-8 After his first quartet of 1770 Mozart wrote three light quartets, K136-8, in Salzburg in 1772. The fact that these have become known as 'divertimentos' is not significant, since this was still the common name in Austria for pieces of chamber music, and was the title chosen by Haydn for his quartets up to and including op.20. However, in substance Mozart's three works are concerned only to divert. The quick movements, particularly, are stamped with the manic quaver energy of the Italian style and its bright tonic–dominant gaiety, and *Mozart K155-60* this goes too for the finales of Mozart's next set, K155-60, written again in Italy between October 1772 and the early part of 1773: one is reminded that for most of this time Mozart was in Sammartini's city of Milan, called there for the première of *Lucio Silla*.

Nevertheless, his decision to follow a cycle-of-fifths key scheme – the quartets are in D, G, C, F, B flat and E flat – is a mark of Austrian seriousness (Hoffstetter had done the same in his op.1), and in terms of imagination and intelligence these works stand far above any contemporaries, and well to one side of Haydn. In Mozart's sonata movements the development is usually brief, rarely develops elements of the exposition in Haydn's manner, and may indeed be concerned with new ideas. Moreover, the recapitulation is usually complete and straightforward, in strong contrast with Haydn's practice in opp.17 and 20, and where this is not so one may be tempted to detect Haydn's influence: in the first movement of the F major quartet K158, for example, as in Haydn's op.2 no.4 in the same key, there is an unexpected use of the subdominant in the reprise. But the aim and the effect are quite different. Mozart's surprise is justified as a recall of the earlier surprise when the tonic key was suddenly replaced by the dominant, and it has to be a new surprise at this point because a repeat of the old one would have been not only no longer surprising but formally misleading, bringing back the dominant where it has no place. Haydn's surprise is not so justified by the context: the difference is to some degree a mark of the difference between the two composers, but it says much more about the growing coherence, range and meaningfulness of the classical style during the decade from the early 1760s to the early 1770s.

Similarly, the sonata inclination of the two minuet finales, those to the quartets in F K158 and G K156 (the others end with rondos), is probably a sign not of Haydn's influence but of the state of minuet composition in 1772, the tendency to make every kind of movement into a sonata. The most revolutionary case of this in Mozart's Italian quartets comes in the finale to the C major quartet K157, which is the earliest known example of a rondo trying to be a sonata form, the progenitor of the 'sonata rondo' which was to become the standard form of concerto finale up to the time of Brahms. Here the structure is comparatively simple, with the first episode, mimicking the secondary material of a sonata form, appearing first in the dominant and then at the end in the tonic:

$$a(C)–b(G)–a(C)–c(c)–a(C)–b(C)–a(C)–coda(C)$$

This has nothing to do with Haydn, who so far had not used rondo form in a quartet, and in the same way Mozart's striking use of the minor key in four movements of the set is a personal adventure, the gesture of an opera composer rather than an imitator of Haydn. Where Haydn adopts the form and the manner of opera in some of his slow movements, Mozart reproduces its essence of extravagant emotion being manifestly acted out, not least in the elaborate contrapuntal E minor adagio which he substituted for a serenade in the G major quartet K156. But if in the quartets in G, C and F the young Mozart is achieving, brilliantly, what lies within his grasp, in the B flat quartet K159 he looks towards the future, not only in the opening idea, which has that polished loveliness he made his own (Haydn is never lovely, though of course he may be beautiful), but also in the hard-pressed G minor sonata allegro that follows, for in this case, as in Mozart's very first quartet, the slow movement comes first.

Mozart K168-73 After completing this group of quartets Mozart returned from Italy to Salzburg and then spent the summer of 1773 in Vienna, where he encountered Haydn's latest quartets. The effect was immediate and quite unmistakable in the next six (κ168-73) he himself wrote in August–September that year, and by no means only in the two of them, in F major and D minor, which have fugal finales in the manner of Haydn's op.20 nos.2, 5 and 6. Haydn's more generally polyphonic handling of the quartet opened avenues which Mozart wanted to explore at once and without circumspection, and that led to some of the most extraordinarily gawky music that he, so rarely in the slightest awkward, ever wrote, like this from the opening of the slow movement of the E flat quartet κ171:

14 Mozart: Quartet in E♭ κ171, second movement

By comparison with this, Haydn's initial contrapuntal ideas, such as ex. 12 above, above, seem wholly natural. But that is to consider only one aspect of the devastating impression that Haydn, now forty-one, made on the seventeen-year-old Mozart. κ168-73 abandon the Italian three-movement form for the Viennese four, and in their sonata structures there is much more development going on within the exposition and the recapitulation, though the development section is still short and the reprise full: indeed, these were to remain essential differences between the sonata conceptions of the two composers, Haydn concerned with process, Mozart with the achieved result, Haydn a composer of change, Mozart one of symmetry. In matters of form, Mozart could assume Haydn's preferences much more complete-ly when writing variations, in the opening andante of the C major quartet κ170, where he follows the pattern of Haydn's op.9 no.5 and op.17 no.3, and where he even includes in the second half of his theme the jolting eccentricity of a silent bar, something much closer to Haydn's musical personality than Mozart's.

Altogether these six quartets suggest that, just for once, Mozart was made deeply uncomfortable by the achievement of another composer, and the most telling work of the set is the one which he composed out of his uncomfortableness, the D minor written last. Concluding again with a fugue, this quartet is hardly less contrapuntal than the other five, but here the counterpoint generates unease instead of being merely expressive of it. The fugue subject opens with a descending chromatic scale fragment of six notes, thus surpassing Ordonez's op.1 no.6 in this as in much else (and of course there is no reason why Mozart in Vienna in 1773 should not have been influenced by others beside Haydn). But the tension introduced by chromaticism is still more acute in the first movement, as bold in form as it is high-pressured in content. Like Haydn in the two minor quartets of opp.9 and 17, Mozart begins with the tonic triad in long note values, and as in Haydn's D minor quartet he makes his first excursion into A minor. In this case, however, most remarkably, A minor is to be used as the secondary key, and so Mozart is obliged not only to ignore almost completely the key of F major, which would normally be the secondary key of D minor, but to launch the music from D minor into A minor with a wild, flamboyant gesture:

15 Mozart: Quartet in D minor K173, first movement

The obsessive repeated quavers then become a feature of the latter half of the exposition, which changes key almost in every bar: they have a needling expressive function, of course, and they also help to substantiate tonality in some very chromatic territory. The development repeats this chromatic appendage to the exposition, variously transposed, and the recapitulation is, as usual, full, with the A minor material brought home properly to D minor. But the movement cannot end with its reprise of the chromatic part of the exposition, and so there is a long coda in D minor, concluding a sonata movement to rival that of Haydn's F minor quartet in its power and originality.

What Mozart does next, though, is even more bizarre. He follows this intense allegro with a blithe 'Andantino grazioso', and here again he eschews the relative major which tradition would dictate, and which would complement the tonality of the first movement: instead he chooses the tonic major, D major, which has the quite different effect of nullifying the preceding D minor. To compound the negation he brings on a rondo after a daring sonata form. Slow rondos are, admittedly, very rare, but rondo form is the most primitive structure available to Mozart at this point, its units short and regular, its quantity of repetition high, and it is primitiveness that Mozart needs here. The contrast could not be more complete, or more bewildering.

After this work Mozart wrote no more quartets for nine years, years filled with concertos, symphonies, sonatas, church music and opera. His experience would not have suggested to him that the quartet was as natural a means of expression as these others: all that would stir him to compose quartets again would be another set from Haydn, and Haydn similarly was silent for nine years. This did not, however, prevent the Paris publishers from rushing into print sets bearing his name. Five quartets by F. X. Dušek appeared as his 'op.18' in 1774, and then in 1778 came the 'op.3' set now generally ascribed to Hoffstetter. There were others. 'Haydn', as a brand name, was evidently market leader in the Parisian string quartet commerce of the 1770s, though not to the total exclusion of others. Curiously, French composers themselves played little part in the industry: sets of quartets were composed by Jean-Baptiste Davaux (1742-1822), François Gossec (1734-1829), André Grétry (1741-1813) and most notably Pierre Vachon (1731-1803), but publishers seem to have regarded the string quartet as proper to the Austrian Empire and to Italians, while their London colleagues preferred the more conservative styles of Richter, J. C. Bach or Charles Wesley (1757-1834), whose six usefully easy works are probably the first quartets by an Englishman. Vanhal had several sets published in Paris during the 1770s, and so too did Boccherini, producing more light pieces in two movements (his opp.15, 22 and 26) than more considered compositions in three. There was also the phenomenon of Giuseppe Cambini (1746-1825), who settled in Paris in the early 1770s, published a first set of quartets as his op.1 in 1773 and during the next three-and-a-half decades brought out 143 more, besides volumes of operatic airs arranged for string quartet and vast numbers of other works.

Cambini's quartets, however, have long been consigned to the oblivion in which they must have been composed, and the history of the string quartet begins again with Haydn's op.33 set, composed in *Haydn op. 33* 1781. On 3 December that year he wrote a batch of letters, of which three survive, offering patrons the opportunity to acquire these works which he had 'written in a new and special way'. This, so some scholars have argued, was mere sales talk, but Haydn's boast is well borne out by his music, and not only by the fact that these were the first works he called 'quartets'. Gone are most of the features that distinguished his previous set, op.20: the fugues and the other instances of strict counterpoint, the challenging use of the minor, the dramatic identification of the four players in simultaneous octaves, the turning of almost every movement into a serious sonata. Drama, vehemence and weight have been displaced as priorities by Haydn's greatest musical asset, namely wit.

Examples of this have already been detected, especially in the false reprises of op.17, but now the wit is pervasive. The nickname 'Gli scherzi' for op.33 is wholly apt – not for the mundane reason that they have the movement heading 'minuet' replaced by 'scherzo' or 'scherzando', since the scherzos of op.33 are generally less amusing than the minuets of opp.1 and 2, and less elaborate than those of op.20 – but rather because these quartets are full of what the Italian word means: 'jokes'. Haydn makes his humorous intentions clear to the dullest hearer in the three of his finales in sonata rondo form, a structure he had no doubt learned from Mozart's concertos of the 1770s. The last movement of op.33 no.2 in E flat has a seeming conclusion followed by four-and-a-half bars of silence, then ends with a pianissimo question. For this the work has come to be known as 'The Joke', though the endings of no.3 in C and no.4 in B flat are hardly less teasing, and the single soft pizzicato with which Haydn completes the operatically passionate G minor largo in no.5 reaches beyond wit to parody.

Beginnings in this set, however, can be just as funny as conclusions. Two of the quartets start in D major: not only the D major quartet itself, no.6, but also no.1 in B minor, and no.5 opens with a turn into its key of G major from the dominant D major. D major was a favourite key of Hadyn's for bright wit, the key of four of the 'London' symphonies and of the only quartet of op.20 notable for its humour, no.4. Its privileged position in op.33 is thus indicative, and in nos.1 and 5 its initial appearance as the 'wrong' key alerts one at once to a kind of musical argument in which the unexpected is shown to be perfectly appropriate, for after all, in both these quartets D major is going to function prominently.

Haydn had always been interested in surprise, but now his attention is on surprise justified, and on surprise which shows itself being justified. There is an instance of this in the latter part of the first movement exposition in the G major quartet, where the at last decisively arrived dominant brings with it a seemingly quite new idea:

16 Haydn: Quartet in G op.33 no.5, first movement

However, via a halfway stage that comes in bars 10-12 of the example, the new idea is shown to have a kinship with the movement's opening theme, which in bars 17ff above is transposed up a fifth into the dominant. At the same time, this use of the identical material in the tonic and dominant sections of the exposition – the 'monothematic- ism' found throughout Haydn, but never before so functional as in op.33 – gives the excuse for the recapitulation to be irregular, since a straightforward recapitulation would necessarily repeat itself: two of Haydn's great sonata-form innovations are thus interdependent. And indeed the recapitulation of the first movement of the G major quartet is full of surprises. Its very beginning is a shock, coming after two silent bars, and soon there is another new melody that the progress of the music and an act of memory have to justify, but most astonishing of all is the sudden leap near the end into the distant key of E flat, a manoeuvre made plausible only by the deft skill with which Haydn moves back to G major, there to end the movement with the shrug of a dominant–tonic cadence with which it had begun.

It is significant that Haydn should have been putting his most sophisticated music into string quartets rather than into any of the other genres in which he was writing around 1781: the symphony, the piano sonata, and opera. To some extent the reasons lie in the nature of the medium. The quartet, with its four increasingly equal parts, offered a greater variety of texture than did the classical orchestra, where the relative importances of the instrumental departments were more firmly fixed. Thus not only is the widespread harmony at the opening of ex. 16 hard to imagine in a symphony (and harder still in a piano sonata), but the quartet also allows for a quick variety of scoring, so that the principal motif here can be played first by the two violins, then by second violin and viola, then by second violin and cello, and finally by solo violin. And given the spirit of op.33, this is not to be seen just as decorative variety: by carrying out the transformation 'underground', in the lower instruments, Haydn makes it clear that transformation is what he is about. Also, the canon at the end of the quotation has become something more than the display of contrapuntal mastery it might have been in op.20, for again the near equality of the four instruments assists a style in which melodic ideas can become accompanimental ideas even from one bar to the next.

In addition, though, there were external reasons why the string quartet should have become in op.33 the prime vehicle of Haydn's wit. Quartets had now been regularly published for more than fifteen years: there was a public of 'dilettanti e conoscitori' who could be expected to play and hear quartets over and over again, whereas symphonies were written for the single experience, perhaps not to be repeated (hence the superiority of chamber over orchestral music as material for recording). Moreover, the 'conoscitori' were starting to have new ideas about what music should be. People of a reasoning epoch would not accept music as a language of sentiments, as the Baroque had understood it, nor did it seem to them necessary to construct such elaborate artificial languages as the art of fugue. 'I would like to know music without having to learn it,' said Diderot, and for such a one Haydn's op.33 might have been composed, its moves open to the listening ear, as in the example above, requiring no special knowledge but only a familiarity with the rules of tonality that an eighteenth-century audience, if not a twentieth-century one, might well have supposed to be a branch of the laws of nature.

This idea that music could be 'followed', understood as a course of sound events without any metaphorical interpretation, was quite new, and it was the main social reason why the late eighteenth century developed a musical style of such lucidity, and why it was at this time that musical jokes became possible for the first time. Just as a child claims command of language by immediately indulging in wordplay, distortion and punning, so Haydn's music celebrates in its wit the arrival of a musical language in which composers could expect their gambits to be closely appreciated. And the pleasure of such acquaintance with the composer's thinking is so great for the listener that music has come to be judged by the extent to which it can be understood in this manner. Always the main cry against new music, from Beethoven's to Boulez's, has been that it was incomprehensible, not ugly or faultily composed or expressively repellent, as if all music had to invite the listener into itself as openly as does the music of the 1780s and 1790s, beginning with Haydn's op.33.

The first movements of that set would have particularly delighted the connoisseurs, able to entertain string quartets in their own houses or hear them in others, while the finales Haydn could have expected to appeal to the perhaps less adept audiences at the quartet concerts that were beginning to take place. For still at this date the string quartet was overwhelmingly a domestic medium: hence the demand for parts indicated by the appearance within two years of four editions of op.33, the first by the house of Artaria, who had recently established permanent music publishing at last in Vienna, and who were to be responsible for many early editions of Haydn, Mozart and Beethoven. Nevertheless, the quartet was starting to become a public medium, and when the Russian Grand Duke Paul Petrovich, son of Catherine the Great and later to be Tsar Paul II, visited Vienna in 1781 it was not thought inappropriate to have op.33 played before him and a distinguished company. It was also to him that Haydn dedicated the quartets, whence their alternative nickname of the 'Russian'.

The man most usefully impressed by op.33, however, was not a Russian prince but an Austrian musician: Mozart. It seems that the first meeting between the two composers took place in 1781, the year of op.33, and there are tantalizing records of their participation together in quartet performances: one in 1784, recalled by the Irish tenor Michael Kelly in his memoirs, had Haydn and Dittersdorf playing violins, Mozart the viola and Vanhal the cello. Mozart thus had the opportunity to gain an intimate familiarity with the 'new and special way' of op.33, and he certainly had the means with which to respond. He returned to quartet composition soon after the appearance of Haydn's set in print, in 1782, beginning with his G major quartet κ387, finished on the last day of that year, continuing the next summer with the quartets in D minor κ421 and E flat κ428, and finishing the set in the winter of 1784-5 with the B flat κ458, A major κ464 and C major κ465. The six quartets were then published by Artaria in 1785 as his op.10 and dedicated, in a rare gesture among great artists, to Haydn, with a letter in Italian affirming that the contents were 'the fruits of long and laborious endeavour'.

Mozart K387, 421, 428, 458, 464, 465

Indeed, for Mozart to spend over two years on a project was most unusual, and his difficulties are evidenced by the abundance of failed sketches and of corrections in the manuscripts. This time, however, the problem was not that he was overwhelmed by Haydn, as he had been nine years earlier, but rather that he had to find his own way along the paths that Haydn had opened up, since by now he had achieved total individuality as a composer, and behind him already lay such works as *Idomeneo*. Thus although Haydn's op.33 was no doubt important to the background of these six quartets, so too were the chamber works that Mozart himself had written during the last decade, especially the Oboe Quartet κ370 of early 1781. Indeed, the two occasions of Mozart's closest homage to Haydn – the minuet of the E flat quartet that mirrors Haydn's in the same key, and the final variations of the D minor quartet that reinterpret the theme of the G major variations at the end of op.33 no.5 – only show how distant the two composers had become, Haydn speaking with clarity and directness to a small audience, Mozart at once more public and more subtle.

But it is in first movements that the difference is most vivid. For example, Haydn's E flat quartet begins absolutely typically with a closed four-bar unit, dividing clearly into two-bar sections and barely clouding the home tonality. It then immediately begins to develop a tiny fragment of this material before repeating it wholesale in preparation for a further phase of development:

17 Haydn: Quartet in E♭ op. 33 no. 2, first movement

Now Mozart was impressed by Haydn's manner of starting to develop even in the early stages of the exposition, but in his E flat quartet, κ428, his manner is entirely different from Haydn's. The opening idea – played, as is rare for Mozart, in bald octaves so that its harmonic sense is made as ambiguous as possible – begins by defining E flat in the clearest terms, in an octave leap, but then swings back through an unsettling tritone, meanders chromatically and ends thoroughly open. The answering music, too, becomes no answer at all but a lead back to a repeat of the opening, now dynamically and harmonically enriched, emphasizing the home key but adding to the tension that must be resolved in what follows:

18 Mozart: Quartet in E♭ κ428, first movement

Haydn's music is carried forward by argument, Mozart's by the need for balance and resolution. And although in these quartets Mozart uses Haydn's technique of development by disintegration and recombination, his tendency is to make everything theme where Haydn makes everything development.

Another point about Mozart's quartets of 1782-5 is that they do not look only to Haydn's op.33 for inspiration. It would be nice to think that Mozart chose his keys to match those of Haydn's op.9, his first set of four-movement quartets, but there is no evidence for this (к421, for instance, has very much less in common with op.9 no.4 than had Mozart's earlier D minor quartet). On the other hand, it is clear that Mozart was still nagged by some of the problems raised by Haydn's earlier batches of quartets, problems which he had not satisfactorily resolved in his Vienna set of 1773. In particular, there was the matter of adapting fugue to the quartet, which must have seemed so natural, with four compatible instruments to take the four parts, but which was in reality so antipathetic to the real nature of the quartet as an ensemble. There was a revival in the art of fugal quartet writing at this time, apparently led by Albrechtsberger, and Mozart himself transcribed five Bach fugues for string quartet in 1782, but in the finale of the G major quartet from the same year he realized, as later in the finale of the 'Jupiter' symphony, that fugue could find a place in works of the new sonata style only if it was altered to fit sonata principles, and that these had to come first. Strict counterpoint had to give way to the new freer counterpoint that the string quartet, above all, was helping to bring to birth.

This was a lesson underlined not only by the G major quartet's finale but by page after page of Mozart's 'Haydn' quartets, and borne out most spectacularly by the celebrated introductory passage that was responsible for the name given to the 'Dissonance' Quartet, the last of the set:

19 Mozart: Quartet in C κ465, first movement

The harmonic uncertainty here is extreme, outdoing even the *Tristan*-like slowly eased dissonances of the slow movement of the E flat quartet κ428 and contrasting boldly with the C major allegro that follows, and that is formally and harmonically the most straightforward, the most Haydnesque, of the set. However, the real dissonance here is that between the strict canonic polyphony with which the quartet begins and the new polyphony of equal but different partners that has been achieved within so few bars. There are, of course, still elements of canon in bars 9ff. of the above quotation, just as there are elements of repetition in any conversation, but what is more significant is that the voices are each of them individual, that they may be joined in different combinations, and that the ear is constantly led among them, drawn by a rising scale in the viola, a sforzato in the cello, a little phrase in thirds and sixths from the two violins.

This new kind of quartet discourse was the great discovery of Haydn's op.33 and Mozart's 'Haydn' quartets, and it had far-reaching consequences not just for the string quartet but for the whole nature of musical composition in allowing composers to deal with parts that are, as noted above, equal but different. And perhaps it would not have happened as it did if the string quartet had not contained within itself aspects of equality and of difference: two violins which have to be made different; three different instruments which have to be made equal. Thus although the make-up of the quartet was on one level a historical accident, due to its origins in trio sonatas for two violins with continuo, it was a happy chance that contributed much to the essential quality of the quartet as an ensemble of in-built cohesion and antagonism. The ear expects to find the melody at the top, and Mozart and Haydn normally respect that expectation, the exceptions being self-consciously rare and special (as when the viola takes the theme in the variations of κ421). But the presence of two potential top instruments makes for variety, and Mozart shows particular discernment in playing with one's expectation that the second violin, if it is given a chance, will always be capped by the first (see, for example, the first movement development in κ387, where the first violin achieves its final victory by undercutting the second).

If homage can dare to outshine, then Mozart's 'Haydn' quartets are in every way a magnificent tribute to the older composer, profiting from much that he had exemplified, but also expanding much. The Mozart quartets are ampler than Haydn's op.33, in terms not only of length but also of substance; they are also more diverse. Where Haydn uses rondo form for three of his finales, Mozart does so only once, in his E flat quartet, and so under-uses what had in Haydn been most Mozartian: elsewhere he uses the form of variations (D minor), fugal sonata (G major and, with a great deal more freedom, A major) and sonata with rondo affiliations (B flat and C major). Where Haydn cuts back to a simple form in his scherzos, Mozart's minuets are small-scale sonatas. Mozart also increases the tonal richness at his disposal by always casting his trios in a contrasting key (Haydn does so only twice in op.33) and by giving all his major-mode quartets a slow movement in the subdominant (again Haydn does this only twice).

No doubt Mozart offered his quartets as a set of six in order to complete the tribute to Haydn and not because he thought they made a coherent group, for in fact the period of their composition was for him one of great growth, not only in the quartet but in other fields too: there were no completed operas, but this was the time of the C minor Mass and of the first Vienna piano concertos. Mozart's father was the first to remark that the last three of the 'Haydn' quartets are 'simpler' than the first, and indeed the writing for the leader becomes less showy as the quartet style becomes more integrated, while the bucolic opening of the B flat quartet, nicknamed the 'Hunt', is at some remove from its three predecessors. However, the quartets do stand together and apart from anything else Mozart was achieving at the time – not to mention any other composer – in the completeness with which the implications of the material are realized in the form. This is something that Mozart would have observed in Haydn, but time and again he outdoes Haydn in adventure. In the final variations of the D minor quartet, for instance, he even makes a dissonance of the notionally most consonant of intervals, the octave, and it is this dissonance, left unresolved even at the end, that impels the movement from one variation to the next and also gives it its needling power. Nor is this the only finale that differs utterly from the comic conclusions of Haydn's op.33, for the last movement of the A major quartet is no laughing matter either.

It was after a performance of some of these quartets in 1784 that Haydn exclaimed to Mozart's father: 'Before God, and as an honest man, I tell you that your son is the greatest composer known to me in person or by name.' And perhaps Haydn himself was taken aback by the giant strides being taken by this young man in the medium he had invented. At Easter 1784 he wrote to Artaria mentioning a set of six simple quartets he was writing for Spain, where Boccherini was composer to the Infante Luis, but nothing of this set, if it was ever composed, survives, unless in the strangely terse and straightforward D *Haydn op. 42* minor quartet op.42 (1785). Haydn's letter indicates that the Spanish quartets were to be in three movements, like many of Boccherini's, whereas op.42 is in four, but it is just possible that one of these was added for Viennese publication after the project as a whole had been abandoned: perhaps the finale, which is an amalgam of fugue and sonata not unlike that of Mozart's G major quartet, but on a much smaller scale.

In the next year, 1786, Mozart too produced a lone quartet, the D *Mozart K499:* major K499, which was printed by Franz Anton Hoffmeister *'Hoffmeister'* (1754-1812), one of the Viennese publishers to follow in the wake of

Artaria. Hoffmeister was himself a prolific composer, not least of
string quartets, but his name lives only in attachment to the quartet
Mozart wrote for him, perhaps in repayment of a debt. Unlike its six
predecessors, this 'Hoffmeister' quartet opens not with an allegro but
with an allegretto, an ambulatory pace for music of amiability and
gentle seriousness that looks forward to Schubert. When the first
movement has been on the slow side, the slow movement proper has
to be something special, and the G major adagio of к499 does not
disappoint, for here Mozart's separation of the quartet into upper and
lower pairs – typical of this quartet more than any other by him – leads
to a point where the paths fork alarmingly. The finale is at last a fast
movement, but of a peculiarly Mozartian kind, where vivaciousness
verges towards anxiety.

Helped by the activities of Vienna publishers like Hoffmeister and
Artaria, the string quartet boom was by now firmly established, and
contributions to it were coming from composers young and old.
Haydn's contemporary Albrechtsberger, by now settled in Vienna as
an organist and greatly respected teacher of composition, returned to
the writing of quartets with his two sets of 'quatuors en fugue' (1780
and 1782) and then, from 1786 for the next twenty years, with
collections of 'sonatas' similarly consisting of a rather Baroque adagio
followed by a fugue: this was the form dignified by Mozart with his
Adagio and Fugue in C minor к546 (1788), the fugue adapted from
one he had written for two pianos in 1783, soon after his Bach
arrangements and the sonata–fugue finale of the G major quartet. It is
also possible that Albrechtsberger's fugal quartets were remembered by
his pupil Beethoven when, thirty years after they had been master and
student, the latter was writing his *Grosse Fuge*.

Albrechtsberger
op. 7

However, not all Albrechtsberger's later works were in the learned
style. Some time around 1781-3 he published a volume of six quartets
op.7 very much in Haydn's manner, or rather Haydn's manners: the
first, in D, leans towards opp.9 and 17, while the third, in F, is close
to op.33, with a condensed recapitulation in the allegro first
movement and a rondo finale, the middle movements being an adagio
and a minuet. The D major quartet is also in four movements, but
with the unusual feature of an andante finale, in variation form, giving
a fast–slow–fast (minuet)–slow pattern. Albrechtsberger's willingness
to experiment with large-scale form, already observed in his quartets
from the early 1760s, is also shown in the A major work from the op.7
set, which begins with a sonata-form andante and then has two
minuets with trios, the second headed 'Scherzando'. But within
movements Albrechtsberger is much more cautious. His ideas are

Haydnesque to the point of imitation, but the development is short and unadventurous, the recapitulation straightforward.

These general comments apply equally to the quartets of Haydn's brother Johann Michael (1737-1806), composer to the Archbishop of Salzburg and a much more sober musical personality. Little of his music was published before modern times, and his quartets were probably written as isolated works over a period from the late 1770s to the early years of the new century. However, he seems to have been fairly consistent in preferring a three-movement form, with an andante in sonata form followed by a minuet and then a quick finale, often a rondo, though he also persisted with the five-movement form of his brother's early quartets and on occasion used one of the standard four-movement patterns.

The quartets of Michael Haydn and Albrechtsberger are honourable if limited attempts to follow Joseph Haydn without subservience, and they were doomed only because Haydnesque ideas quickly become boring in their simplicity – and of course it was the simplicity of Haydn's ideas that made it possible for him to be imitated, unlike Mozart – if they are not treated with the wit and daring that belonged to Haydn alone. Other, younger composers would seem to have emulated Haydn simply because the Haydn-style quartet had become a profitable commodity, and none was more productive than Haydn's own pupil Ignace Pleyel (1757-1831), who began his operations at the beginning of the 1780s and by the end of that decade had overtaken Haydn with an output of fifty-seven quartets. Only his subsequent activities as a publisher and music dealer stemmed the flow.

But if the commercial market distorted the composition of quartets in the 1780s, except by the two composers unable to be anything but original, then so too did the patronage of Friedrich Wilhelm II of Prussia, who played the cello and had an insatiable appetite for quartets. He put Boccherini on a salary and in 1786, the year of his accession, received a dozen quartets from Pleyel, but it was again Haydn and Mozart who succeeded in obeying the royal wishes and also their own. In particular, Haydn's quartets for Berlin, his op. 50 set of *Haydn op. 50* 1787, do not notably set out to flatter the kingly cellist, except, typically, in terms of gentle comic irony, as when the first of the six, in B flat, begins with a repeated one-note solo for the cello and ends with that instrument caught in a humorously hurried, vigorous upward scale. Otherwise, and much more generally and importantly, the op. 50 quartets profit from the discoveries of the op. 33 set, making the string quartet a still more intimate and faithful transcript of creative thought processes.

The distinction from the symphony is now complete. Haydn's
'Paris' symphonies, written only in the preceding two years, are full of
characterful ideas, whereas the op.50 quartets mark an extreme in the
submergence of themes so that arguments can be the richer and more
prominent. Especially is this the case in no.3, in E flat, where the slow
movement is a set of variations (like two other slow movements in this
ultra-variational collection), where the trio audibly grows out of the
minuet's material, and where a single idea sparks off two whole sonata
movements, since both the opening allegro and the final presto are
based on similar themes serving as both primary and secondary
material:

20 Haydn: Quartet in E♭ op.50 no.3

As has already been remarked, Haydn's monothematicism permits his
irregular recapitulation, and when the monothematicism is as
wholesale as this, the formal effect is similarly alarming. Already
replete with repetition in its exposition, the first movement of op.50
no.3 can afford to chop a first section of forty-four bars down to twenty
bars in the recapitulation.

However, the reductionism of op.50 is not simply a matter of
making one theme do duty for four. Even more crucial is the fact that
the theme contains the determining power for the whole movement,
as had always been the case in Haydn. Where his movements are
simply structured, in the opp.1 and 2 quartets, his themes are often
near relations to the arpeggio or scale of the tonic key. And now that

his movements are more complicated, though also more lucidly set forth, their germinal ideas naturally give the excuse for complication, like that of the first movement of the C major quartet no.2, whose halting upward progress begins a movement which similarly moves by small but unexpected degrees, or again that of the first movement of the D major quartet no.6, which slithers down into the home tonality from an E and gives likewise a characteristic shape and gesture to the movement that contains it (and how typical it is of Haydn's variety that whereas in op.33 three quartets began 'in' D major, here none does, not even the D major quartet).

It is rather as if Haydn had taken the daring inventiveness of his op.20 quartets and made it more perfect, whole and comprehensible by the means he had found in op.33. The minuets – now again called minuets and not scherzos – return to the larger form of the earlier quartets, but with the integration bestowed by op.33: the trio is either in the same key as the minuet or, in two occasions, the tonic minor. Sonata form is again the guiding feature in those slow movements which are not cast as variations, and the finales are in sonata form or, in the case of the F sharp minor quartet, fugal. The rondos of op.33 have completely disappeared, and so has much of that set's comedy, but though op.50 is once more a collection of 'serious' quartets, it does not declaim its profundity in the manner of op.20, and Haydn remains occasionally capable of pure silliness, as in the finale of the D major quartet, whose bouncing on one note has given the work its nickname of the 'Frog'.

Naturally the quartet from op.50 that most recalls op.20 is the F sharp minor, by virtue not only of its tonality but also its fugal finale. But in both areas Haydn has made great strides in fifteen years. The opening movement – like the only other sonata movement of op.50 in the minor, the Poco adagio of the D major quartet – is not allowed to end in the minor mode, but instead the secondary material is recapitulated in F sharp major. This recapitulation is divested too of the most extraordinary sound in the whole quartet, indeed the whole series: that of the violins in octaves above the stave. The slow movement that follows, like the finale of op.33 no.6, is in a favourite form of his later years, that of double variations, here alternately reconsidering themes in A major and A minor, and there is then an abrupt switch back to F sharp major for the minuet, with its trio in the minor: possibly Haydn intended originally that the minuet should here come second, so abutting the end of the first movement in the same key, but in the published edition all six quartets of op.50 have the pattern inherited from the last two quartets of op.33 and the D major and A major quartets of op.20, with the opening allegro followed by a slow movement, then a minuet, and then a quick finale.

In the case of the F sharp minor quartet this last movement is a fugue, the most open display of a contrapuntal impetus that had, as a further memory of op.20, re-entered Haydn's quartet style (in the first movement of the C major quartet, for example, the two development sections, one in its correct place and the other interpolated into the recapitulation, both make a show of strict counterpoint). However, the F sharp minor fugue of op.50 is quite different from its three predecessors of op.20. Twice the fugal texture is allowed to blend into untroubled homophony for long stretches, and this textural combination of the Baroque and the classical helps to articulate a similar formal mix, with sections corresponding to exposition (fugal), development (fugal changing to homophonic), recapitulation (fugal) and coda (homophonic). The synthesis differs from that of Mozart's G major quartet only in leaning more towards fugue than sonata: Haydn's is a sonata-style fugue, while Mozart's is a sonata movement with fugal sections.

One might expect there to be other, clearer indications in op.50 of the seven great Mozart quartets that had been written since op.33, but they are remarkably few. After all, Haydn was now in his mid-fifties, almost as old as Beethoven at his death, and his musical imagination had quite enough stimulus in his own past achievements, as op.50 well demonstrates. The only totally new feature here is his use of C and ₵ time signatures in the initial allegros of the first and last quartets of the set, where all his earlier fast quartet movements had been in the quicker-moving metres of 2/4, 3/4 or 6/8. And this broader speed is something that can be traced to Mozart, who had thought in such terms right from his first quartet. Nevertheless, the music that Haydn launches at the new pace is entirely his own, even self-consciously so, the first movement of op.50 no.1 building on the simplest *donnés* of a repeated note and a six-note curlicue, and that of op.50 no.6 stumbling by surprise in a manner quite alien to Mozart.

By now, in the late 1780s, the practice of string quartet playing was obviously widespread, as is evidenced by the activities of publishers in Vienna and Paris, and the quartet had come to hold a place occupied in the nineteenth century by the piano and in the twentieth by the radio and the gramophone: it was a prime means by which amateurs could acquaint themselves with the repertory. As such it became the vehicle not only for original works but also for arrangements and pot-pourris. Among Cambini's publications were several volumes of 'quatuors d'airs variés', using popular operatic numbers and other songs (it was this kind of production that Mozart mocked in his flute quartet K298 of 1786-7), and Haydn's 'Paris' symphonies, for instance, appeared within a little while in quartet versions, as later did several of his 'London' sets. Haydn himself may have been responsible for quartet arrangements that were made, but not published, of items from two of his operas, and it is quite certain that in 1787, the year of op.50, he prepared a quartet version of the orchestral interludes he had written two years earlier for a Lenten ceremony in the Cathedral of Cadiz.

This work, generally known as the *Seven Last Words* and published as op.51, consists of an introduction (in D minor), a septet of sonata-form slow movements, each designed to follow a sermon on one of Christ's sayings from the Cross (the keys are B flat, C minor, E, F minor, A, G minor and E flat), and finally a depiction of the earthquake that marked Christ's death (this also in C minor). The key sequence – not to mention the succession of seven slow movements with a presto only at the end – must suggest that Haydn had no intention that the nine pieces should be played together as a 'work': rather the quartet medium gave him an outlet for music that otherwise could never have become widely known. And the fact that he took this trouble with the *Seven Last Words* indicates its importance to him, while the fact that he arranged it for quartet is a token only of the popularity of the medium and of his allegiance to it. Indeed, leaving aside works with keyboard, which belong to a somewhat different category, Haydn had written no chamber music for other combinations since well before his op.9 quartets, except works commissioned for the baryton by his Esterházy patron and for the hurdy-gurdy by the King of Naples.

Haydn op. 51: Seven Last Words

Other composers, though, cast their favours differently. Mozart, Vanhal and Carl Stamitz (1745-1802) all wrote quartets with flute, oboe or clarinet replacing one of the violins, especially during the 1770s, when the Paris publishers were eager for such works. Boccherini wrote fewer quartets than he did quintets, with two cellos as well as two violins, and this combination was also used often by Cambini, whereas their Austrian contemporaries, including Pleyel and above all Mozart, preferred the quintet with two violas. Most intriguingly of all, the possibility of a string quartet with two violas instead of two violins was raised in the 1770s by Carl Stamitz and in the 1780s by Pleyel and Cambini, among others. In a sense this is a more logical formation, since the upper viola can shine as alto whereas a second violin is necessarily subdued, but composers had too long been familiar with first and second violins in the orchestra, and the element of competition in the quartet is more persuasively placed at the top than in the middle.

The beauty of the Mozartian string quintet, of course, is that it provides both arenas, apart from which, for Mozart, it also satisfied his wish for a rich inner life in his musical textures and gave him more opportunity to show off the viola, the instrument he himself played in the celebrated quartet with Haydn, Dittersdorf and Vanhal. His fondness for the viola naturally colours his quartet writing, not least in the 'Hoffmeister', where the first movement recapitulation hands to the viola a theme previously played by the first violin; and the gesture is all the more remarkable in a recapitulation which, like Mozart's generally, is otherwise quite straightforward. However, the 'viola quintet' obviously made viola prominence even more excusable, and Mozart took full advantage of this in the four quintets he wrote after the 'Hoffmeister' quartet, during those last years that also saw the composition of the clarinet quintet (with another favoured instrument of warm alto range) but only three string quartets: κ575 in D, κ589 in B flat and κ590 in F.

Even so, Mozart's comparative neglect of quartet texture has to be understood in the light of factors other than his liking for full sonority and viola tone, since he was quite as capable of impoverishing the ensemble as of enriching it, as witness the E flat divertimento for string trio κ563. Variations on the quartet formation were possible and even stimulating, but the quartet itself had presented problems ever since the Vienna set of 1773: first the bewildering influence of Haydn, then the 'long and laborious endeavour' that bore fruit in the 'Haydn' quartets, and finally, in the last quartets, similar difficulties of which Mozart complained in his letters and of which evidence remains, as in the case of the preceding six, in the form of sketches and discarded beginnings. Clearly the quartet was not a natural medium for him in his maturity, and the timing of the start of his difficulties with it suggests strongly that Haydn was a prime cause. Haydn had created the string quartet in his own image (or created his musical image to match that of the string quartet: it amounts to the same thing), and so other composers could only copy, in the manner of Pleyel, or else tug at the medium until it fitted a different usage.

The boldness and imagination of Mozart's 'Haydn' quartets come out of his struggle with the medium, and the more polished feel of the last three of them is a mark of the success of that struggle. In the 'Hoffmeister' and the three quartets that followed, the tension with Haydn has ceased: Mozart moves into his own quartet style, and from that vantage point he can even, in his last quartet, pay frank tribute once more to Haydn. Unfortunately, though, this achievement of independence is somewhat compromised by a new dependence on the needs of the cello-playing Friedrich Wilhelm II, for whom Haydn had written his op.50 quartets in 1787 and whom Mozart visited in the spring of 1789. On his way back to Vienna he began a quartet for the monarch, к575, and was much more assiduous than Haydn had been in providing opportunities for the display of royal virtuosity. Every movement of this D major work includes prominent cello solos with the instrument at the top of its range, and to accommodate these Mozart is obliged to give similar solos to each of the other three members of the quartet, which can make the ensemble sound like a committee in which all must have their say:

Mozart K 575

21 Mozart: Quartet in D к575, first movement

The manner here is that of the 'quatuor concertant', as practised by Cambini and many of his Parisian colleagues, and its inherent repetitiveness is only just redeemed by Mozart's variation of line and texture. It is still inevitable that the concertante style dilutes the music, since so much has to be stated four times over, but the challenge to alter and conceal brings its own rewards, notably in the finale, a sonata rondo further infused with variation form, since the rondo theme is differently presented on each appearance.

Concertante texture also predisposes music to a moderate tempo, since hurried little solos would be absurd and repeated slow ones wearisome, and indeed all the movements of κ575 proceed at middle speeds, the outer movements and the minuet being marked 'allegretto' and the second movement being an andante. This evenness of tempo

Mozart K589-90   remains a feature of κ589 and κ590, as does too the dominance of the major key in every movement: there is no successor to the adagio of the 'Hoffmeister' or to the extravagance of its D minor trio. However, these are signs not of a weakness of invention but of a depth of thought that grows from each of these late quartets to the next, exactly as the image of the kingly cello recedes. In the B flat quartet κ589, which may have been started, like its D major companion, during Mozart's journey back to Vienna in the spring of 1789, solo writing is a feature only of the first two movements, and in the F major quartet κ590 it appears only in the first movement, and there in a much more integrated fashion than in the D major work. Both quartets were probably finished in the spring of 1790: certainly the period of their composition spans that of *Così fan tutte* (winter 1789-90).

The nearness of the opera seems especially pertinent when so much of these last two quartets is subtle and mocking in mood – and again it is the movements that Mozart wrote later, the last two of κ589 and the whole of κ590, that are most elusive, wry and ironic. In κ589 the minuet stands out in a work of otherwise modest scope, where the key of B flat, as three times earlier in Mozart's quartet output, brings forth his most natural quartet invention. The E flat trio has the first violin startlingly thrust up into an uncomfortably high register by the canonic entry of the second, and the minuet itself has a first section squarely set out in two four-bar phrases followed by a second of extraordinary irregularity and drama.

In κ590 the minuet is again remarkable, the first section in two seven-bar phrases, of which the first is in pure but aerial F major, scored for the two violins alone, while the second brings a sudden charge of D minor, fully scored and now forte instead of piano; the longer second section then considers the implications of this conflict – harmonic, textural and dynamic – over some very unsettled territory. In this quartet, though, the minuet is not alone in presenting unexpected changes that force one to revise one's views about what has happened – in contrast with Haydn's normal deception of confounding one's expectations about what is to come. The first movement, one of Mozart's most Haydnish in the elemental quality of its material and its degree of monothematicism, starts out from the simplest idea, that of a rising tonic arpeggio sounded in minims by all the instruments in octaves, but the soft F and A are followed by a loud C, and the opening skitters off-balance in a downward scale. Only later can it expand into a melody, and grow into the vocal tunefulness characteristic of all Mozart's last four quartets.

At this point, too, Mozart profits from the concertante conception, for the F major violin melody is immediately imitated by the cello in the dominant, the transition to the new key and the monothematicism eased by the instrumental dialogue. This also brings the opportunity for a telling moment in the recapitulation. If the cello were now to follow the violin in its own F major, as it properly should, the effect would be one of excessive redundancy, and so the imitation is transferred to the viola, and to the tonic minor: as in Haydn, monothematicism is naturally allied with an altered recapitulation, but where Haydn, by the time of op.50, is thoroughly revising the final sections of his sonata structures, Mozart simply transfers a section from one key into another. Once more, Haydn is looking to the future, to frustrating the expectations he has set up, whereas Mozart's more identifiable change at first shocks and then alters one's perspective as much on earlier as on present events.

In comic terms, the difference is that between wit and mockery, and Mozart's mockery comes most to the surface in the development section of the same movement and again in the coda, which is a development of the development. The idea to be reinterpreted here is a cadential fall at the end of a drunken slide from one key into another, this possibly stimulated by the example of Haydn's D major quartet op.50 no.6:

22 Mozart: Quartet in F K590, first movement

The coda, shown complete in this quotation, blithely strips the two-crotchet fall of all decisiveness by changing its dynamic, and plays with it in various harmonic contexts, linked by a commonplace and set against a self-consciously banal background. Something stern becomes something quite insignificant, a plaything to be inverted and toss the movement aside with Fs bouncing up through four octaves. If the andante is a pensive fusion of feeling too tender for interpretation, the finale repeats the victory of lightness over minor-key drama and contrapuntal legerdemain. Mozart's 'Prussian' quartets – so called though only the first was explicitly dedicated to Friedrich Wilhelm – have often been rated below his 'Haydn' set, but although they are indeed less spectacular in the range, beauty and daring of their ideas, the F major quartet in particular contains an emotional and musical complexity he never equalled in the medium, and rarely beyond it.

Often it has been supposed that Mozart broke off work half way through a set of six quartets and turned to the more congenial media of the string and clarinet quintets, but by 1790 it was quite common for quartets to be published in threes: this was the way with Haydn's latest set of six, printed in two volumes and so carrying two opus numbers, 54 and 55. These quartets, dating probably from 1788, had some unclear commercial connection with Johann Tost, a violinist in the Esterházy orchestra and later a wholesaler in Vienna. In any event,

Haydn opp. 54, 55

like the op.64 quartets which were certainly written for and dedicated to Tost, the opp.54-5 set once more gives prominence to the first violin. It is tempting to imagine that Haydn was here thinking back to his 'Tomasini' quartets of twenty years before, and certainly in one of these quartets there is a feature that had not appeared since opp.9 and 17: the F minor quartet, op.55 no.2, begins with a slow set of variations. However, the concerto character of the earlier quartets is almost wholly absent. Many movements, including most of the minuets and finales, offer no special glories to the leader, and elsewhere brilliance is made to serve a formal and expressive need. For instance, in the opening movement of the quite extraordinary C major quartet, op.54 no.2, the first violin's high-reaching virtuosity is just one means of achieving an extravagance of gesture: others include sudden harmonic shifts into distant territory – not least a leap from C into A flat after the first dozen bars – and the concatenation of a great variety of thematic ideas, so many that the development has to be unusually short in order that the basic material itself can be further considered in the recapitulation.

The slow movement of this quartet shows another way in which Haydn uses violin dominance to achieve a quite interior result, something far removed from outward display. The key is the dramatic one of C minor, but by contrast with the adagio of op.20 no.2, also in C minor, there is no suggestion of operatic emotion. Instead the piece takes the form of a short passacaglia, on a bass whose chromaticisms are exquisitely reinforced by the harmonic delayings, prefigurings and decorations of the first violin, which acts similarly, though never so devastatingly, to increase tension in other slow movements in this set, especially those of the G major op.54 no.1, the E major op.54 no.3 and the A major op.55 no.1.

Since slow movements tend naturally more than quick movements to approximate to song, it is thoroughly reasonable that the first violin should move towards a solo role here, particularly when Haydn prefers an adagio tempo, not the andante of Mozart. And indeed several earlier quartets show a spotlight held on the leader's prevarications, notably op.50 no.5, whose poco adagio in B flat gained the nickname 'A Dream' from the way in which the first violin wanders and soars against the soft chordal background of the other instruments. But in opp.54-5 such things become more important because the slow movements generally have more weight. For though the adagio of op.55 no.3 is a straightforward set of variations, the largo of op.54 no.3 is a sonata rondo with touches of variation in the treatment of the rondo theme, and in op.55 no.1 the fusion of sonata, rondo and variation elements is so complete that there is no point in describing the movement as being 'in' a particular form.

Of course this is so with the vast majority of classical movements: the discussion here of Haydn's and Mozart's quartets has already indicated how very little is prescribed by the term 'sonata form', and the lesson is re-emphasized by the sonata movements of opp.54-5, where the recapitulation may be extended into a weighty coda, as in the first movement of op.54 no.3, or greatly curtailed, as in the second movement of op.55 no.2. But the richness of Haydn's material in opp.54-5, which generally lack his regular answering phrases (the first movement of op.55 no.3 stands out as an exception) and which are freer and quicker in harmonic change, this richness has to be contained in forms of greater complexity. The finale of op.55 no.1 and the second movement of op.55 no.2 both include fugal episodes, in both cases much more smoothly integrated into the sonata design than in any earlier quartet by Haydn or Mozart, and in both cases occurring in the development. They represent, though, two quite different uses of fugue. In op.55 no.1 the fugal material is associated with a rondo theme, which creates delicious uncertainties about the point at which this lively idea will succeed in extricating itself from counterpoint. On the other hand, in op.55 no.2 the canonic entries are weightily proposed, and the recapitulation is clearly marked off by a heavy cadence and a change of key.

This is necessary because the first movement of the same F minor quartet is the longest in playing time of all Haydn's quartet movements: it is a set of double variations, alternating related themes in F minor and F major, and so having some similarity with rondo form. Although there is a connection with opp.9 and 17, each of which had included a quartet starting with a slow variation movement, in using this pattern for one last time Haydn extends and broadens it, and instead of introducing a second slow movement later on, he is able to follow the variations with a sonata allegro, since he now has the means to make such movements sufficiently grave and imposing, even though, like the minor-key sonata movements of op.50, this one moves into the major at the end, and indeed does so for the whole recapitulation (which is one reason why it makes sense that the recapitulation should be abbreviated, or otherwise it might unbalance the structure). To hold its own in such company, the minuet (in F major with an F minor trio) has to have an unusual density of interest: its first section, for instance, is a two-part conversation for first violin and viola, with an exchange of ideas half way through, and instead of the normal repetition the entire section is rewritten for second violin and cello, with new counterpoints from the other two. Then in the finale, which could not in the circumstances be wholly lighthearted, Haydn's wit turns to mock pedantry, and the four players are engaged in a tussle of hair-splitting arguments over the movement's minute substance of three quavers and a semitone step:

23 Haydn: Quartet in F minor op.55 no.2, fourth movement

This work owes its nickname of 'The Razor' to a story that Haydn promised he would give his best quartet for a decent pair of razors, and duly handed over op.55 no.2. Undoubtedly the anecdote is apocryphal, but the choice would have been entirely apt.

Of course, though, the other quartets of this set are not completely overshadowed in terms of richness of material, complexity of form, individuality and breadth. Haydn's quick-moving harmonic range has already been mentioned in connection with op.54 no.2, and it is a feature throughout; except in the E major quartet, where the possibilities are somewhat limited by so sharp a key: interestingly, Haydn never used it again. And by contrast with op.50, the sonata expositions of opp.54-5 delight in variety, once more like those of opp.9, 17 and 20, though usually it is the opening theme that is most important, often appearing again in the dominant and normally launching the development (however, the development of the first movement of op.55 no.1 surprises by seizing on a dotted idea introduced only in the last two bars of the exposition). As for formal complication, there is nothing to compare with the finale of the C major quartet – that bizarre work again – where a sort of fast rondo is interpolated into a sort of slow rondo. To find a parallel for that kind of experiment one has to go back to Haydn's earliest quartets, to the finale of op.1 no.4, or to the first movement of Mozart's E flat quartet κ171. Like the 'old-fashioned' pattern of the F minor quartet in this set, it is perhaps Haydn's reminder that even within the classical quartet style at its peak (and he must have been aware that in opp.54-5 he had created a set to stand beside Mozart's 'Haydn' quartets) there was room for something quite unexpected.

Haydn op. 64   Nothing of this kind is to be found in the second set of 'Tost' quartets, op.64, where instead Haydn looks back to the eminently classical wit of his op.33. And one may suspect he was doing so consciously. The keys of op.64 are those of op.33, and two of the quartets, the ones in C and G, revert to the old pattern of placing the minuet second, a pattern unused since op.33. Also, the B minor quartet op.64 no.2 opens as if it were going to be in the relative major, just as had op.33 no.1 in the same key, and generally there is a return to brevity in the sonata-form movements of op.64, after the comparatively extended and more richly endowed movements of opp.54-5. However, Haydn's manoeuvres within the basic expectations of sonata form continue to be more surprising while remaining wholly justified by the nature of his material, and though the same formal intelligence is at work in the symphonies of the same period, such as no.88 and the 'Oxford', Haydn can be more intimately clever in his quartets, more at home and more dangerous.

It would be difficult, indeed, to find a set of works to outdo op.64 in variousness of sonata form. In the first movement of the C major quartet, no.1, the surprise is the absence of surprise: almost half the exposition, a segment of 23 bars, is recapitulated without any change whatever, making a repeat more literal than in any Haydn quartet since opp.1 and 2. But, as always, there is a reason for this. The development ignores the primary material entirely, and so a wholesale repetition of it is not as redundant as otherwise it would be, especially when this material contains within itself a fair degree of development. However, the same cause can have different effects. In the first movements of the B minor and G major quartets the development also manages without the opening ideas, but instead of a straightforward recapitulation this stimulates one which develops almost at once.

Of course, Haydn had long been prone to include development in his reprises: more unusual is the presence of recapitulation within the development, yet this is what happens in the first movement of the B flat quartet, op.64 no.3. A four-bar tune in the dominant section of the exposition, heard in F major and then repeated in F minor, appears twice over in the development in B flat minor, and so there is no need for it to be heard again in the recapitulation, nor, since the minor mode is used, is there any risk that it will be taken as a proper reprise: both functions are adequately and unconfusedly served.

The D major quartet, no.5, also sports a tune which can be developed only by repetition in different circumstances, but this time the melody comes in the first part of the exposition, a soaring theme above a staccato accompaniment that has given this work its nickname of 'The Lark' (curiously, there is also an avian quartet in op.33, the C major piece known as 'The Bird', though there the name is owed to the finale, and to an analogy with beaks rather than wings):

24 Haydn: Quartet in D op.64 no.5, first movement

As in the B flat quartet, the tune appears in the development transposed a fifth down, in the subdominant, but this cannot count as a sufficient recapitulation of the movement's principal theme: it is development, albeit of an unusually stable character, and no more. However, when the recapitulation does arrive, with a repetition of the melody in D major, it is still not sufficient, since the eight-bar introduction is lopped off and so the tune feels hurried, not hanging in space as it had originally. This creates a problem. A firm repeat is needed, but if the tune were to come back again complete with its introduction there would be an excess of repetition. So Haydn, most ingeniously, provides instead a second half-reprise, speeded up like the first, but in a different way. Where the first recapitulation was hastened by arriving too precipitately, the second is accelerated by a new accompaniment that changes the crotchet to a quaver pulse, and the two together add up to a satisfactory balance for ex. 24.

This is just one example, perhaps the most developed, of a subtle control of pace that Haydn wields throughout op. 64 by his choice of note value and context. In the first movement of the B minor quartet an effect of acceleration is achieved by a change in successive bars from minims to crotchets to quavers to semiquavers. At the very end of the E flat quartet, no. 6, the rondo theme is teasingly held back by interpolated quaver rests. And in the slow movement of the same work the central section in the minor is brought forward not only by the first violin's flamboyance, stepping out of the ensemble to become suddenly a soloist, but also by the abrupt shift from quaver to semiquaver values.

The slow movements of op. 64, in contrast with the sonata-form movements, are very much structurally alike. All are rooted in the variation principle and at the same time in palindromic symmetry: the combination is common in Haydn, and is at the root of his double variation forms, where the alternation of material gives a rondo aspect, as in the finale of op. 33 no. 6 or the first movement of op. 55 no. 2. The F major Allegretto scherzando in op. 64 no. 1 is of this kind and has an ABABA structure; in the last four works of the set Haydn accentuates more the symmetry by putting the central portion into the minor, though in each case this middle section is a disguised variation of its frame. And once more the majority of the slow movements are adagios, four out of the six, all based on private and ornamented song for the leader.

In general, though, solo writing for the leader is not as prominent in op. 64 as in the earlier set of 'Tost' quartets, according with the less extravagant, more scherzando character of this group. In opp. 54-5, perhaps with a view to publication in Paris, Haydn had leaned some way towards the 'quatuor brillant', as practised by the indefatigable Cambini and others in France, though without going anything like as far as they did in making the string quartet a genre for solo violin with string trio accompaniment. But with his thoughts returning to op.33, in op.64 the load is more evenly shared. The slow movement of the C major quartet has the first theme progressively passed down the line as it recurs, from first to second violin, then to viola and finally to cello. And the perpetuum mobile that ends 'The Lark' has the leader relieved at intervals by the other three players in order to preserve a continuous semiquaver motion.

In this finale, as also in the other rondo that ends the quartet in E flat, Haydn capitalizes on the exquisite uncertainty inherent in the form, the uncertainty about what will follow each reappearance of the rondo theme, and about how each reappearance will be achieved. But just as the rondo forms of this period are permeated by sonata principles – in that of 'The Lark', for instance, a section in dramatic D minor has the function of development – so too the sonata finales of op.64 are infected by the rondo's innately humorous transitions into and out of the unknown. The last movement of the B flat quartet, no.3, is outstanding in this respect, outstanding too for its wit, and in rondo fashion the ten-bar opening comes back at the end to lead into a comic conclusion.

Even the minuets of op.64, though not called 'scherzos' as they were in op.33, have a new share in the generation of humour. The characteristic form of the minuet has a short first section followed by a longer second section which includes a repetition of the first, often at the end: this was a form to which Haydn had subscribed since the op.1 quartets. But in op.64 he introduces a twist, most strikingly in 'The Lark' but also in the first and last works of the collection. Instead of repeating the first section complete, or very nearly so, in the second, he breaks off part way through and only completes the phrase later, so introducing into the minuet his sonata technique of broken recapitulation. Also remarkable here, though not so new, is the thematic link between minuet and trio, which becomes all the more effective when, as again in 'The Lark' the trio is in the alternative mode. Altogether the minuets of op.64 are more substantial than those of any set since op.20, and they are also generally longer.

In 1791, the year after he wrote op.64, Haydn arrived for the first time in London, and some at least of these latest quartets were performed at the concerts he gave for Johann Peter Salomon: a London edition of the set refers to them as 'composed by Giuseppe

Haydn and performed under his direction, at Mr. Salomon's concerts'. So by this date the boundary between drawing room and concert hall, between quartet and symphony, was beginning to disappear in practice, just at the point when, in compositional terms, it had become most acutely felt, for 1790 was the date not only of Haydn's op. 64 but of Mozart's last two quartets. Naturally Haydn responded to this new challenge, to create music that would appeal to the less intensely committed concert public as well as to the 'dilettanti e conoscitori', and he wrote his next six quartets with an eye to their being performed at the 1794 Salomon concerts, while also keeping in view the still predominant use of quartets as private entertainment.

Haydn opp. 71, 74 Like the first set of 'Tost' quartets, this new group was published originally in two volumes as opp. 71 and 74, both carrying a dedication to one of Haydn's Viennese patrons, musical friends and fellow Freemasons, the Count Anton Apponyi.

But the truly public address of opp. 71 and 74 is clear right from the start of each work. Five of the quartets start with a loud and slow introduction, and the sixth, the G minor op. 74 no. 3, is an exception only because its opening theme is chordal and so vigorous that an introduction would be presumptuous. Obviously these beginnings would serve an immediate function in seizing the attention of a large audience, but equally, in binding the four instruments closely together from the start, they point an emphasis towards ensemble playing rather than solo and dialogue. There is, in other words, less of the musical conversation that had emerged in Haydn's quartets as early as op. 9 and become a major feature of the 'Tost' twelve, for a private conversation conducted in public is likely to be embarrassing. So Haydn does not here write for four individuals but for a group, and though in any chamber music we may be aware of two levels of communication, the composer's voice in the whole and the player's in each part, in these London quartets the latter has less scope and we hear more prominently, as in a symphony, the composer operating through his chosen medium.

This does not, of course, mean that opp. 71 and 74 are necessarily simpler than their predecessors in form or expression. For while expressive intensity or complexity is not easily measured or compared, the slow movement of the G minor quartet does sound a new note of gravity:

25 Haydn: Quartet in G minor op.74 no.3, second movement

This is the first slow movement in Haydn's quartets that does not start with a tune for one or other of the instruments, usually the first violin; and it cannot be considered either as an introduction to something else. It is whole and sufficient, and it owes its power not only to its searching harmonic movement but also to the absence of a soloist, hence to the absence of any outward display and of any other voice to distract from that of the composer. Indeed this can be demonstrated, for when this music is brought back at the end of the movement it has gained shows of brilliance from the leader, and though the harmony is further stretched, the feeling more extreme in its quality, its scope is reduced: tragedy becomes pathos.

Admittedly, this largo from op.74 no.3 is extreme. All the other slow movements of the set do open with tunes, often with tunes clear enough to serve as subjects for variations, and all the others too are closer tonally to the first movements they succeed: the first four are back in the dominant, used only twice in op.64 and not at all in opp.54-5, and the fifth is in the subdominant Haydn had favoured in his preceding three sets of quartets. The submediant relationship (a major third below) of the G minor quartet is new, and it appears also in the trios of the other two quartets of op.74, the C major having a trio in A and the F major one in D flat. In all three cases its effect is to enhance a turn inwards, to give a public face to a private circumstance.

In other respects, though, the slow movement of the G minor quartet is typical of the collection as a whole, and not least in its avoidance, at least at first, of a dominating first violin. By comparison with the 'Tost' quartets, particularly opp.54-5, or with the earlier sets written for Tomasini, opp.71 and 74 have less flamboyant and less exposed parts for the first violin, in accordance with their increased ensemble character. Naturally the leader still leads: Haydn could not gainsay such a basic precondition of the medium he had invented. But in place of the poetic individualist of many of the earlier slow movements, or the dazzling virtuoso of the allegros and prestos, opp.71 and 74 expect one who commands, one who does the same things as his companions but does them with more significance and élan. Again this must have something to do with the integration of the quartet in these works, but it may perhaps also reflect the different personality of Salomon, whose playing, with which Haydn will have been thoroughly familiar after his first eighteen months in England, one might expect to have influenced the nature of these quartets written for him. Certainly the new role of the leader is responsible for – or, less likely, the result of – a sturdier, more boldly featured kind of music, where the ideas are unusually compact and the strategems clearly set forth, involving less of Haydn's favourite indirection.

Once more the public purpose of the quartets may be at issue here, but the greater clarity of the structure does not make it inevitably less surprising, wayward and far-ranging. The first movement of the D major work, op.71 no.2, is a case in point. Its proportions are uncharacteristic and deceptive: an exposition of forty-eight bars is followed by a development of only eighteen, whereas in most Haydn quartets the ratio within sonata movements is of the order of 3:2 (op.64 had even introduced two movements in which the development was longer than the exposition, the finale of the B minor and the first allegretto of the E flat major). But the comparative brevity of the development in the D major allegro does not mean that Haydn's structural imagination is untypically relaxed, for the whole movement is filled with development, especially of the brilliant cascade of octave leaps which is the main feature of both primary and secondary material. Moreover, this continuous development makes the recapitulation notably irregular yet satisfying, even by the standards of late Haydn. As in many of Haydn's sonata movements from this period, there is a short, carefree closing tune at the end of the exposition, and since this becomes a principal subject of the development, it cannot be ignored in the recapitulation until the end: instead the 'second subject' proper is ignored (it was, in any event, a close relative of the first) and its function is taken over by the closing tune, which continues prominent in the coda, now joined by the octaves. Just as in so many earlier Haydn quartets, a completely readjusted recapitulation comes about partly because of the needs of the material, and also partly because Haydn cannot help looking, sometimes with humour and at other times with a more exploratory intent, at paths that he did not explore first time round. In this reprise it happens close to the beginning, where the octaves, instead of repeating the message of D major loud and clear, look through other possibilities: B flat, dominant seventh of F major, diminished seventh chord on F sharp, G minor. Any sonata recapitulation is a symmetrical pulling back of the shutters on landscapes of theme and harmony opened up in the exposition. Haydn's great skill is to preserve the symmetry while also straining his view in new directions, and to bring the experience of the whole past into the act of reprise.

The leaping octaves of the D major quartet have often been cited as an instance of Haydn's preoccupation with new textures in the 'Apponyi' set, but in fact the 'Tost' quartets had been just as well stocked with new effects, such as the brilliant runs of triads in the first movement of op. 55 no. 3 and elsewhere. Nor is it cause for comment that four decades of quartet writing should have made Haydn more inventive and not less. If the surface of opp. 71 and 74 does have a greater glamour, that is Haydn's showmanship, justified not only in historical terms, as a concession to conditions in London concert rooms of the 1790s, but also by the new sort of quartet composition that became possible here and afterwards, one that presupposes at least a fifth person in the room and addresses him quite separately but as pointedly as the other four. And if the new tone of the London quartets turns out to be not so very far from that of Mozart's op. 10 of a decade before, that is surely because Mozart was already imagining a pair of ears beyond his players, namely Haydn's.

Haydn's opp. 64, 71 and 74 were not the only quartets included in Salomon's programmes in the early 1790s: Pleyel's name appears, and so does that of Adalbert Gyrowetz (1763-1850), a Bohemian composer who was living in London at the time of Haydn's first visit. To judge from contemporary reports, Gyrowetz's quartets were as well liked as Haydn's – the comments on both are disappointingly rudimentary – but history has been unkind to one who, like Hoffstetter before him, was devoted to demonstrate that devotion constantly in his own works. Nor was he alone in this. His Bohemian contemporaries Franz Krommer (1759-1831) and Paul Wranitzky (1756-1808) similarly published dozens of quartets in the 1790s and early 1800s, and indeed the great quantity of publications in this period must indicate that quartets were still much in demand for amateur use. But, as with the quartets of Albrechtsberger and Michael

Haydn, the most well-intentioned composer cannot make the Haydn style work if he lacks Haydn's wit. Even Emanuel Aloys Förster (1748-1823), renowned for his bold imagination and claimed by Beethoven as a model of quartet composition (though probably only because Beethoven at the time was loath to admit his real father was Papa Haydn), even Förster was capable of little more than reproducing Haydn's mannerisms but not his structural substance: the F minor quartet from his op.16 (published in 1801) has a remarkably long finale, stretching to 433 bars of 2/4, but within it the pacing, development and ordering of events hold no surprise.

It must be admitted, though, that any final judgment on these contemporaries of Haydn's last years must wait until more of their music is available – and it is rather remarkable that, in an age when hundreds of less than astonishing Baroque sonatas can be had in good editions and recordings, the chamber music of the late eighteenth century remains so little explored. But of course there is a market among instrumentalists for flute sonatas by Loeillet, just as there is for clarinet quartets by Carl Stamitz, whereas the fund of string quartets is already sufficient, especially given the particular kind of music making expected from a string quartet. For because Haydn invented the genre with a built-in predisposition to musical conversation, no ensemble would think of going before the public until each player had thoroughly absorbed his part and deeply considered its possible relationships with the others. Nor is there any reason for the playing amateur to look beyond the familiar repertory, since it is within this that he will meet his fellows. The conservatism of the string quartet repertory is thus a corollary of the nature of the medium, and it is not at all surprising that, for instance, the quartets of Joseph Leopold Eybler (1765-1846) should have disappeared long since from active musical life, much as one's interest may warm to a man approved by both Haydn and Mozart, and one who restricted his quartet output in a prolific age to just two sets, the first, like Gyrowetz's op.2 and of course Mozart's op.10, dedicated to Haydn.

One set which has, like certain of Boccherini's quartets, enjoyed a continuing existence on the fringes of the repertory is that by Dittersdorf, another commendably modest producer in the genre. He published his six quartets in 1788, and though they are various in achievement – those in D and E flat are outstanding – they are all in an unusual three-movement form: sonata allegro, minuet and trio, finale. With no slow movement, Dittersdorf is obliged to find somewhere else in the scheme for softer contoured song-like material and variety of tonality, and in the E flat quartet he finds room in his first movement, where the dominant section of the exposition opens out for this:

26 Dittersdorf: Quartet in Eb, first movement

The key of G flat is the flattened submediant of the dominant: when this music returns in the recapitulation it is doubly brought home, to the submediant of the tonic, C major. In other respects, too, this work has an imaginative range rare outside the quartets of Haydn and Mozart. As for them so for Dittersdorf E flat is a strong, warm key, inhabited as proudly by the expansive first movement as by the brilliant finale, which ends with reiterated and variously scored affirmations of the tonic triad taking the leader to the very top of his eighteenth-century range. If, as Michael Kelly remembered, Dittersdorf played second fiddle to Haydn in the Viennese composers' quartet of the 1780s, this ending is an exultant admission of the older man's dominance.

That dominance was confirmed by Haydn's last completed set of quartets, the six op. 76 of 1797, written not for public concerts but once more for distinguished salons: the set was commissioned by another Viennese–Hungarian nobleman, Count Joseph Erdödy, who

Haydn op. 76

kept the quartets to his exclusive use until they were published in 1799, with a dedication to him. However, the experience of writing for a larger audience had left its mark. Perhaps Haydn was aware that the string quartet was entering a new phase, that it would no longer be the preserve of a small group of players and admirers: certainly op.76 follows on directly from opp.71 and 74, and makes all the more decisive the break with the 'sociable' quartets from op.33 to op.64.

For one thing, the slow movements are again of special weight. Five are in the particularly slow tempo of adagio or largo (no.2 in D minor has, exceptionally, an andante, but even this stands out for slowness in a work otherwise so hard-driven), and in the last two quartets of the set the slow movement is given extra gravity by being made to follow an allegretto, not a sonata allegro. In earlier opening slowish movements Haydn had used variation form, and he does so again here in the E flat quartet, no.6, but the D major quartet, no.5, begins with an original structure having some variation features within an ABAB form. Nor are the E flat variations exactly straightforward. As in the more famous set of variations in op.76 – those in the C major quartet, no.3, on the imperial paean Haydn had himself composed in the winter of 1796-7 (now the West German national anthem) – the tune is passed from instrument to instrument, and in the same order: first violin, second violin, cello, viola. But more important is the fact that the long second wing of the theme includes within it a re-examination of the first, rather in the manner of the minuets Haydn had been writing since op.64. These different formal peculiarities make the first movements of the D major and E flat quartets unusually searching, and the slow movements that follow have to be unusual as well if they are not to seem relaxed.

Haydn answers his own challenge by quite extraordinary means in the 'Fantasia' of op.76 no.6. It would be charming to believe, as has been suggested, that Haydn was here influenced by the fantasias of Purcell he might have perused in London, but this movement points as much forward as back, and perhaps here Haydn reached a point that Beethoven was to reach a generation later, a point where learned counterpoint and old modality have to come to the assistance of a tonal structure stretched to its limits. As so often, the most obvious sign of a new order is notational confusion. There are no sharps or flats in the key signature at the start of the movement, yet the key is clearly B major (more logically interpreted as C flat major, the flattened submediant), and in the latter half the key signature of B major is established. Also, as not infrequently in op.76, Haydn works with enharmonic change, moving gradually in the example below, almost one part at a time, from B flat to B, via its enharmonic equivalent of C flat:

27 Haydn: Quartet in E♭ op. 76 no. 6, second movement

The contrapuntal virtuosity that this movement later develops is to be found also in the finale of the same quartet, but it is uncommon in Haydn's quartets of this period: opp. 71 and 74 had been his most fugueless quartets since before op. 20, and the development section of the final rondo of op. 76 no. 4 in B flat makes as if for a fugue, which doubtless would have come at this point in op. 64, but then curiously and humorously both disappoints and fulfils expectations by having the instruments imitate one another not in fugal response but in simple monody:

28 Haydn: Quartet in Bb op. 76 no. 4, fourth movement

In other respects Haydn's musical wit is subdued in op. 76, as in opp. 71 and 74, by comparison with the 'Tost' quartets, and this again is in line with the change in the nature of the medium. The public quartet made possible an increase in expressive depth in the slow movement because an ensemble can say things which would be embarrassing or ridiculous if vouchsafed by four individuals, each of whom had to seem to be speaking for himself. But equally, the comparative atrophy of discourse in the later quartets makes it difficult to achieve the sort of humorous argument represented, for example, by the finale of op. 55 no. 2. Moreover, wit is a commodity more easily enjoyed when the company is small. There is, however, one finale in which Haydn brings back some of his earlier traps, and that is the final Allegro spirituoso of the E flat quartet, where the unwary are persuaded to accept a recapitulation in the subdominant as the real thing, then put to scorn before the true reprise begins.

More characteristic of the late Haydn is the Mozartian suavity of the final rondo of the B flat quartet, or the exultation of the presto finale to the D major, a sonata form which has no patience for repeats. And even more characteristic of op. 76 is a weightier kind of finale that opens in the minor and reaches the major only in the recapitulation: this is the pattern not only of the D minor quartet's finale but also of those to the quartets in G and C. Since op. 50 it had been Haydn's practice to bring minor-mode quartet sonata forms into the major well before the end, usually at the point when the secondary material is recapitulated, but he had not before taken up the opportunity of placing such a movement within a major-mode work. This pushes the centre of gravity towards the end of the work in a way Haydn had previously achieved by means of fugue, and the prominence of major and minor within a single movement can be used to achieve expressive extremes: in the G major quartet's finale, quite astonishingly, the deeply troubled first theme, announced in bald octaves, is changed with the change of mode into a piece of nonsense, making irony into parody.

This is one of several points in op. 76 where Haydn's intentions become puzzling in a way they have generally not been since op. 20, for his aim in op. 33 and its successors, thoroughly achieved, had been to create music which is as open as may be. The ending of op. 76 no. 1, though, may be devastating parody or it may just be a final dissolve of care, accepted as such by a less questioning age. And it is often, as here, when Haydn is most folk-like that he becomes most difficult to follow, for op. 76 includes peasant material with a directness unequalled in his quartets since the gypsy incursions into the finale of op. 17 no. 6: there is, for example, the drone fifth E–B that stares out baldly and leads a Hungarian dance in the middle of the first movement of the C major quartet.

But if such passages remain difficult to interpret as part of a coherent musical continuum, undoubtedly they have great force in creating the specific character that is so much a feature of the individual movements of op. 76, more than of any other set since op. 20, with the single exception of Mozart's op. 10. Some examples have already been mentioned: the solemn 'Fantasia' in the E flat quartet, the jubilant finale to the D major, the majestic variations of the 'Emperor' quartet in C major (though they are nettled out of complacency on occasion). It is as if Haydn had set out in this last set to explore as many possibilities of his invented genre as possible, to range in scoring from a solo violin (finale of no. 4) to a full ensemble in rich chords, to complete his odyssey of the minuet and point it firmly, in the G major example, towards the Beethoven scherzo, to bring to a peak the forms of sonata and variations and to search for new patterns, to look back on the quartet's past, a past created so much by him (the D minor quartet clearly remembers its predecessor from op. 9), and to look forward to late Beethoven and, again in the D minor quartet, late Schubert.

We are near the end of the longest chapter in the history of the *Haydn op. 77* string quartet. In 1799, the year op. 76 was published, Haydn began a new set for yet another Viennese patron, the young Prince Lobkowitz, who gave much support at this time to Haydn and to the young Beethoven. But only two quartets were completed, to be published in 1802 as op. 77, and when Haydn began a third, in or before 1803, he was able to complete only the middle movements, not the sonata structures, that would have required more concentrated effort. Within what he did complete, however, there is no sign of diminished power. These are again private quartets with a public voice, and as in op. 76 the slow movements are weighty, cast in the submediant (op. 77 no. 2, and also the unfinished op. 103, whose B flat andante would have been preceded by a first movement in D minor, since this is the key of the minuet) or flattened submediant (op. 77 no. 1). The E flat adagio in the G major op. 77 no. 1 is a solemn meditation comparable in its harmonic venturings with the slow movements of op. 74 no. 3 and op. 76 no. 6; the other two quartets have sets of variations that, like those that open the last two quartets of op. 76, stray some way from the normal regularity of the form, which had been represented for the last time in the imperial variations of op. 76 no. 3.

The sonata movements of op. 77 also show Haydn taking on fresh challenges. It had always been his general practice to make the recapitulation roughly equal in length to the exposition, but in the first movements of op. 77 he not only achieves these proportions exactly but also enlarges the development until it too is of the same length. In the majestic F major movement this entails extra discussion before the unmistakably heralded reprise, but in the march-like G major movement (both are in common time and at Allegro moderato pace) the development includes halfway through a recapitulation of secondary material, which then does not have to be heard again in the recapitulation proper, so leaving room for a full coda. The finales are again curious. That of the F major quartet has an introduction, which Haydn may have felt to be necessary after the D major slow movement, for here he reverts again to the 'minuet second' pattern last used in op. 64. And the G major presto starts with a peasant tune:

29 Haydn: Quartet in G op. 77 no. 1, fourth movement

The notes here are those of the D major scale, but the sharpened C serves only as an appoggiatura and the theme is unquestionably in G major, like the not dissimilar folk melody that starts the G major quartet op.76 no.1 – and even more than in that case the tune provides motifs for intensive development, so that something seemingly naive suddenly becomes material for fierce argument. The theme's closeness to the dominant, however, allows Haydn to repeat it as his secondary material, transposed up an octave and with new harmony to adjust its meaning.

There remain only the minuets, which in op.77 are most remarkable of all (that of op.103 is not so unusual in its basic nature, only in its harmonic and expressive intensity). Both are long; both have trios in the flattened submediant; and both bound with the vigour of a scherzo by Beethoven, or – a closer parallel, given the emphatic ostinatos and the utterly contrasted, subdued trios – one by Bruckner. This is not, of course, to suggest that the elderly Haydn had presentiments of Bruckner's symphonies, any more than that Bruckner was influenced by op.77, or Schubert by op.76 no.2 or Beethoven by op.76 no.6. It is rather that tonal music contains within itself favoured pathways of progress which different composers may travel at different times: the point that Bruckner reached in the 1870s had already been visited in 1799 by Haydn in the last two of his sixty-seven completed quartets, at the end of a journey that had begun with the birth of the classical style and now concluded with forays into that style's furthest possible extensions. Any subsequent quartets, unless they were to reinvent the genre entirely, would have to be obliged to at least one of the several different Haydns who had opened so much territory in the course of four decades.

Development and Recapitulation
1800-1826

No excuse is needed for making this section serve two functions in the first movement of the quartet's history, since examples have already been given of Haydn's confusion of the two, his placing of development within the recapitulation and, more rarely, recapitulation within the development. Moreover, the period under review, roughly the first quarter of the nineteenth century, was one in which the creation of new string quartets took place in a culture increasingly aware of past achievements in the genre. The life of the quartet was becoming centred in its history. In 1801 Pleyel published his *Collection complette des quatuors d'Haydn dédiée au Premier Consul Bonaparte*, including all the genuine quartets up to op. 76 (except 'op. 0') and also giving respectability to the cuckoos in opp. 1 and 2, and to 'op. 3'. Like all previous quartet publications, this printed the works in parts, for the use of players, but Pleyel soon followed it with an edition of miniature scores in ten volumes, suggesting the growth of an audience wishing to study the music at home or follow it at the newly developing quartet concerts. This new attitude to the string quartet as an object of study, coupled with the already mentioned scrupulousness of publicly performing ensembles in requiring long periods of preparation, would help to circumscribe the repertory. Thanks to Pleyel, performers and listeners became aware of the abundance of masterpieces already composed in the medium, and if more were needed they could be drawn from existing celebrated sources: Haydn's 'London' symphonies, six of which were published by Pleyel in quartet versions in the 1790s, or Mozart's operas, which similarly were regarded as fair game by publishers. There was even an antiquarian revival of early quartets other than Haydn's: six by Gassmann, for instance, were published in 1804, thirty years after the composer's death, and lengthily, seriously reviewed in the leading musical periodical of the day, the *Allgemeine Musikalische Zeitung*.

This overloading of the present with the past, nowadays familiar in all the arts, seems to have affected the string quartet first, partly because its whole development had been swift, so that its history could be easily comprehended (after all, elderly players who welcomed Pleyel's 1801 edition might in their youth have greeted the publications of Chevardière and Hummel), partly because of the inherent conservatism of anything stable enough to be called a medium, and partly because the repertory was already so well stocked, with nearly a hundred works by Haydn and Mozart alone. The situation was one to make any young composer think long and hard before embarking himself on quartet composition, and it is not surprising that Ludwig van Beethoven (1770-1827), the rising star of Bonn ambitious to shine in the musical capital of Vienna, should have prepared his début in the quartet, as in the symphony, with great care. After his arrival in Vienna in 1792 he concentrated on the lesser genres of the piano trio and the string trio, and only in 1798 began the set of quartets which he finished in 1800 and published the next year, his op.18.

Beethoven op. 18

Beethoven was thus working on his first quartets while Haydn was composing his last, and Robbins Landon has suggested that the older master's failure to complete his 'Lobkowitz' sextet was a withdrawal in the face of his pupil's achievement (one need feel no sorrow for the frustrated patron: he became the dedicatee of Beethoven's op.18, his op.74 quartet and other major works). Certainly it does not seem realistic to blame failing creative powers when after op.77 Haydn wrote *The Seasons* and the *Harmoniemesse*. But if Haydn was overawed by Beethoven's early quartets, Beethoven was far from blind to what had been done in the medium by his two great predecessors, so that within op.18 the development of a new voice – the first authentic new quartet voice for thirty years – is itself intimately connected with aspects of reprise.

Yet one should be cautious about pointing influences, for if Haydn can contain foreshadowings of Bruckner, then certainly Beethoven can include remembrances of Haydn and Mozart without these having been copied as such. For example, the use of short answering phrases at the start of the F major quartet, no.1, and at that of the G major quartet, no.2, is distinctly Haydnish, but it is also a perfectly natural way of setting forth elementary material, and in neither case is the consequent movement under Haydn's shadow: Beethoven is far from the imitation practised by so many composers from Albrechtsberger to Gyrowetz. For even though, like those followers, he makes little attempt to emulate Haydn's adjustment of the recapitulation, he introduces his own kinds of structural complication, not least a persistent binding of a movement with a small motif (notably in the first movement of the F major quartet) and a great expansion, even by comparison with Haydn's last quartets, of the variety of material to be exposed. And, significantly, the one movement that does toy with the reprise in something like Haydn's manner, the opening allegro of the G major quartet, is also one in which Beethoven's own personality comes most forcefully to the surface, the recapitulation being summoned by an insistent monotone figure and then entwined in new counterpoints:

30 Beethoven: Quartet in G op. 18 no. 2, first movement

This is something very different from Haydn, for whom the reprise is a humorous necessity, for in Beethoven's example it is transformed, newly urgent, helping to make the sonata not a return journey but a voyage of discovery.

As one might expect, this new, quintessentially Beethovenian conception brings a new importance to the coda, of which there are notable examples in all the outer movements of the first four quartets. In the C minor quartet, no. 4, for instance, the coda restores the minor mode after the recapitulation has, following a common convention, brightened into the major at the point where the secondary material returns. Unlike other recent first movements with minor endings (Mozart's K421 in D minor and Haydn's op. 76 no. 2), the already troubled nature of the key is exacerbated by the fact that the music has once broken through into the major. Hence the uncertain atmosphere in which the next, uncertain movement begins, bearing the title 'scherzo' but in fact turning out to be a C major Andante scherzoso in fugal sonata form, a piece hanging in the air between different movement types, different means of construction. Then comes the real scherzo, though it is called a minuet, in the proper key of C minor, but moving into distant keys as Beethoven's scherzos already do, and containing a soft trio in A flat.

This use of third-related keys is again a feature of Beethoven's op. 18 even more than of Haydn's opp. 76 and 77, and it is specially prominent in the D major quartet, no. 3. Here the slow movement is an andante in the flattened submediant, B flat, and third relations are present in all the other movements. The first limb of the scherzo modulates not to the dominant but to its relative minor, F sharp minor, bringing a quite particular feeling of constraint. The finale includes an episode in F, recapitulated in B flat again, and in the first movement there is a similar phenomenon, though more prominently displayed and more powerful in its effects. Instead of settling in the dominant for a clear tune – as, Mozart-fashion, sonata movements in op. 18 generally do – this one swings on to its flattened mediant, C major, and there provides a theme. This is duly recapitulated in F, but there are still structural debts to be repaid, and in the coda, within a context of G minor, it appears again in E flat, the flattened submediant of the subdominant to balance the flattened mediant of the dominant. Once more, then, this is a coda of crucial function, by no means just a re-emphasis of the tonic and the primary material as the coda usually is in Haydn.

But the favouring of the third relation, though heightened in this D major quartet, is more a feature of the time, already more than adumbrated in quartets that Haydn and Dittersdorf had written in the preceding decade or so. It is as if the new sonata style were recapitulating the history of western music. When that style was new, in the 1750s and 1760s, the fifth was the only possible relationship between points of stability: events within a movement had to take place in the tonic or the dominant, anything else being transitory, and movements within a work had to be similarly related. Then the fourth became a new structural consonance, to be followed by the third, making possible in Beethoven's op. 18 quartets a much more varied and richly expressed exposition than in any set of Haydn or Mozart.

To some extent, though, this was also a matter of personality. Beethoven was the first quartet composer to enter the medium in the full knowledge of his inheritance, and of what was expected of a quartet in the 1790s – something very different from what was expected in the 1770s, when Mozart began. So although it is risky and anyway unrewarding to speculate about specific influences, even in the case of the A major quartet, no.5, which has often been seen as an answer to Mozart's κ464 in the same key, certainly Beethoven felt pressed to produce only his best, and all of his best. Also, unlike Haydn and Mozart, he appears not to have served as a quartet performer, his own instrument, after his arrival in Vienna, being exclusively the piano. Thus the quartet was for him what it has been for most later composers: a medium apart, and richly endowed. It is no wonder, then, that he should have saved for it sonata designs as broadly conceived as that of the B flat quartet, no.6, with its spacious, beautiful lead back out of development into reprise, and with its range of material from accompanied melody to sforzando chords of the kind that appear in all these quartets and have sometimes been criticized as 'orchestral', though in fact Beethoven's use of such effects is too fine and occasional for the orchestra: the bigness is all bigness of substance, not means.

It is evident, too, as much in the make-up of whole works as of single movements. In the first four quartets of op.18 Beethoven places the slow movement second, following Haydn's general practice from op.50 onwards, but he plays with the balance of the quartet by altering the weight of this second movement: first an adagio, then an adagio which incorporates an allegro digression on a little motif, then an andante, then the scherzoso sonata fugue of the C minor quartet. The A major quartet places its andante D major variations third, and in this respect indeed does follow κ464. The B flat work goes back to the other pattern, and at last attains the sober pathos of Haydn's quartet adagios not once but twice, first in its E flat second movement, then again at the start of the finale, which Beethoven heads 'La malinconia' and asks to be played 'with the greatest delicacy'. Like the slow movement of the G major quartet, this remarkable movement is a dialogue of adagio and allegro but in an altogether more searching manner, the chromatic 'La malinconia' appearing briefly twice within the main body of the movement as well as at the start, seeming to be both the natural spur and the inevitable consequence of the fast music's racing gaiety.

With this first collection Beethoven had changed the nature of the quartet, quite apart from his response to changes that were becoming almost inevitable, and he had also changed the sound. There are numerous passages where he engages the two violins as partners, but more commonly he associates the second violin with the viola as an alto instrument, as Haydn had done on occasion, notably in the first movements of op.54 no.3 and of the 'Lark'. This, added to Beethoven's antipathy towards virtuosity except in the piano music he was to play himself, makes for a quartet sound weighted in the centre, a centre across which, as in the first movements of the F major and B flat quartets, it may be possible for first violin and cello to exchange ideas in a resurgence of the conversational mode that had gone into the shade in the public quartets Haydn had produced in the 1790s. And that sort of dialogue, like the new formal possibilities that Beethoven begins to investigate here, was to remain and develop beyond all recognition in the quartets he was to write in the 1820s. He had approached the quartet medium only after intensive preparation. He left it, after this first encounter, with every indication that it would be the vessel of his most exploratory thoughts.

But such a special regard for the quartet was by no means peculiar to Beethoven at this time, when indeed we find the earliest expressions of that reverence the medium has continued to enjoy. Curiously enough, it is Cambini, composer of quartets by the dozen, who provides the most vivid evidence of a new attitude in an article published in the *Allgemeine Musikalische Zeitung* in 1804. He starts out from the view that 'if music should not stir up or soothe the emotions, then it should at least draw our attention to itself and so divert us from the cares and griefs of our everyday life'. After giving Haydn's symphonies as examples of works that achieve this, he suggests that chamber music is even more likely to do so, since it is heard in smaller halls and played by smaller ensembles. However, 'perfect performance of this sort of music is as difficult as it is rare', for to perform a 'true' quartet – by which Cambini means a quartet 'in dialogue' – requires exhaustive rehearsal both by each player alone and by the quartet as a whole. Cambini then recommends such dedicated quartet playing as the highest form of musical life.

But what were the works that were to justify this new approach to music as an object of contemplation, study and practice? Cambini refers only to the past, when together with Manfredi, Nardini and Boccherini he played Haydn's opp.9, 17 and 20, and contemporary quartets by the last-named of the ensemble. Indeed it is possible that in 1804, with Haydn no longer active and Boccherini on the threshold of death, the string quartet repertory might have been about to freeze, just as the operatic repertory froze in the 1920s, admitting no new works and gradually winnowing the accepted body of master-pieces. Of course this did very nearly happen: still today the quartets

Beethoven op. 59: the 'Razumovskys'

of Haydn and Mozart must account for a good half of the living repertory. But the gates were not completely shut to newcomers, and for that the credit must go to Beethoven, who in 1805 began the set of three quartets op.59 he dedicated to the Russian ambassador to Vienna, Count Andrey Kyrillovich Razumovsky.

Beethoven's style had changed massively since his last string quartets, the op.18 set and the unhelpful arrangement in F of the Piano Sonata in E, op.14 no.1 (this arrangement dates from 1802). In between had come, most importantly, the 'Eroica' Symphony, which had brought into music a new largeness and unity that Beethoven quickly felt impelled to explore not only in further symphonies but also in opera (the first version of *Fidelio* dates from 1804-5) and concerto. On the surface, the string quartet was a much less obvious medium for the new manner, one of distinctly public rhetoric, but in fact Beethoven seems to have relished the challenge of using his new grand manner in an intimate medium: the 'Razumovsky' quartets are notably less orchestral in sound than those of op.18, less dependent on brusque sforzando effects and more richly filled with textural inventions which, though quite new, are ideally suited to the quartet. There may also have been external reasons for his return to the quartet. In the winter of 1804-5 Ignaz Schuppanzigh, already thoroughly familiar to Beethoven as the outstanding quartet leader in the Vienna of his day, began to give subscription concerts of quartets, and in 1808, the year of the publication of the 'Razumovsky' quartets, Schuppanzigh's ensemble was to receive a salaried appointment to the household of Count Razumovsky. It was certainly for Schuppanzigh that Beethoven wrote op.59 (as he did all his later quartets), and in doing so he was writing for a violinist who, unlike those for whom Haydn had composed, was primarily a quartet player. Thus op.59 presumes not merely brilliance, though on occasion the three works do require that of the first violin, but also dedication and understanding.

On the basis of that dedication and understanding, Beethoven was able to create a set of works more radically new in matters of form and feeling than his contemporary symphonies and concertos. The first movement of the first 'Razumovsky' quartet, in F major, is famously the first sonata allegro to dispense with the customary repeat of the exposition, but this is no gratuitous innovation. On a simple level it is necessary because the movement is already amply long enough without any repetition, extending for nearly four hundred bars in common time. On a more deeply structural level, the absence of repeats makes the movement a single broad sweep, since the beginning is now only a beginning, never to be rediscovered (the momentary rediscovery at the start of the development merely emphasizes the fact that a repeat is to be expected here but not granted). The new formal balance also throws greater weight into the development, which here is half as long again as the already well developed exposition. Finally, repetition of the first section simply becomes less essential when a composer can be sure of reaching, as Beethoven here was sure, an audience of cognoscenti.

The increased size of the first movement of op.59 no.1 is fully characteristic of the set: all three works last for forty minutes or so, compared with the twenty or thirty of Haydn's and Mozart's quartets (and indeed Beethoven's own op.18). Whatever may have been the performing practice at the time, and on this subject the records are too piecemeal to admit of any general conclusions, the difference in length is crucial today. A Haydn or a Mozart quartet needs something else to complete half of a recital programme or the whole of a disc, whereas one of Beethoven's 'Razumovsky' quartets can legitimately stand alone. The works have attained a size where they become independent, self-sufficient entities.

But of course this is not just a matter of duration. The singleness of each of these quartets is guaranteed, as in the fifth symphony that succeeded them, by a sustained psychological impetus throughout the four movements, an impetus assisted by actual joins: in both the F major quartet and the C major (no.3) the third movement leads directly into the finale. In the F major quartet this is not so very unusual, since the third movement is an adagio and slow movements had often been connected directly to finales, but in the C major quartet Beethoven links the minuet to the last movement, just as on a broader scale he was to combine scherzo and finale in the fifth symphony. The effect, both in the quartets and in the symphony, is to give the finale the force of a recapitulation, which tonally, of course, it necessarily is, so that the principles of sonata form begin to apply not just to each movement but to the four-movement cycle as a whole.

Such a conception requires the first movement to be newly spacious, opening a musical arena sufficient for the whole work, which Beethoven achieves in the first 'Razumovsky' by beginning with an F major that remains without its feet on the ground throughout the introduction and elaboration of the first theme:

31 Beethoven: Quartet in F op. 59 no. 1, first movement

Here Beethoven continues the answering of first violin and cello that had been a feature of his op.18 textures, and more generally the 'Razumovsky' quartets are very much dialogue quartets, whether the instruments speak in terms of crazily humorous interchange, as in the second movement of the F major, or grave concurrence, as in the same work's adagio. The nearest parallel is with the 'Prussian' quartets of Mozart, though the concertante imperative is not for Beethoven the embarrassment it was for Mozart. Instead his quartet writing positively thrives on discourse, on solo melody and on pressing the first violin, in particular, to the limits of its power, for the bigness of the 'Razumovsky' quartets depends not only on harmonic breadth and sheer size but also on the scope that is made available to four distinct personalities who are prepared to argue or sink their differences. Again this is clear in the first movement of the F major, where the main material is handled by the cello and the first violin, as in the example above, but where the fugal episode in the centre of the development is led by the second violin and the viola. The introduction of a new kind of musical structure comes with the introduction also of new principal voices, the one justifying the other. And at the same time Beethoven suggests that only in a fugal texture will a real quartet counterpoint be possible.

It is interesting, therefore, that part of his preparatory work for the 'Razumovsky' quartets involved making quartet arrangements of fugues by Haydn, Fux and Muffat, and that he had already, at the time of op.18, written out a copy of Mozart's quartet with a sonata-fugue finale, κ387. Moreover, since Albrechtsberger was still alive and composing actively, the tradition of writing fugues for string quartet was far from dead: Beethoven himself had contributed to it while he was a pupil of Albrechtsberger in the mid-1790s, from which period survive preludes and fugues by him in F and in C. He would also have been familiar with quartets incorporating fugues by his acquaintance of the time Antoine Reicha (1770-1836), such as the latter's *Quatuor scientifique* (?1806) in three fugal movements. Fugue, though, as has been remarked before, is essentially alien to the quartet, since it implies several voices saying the same thing whereas the quartet is at its greatest concerned with four voices saying different things, and it is significant that, after opening the possibility in the first movement of op.59, Beethoven has no recourse to fugal writing until the show-fugue in the last movement of the set, which is really a canonic sonata.

And this is only one way in which Beethoven goes beyond unifying each work and asks us to accept op.59 as itself a totality, a triptych. It was, after all, by this stage unusual for him to publish instrumental works in batches, and it is hardly enough to suppose that he was merely following the convention of such contemporaries as Krommer and Wranitzky: he could easily have broken with them in this, as in so much else. No, the publication of the 'Razumovsky' quartets as a set must suggest that the vast plane brought into sight by ex.31 will not have been completely covered until the last bar of the C major quartet.

Starting this cycle, the first movement of the F major quartet is so large and fully developed (as in many Beethoven sonata allegros, the development continues in the coda) that it could not possibly be followed by a slow movement of any gravity – and Beethoven is planning for this quartet an adagio of great expressive warmth in F minor. So the two are separated, but not by a straightforward scherzo, which would not fit into the enlarged scale of the work: instead there is an allegretto of scherzo character but sonata form, cast in B flat and avoiding, like the first movement and indeed the adagio, any literal repetition. Coming after all this, the sonata-form finale is too trivial to be an adequate conclusion, dancing as it does to one of the 'thèmes russes' that Beethoven introduced in tactful homage to his patron.

The second quartet, in E minor, answers its predecessor by contrast. Where the earlier work had done away with repeats, this one repeats as much as possible: not just the exposition in the first movement but the second half as well (thus enforcing a practice that was starting to die out), and not just the usual da capo in the scherzo but a further repetition of both parts to make an ABABA pattern. Also, where the initial allegro of the F major quartet had been well settled in its expansiveness, like that of the 'Eroica' Symphony, in the E minor quartet there is a furious driving force, and, as in the C minor quartet of op. 18, the taut minor mode is decisively reaffirmed in the coda after a recapitulation that turns into the major. This time the work's next stratagem can and must be a slow movement, but the E major adagio here has none of the personal grief of its F minor counterpart in the previous quartet. Indeed, it is tempting to give credence to the old tradition that Beethoven wrote this music in contemplation of the night sky and of the harmony of the spheres, whereas in the margin of the manuscript of the F minor adagio he had written: 'A weeping willow or an acacia tree over my brother's grave', referring to the other Ludwig, born a year before the composer and dead at the age of a week.

Instead of gracing the finale, the 'thème russe' of the E minor quartet comes in the E major trio, which it makes into a parody of the 'quatuor concertant', the absurdly jaunty tune passed from one instrument to another. The finale can then unfold on more powerful lines, as a sonata rondo with the curious feature that the rondo theme is in C major, which thus has to swing repeatedly and forcefully into E minor. This movement, then, is looking forward to the key of the next quartet, just as the first movement of the E minor, by involving F major as a significant sphere of interest, looks back to the key of the last.

However, like Mozart in his C major quartet k465, Beethoven withholds this most innocuous of keys at the opening of the work. In fact there is a double delay, because the introduction, equally as deserving as Mozart's of the nickname 'Dissonance', is followed by an allegro which starts with a further detour before what is unmistakably the first theme, in the most unsophisticated C major, starts on its way. And in complete contrast with the first movement of the F major quartet, which begins on the fringe of its key and is very ready to leave it for the dominant, here the music is reluctant to leave its home tonality. Indeed, the whole work has the greater stability and simplicity proper to a finale: it even has a minuet in third place, though this is an awkwardly prodded dance.

The second movement of the C major quartet, like that of the F major, is unconventional in form, the point of departure this time being the variation set. Since the two earlier quartets have staked claims to the polar extremes of the adagio – the subjective and the objective, the pathetic and the solemn – this movement is an andante, and in its meandering into and out of A minor, as also in its plucked cello drones, it seems to supply the need for Russian folk material satisfied by the finale of the F major quartet and the trio of the E minor. The work moves once more into the minor in the coda to the minuet and trio, which is in C minor, the key that Beethoven had used for his secondary material, instead of the more normal A flat major, in the F minor adagio of the first 'Razumovsky'. Of course this is only one of the tonal linkages across the set: for instance, G major is the secondary key for both the C major of the third quartet and the E minor of the second. And if the last 'Razumovsky' ends with a long, canonically reinforced celebration of C major, that just serves to make it the dominant preparation for our next experience of the F major.

Beethoven's op. 59 quartets altered the medium as profoundly as had Haydn's op. 33 or his opp. 71-4, but there was no great contemporary to be impressed into emulation. For though the weight and scale of these works suggests that they were written at least as much for public as for private edification, the growing vogue for quartet concerts generally stirred composers to make their quartets concerto-like rather than symphonic, following the tradition of the Parisian 'quatuor brillant' rather than that of the 'Razumovsky' quartets. Naturally this tendency was particularly pronounced among composers who were themselves violinists, and indeed it was violinist–composers who were the chief composers of quartets in the early nineteenth century: men like Pierre Rode (1774-1830), Andreas Jakob Romberg (1767-1821) and, most productive of all, Louis Spohr (1784-1859), who, in an active career of half a century, published thirty-six quartets. Spohr distinguished some of his works specifically as 'quatuors brillants', and in them the lower three members of the ensemble do no more than support the leader's bel canto:

32 Spohr: Quartet in D minor op. 11, second movement

However, this kind of writing is found also in Spohr's other quartets. Nor was it likely to be otherwise, given the decisive changes in musical culture around the turn of the century.

Since string quartets were still being published in parts for performance, one must assume that there continued to be a demand from the amateurs and connoisseurs who fifty years before had been served by early Haydn and Boccherini. But music of the sort just quoted was obviously not written in the first place for the domestic musician. Rather the vogue for quartet concerts had made the genre hardly more than a branch of the concerto, for generally such concerts were not given by regular ensembles (Schuppanzigh's quartet seems to have been rather unusual) but by touring virtuosos who would hire a string trio to accompany them. Alternatively the whole quartet might be obliged to take on the role of concerto soloist, as in Spohr's A minor concerto for string quartet and orchestra (1845) or in his four double quartets, which are effectively concertos for one string quartet accompanied by another.

It was against the background of such a trivialization of the medium that Beethoven was, in his 'Razumovsky' quartets and their successors, insisting that the string quartet was still the appropriate medium for the most challenging musical thinking. And though nowadays his works stand virtually alone in the repertory to represent the first two decades of the nineteenth century, at the time they stood in the face of a flood of fripperies. No doubt it was to distinguish himself from *Beethoven opp.* what the quartet had become that he called his F minor work op. 95 *74, 95* (1810) 'quartetto serioso', though this has had the unfortunate effect of suggesting that its immediate predecessor, op. 74 in E flat (1809), does not have to be taken so seriously.

In fact the ostentatious seriousness of op. 95 is implicit in op. 74, and the two works together inhabit a quartet style quite different from that of the 'Razumovsky' triptych. They are distinctly shorter, returning to

Haydn dimensions, and they take a further step, quite against the spirit of the times, in making the quartet a convening of different equals. In the first movement of op.74 this makes possible an exhilarating display of wholly new textures: not just the pizzicato arpeggios which have given the quartet its nickname of the 'Harp', but also bowed scales and arpeggios running from one instrument to another and occasionally filling the whole space. And in the adagio that follows attention is often drawn to the fact that four individuals are involved, with quite separate things to say even if harmonically they are happy to concur:

33 Beethoven: Quartet in Eb op. 74, second movement

The scherzo is once more in ABABA form, with the A sections in C minor and the B in C major, and as in op.59 no.3 it leads directly into the finale, a perfectly well behaved (though again texturally diverse) allegretto set of variations in E flat.

The shock of this, coming after the hard-driven presto scherzo, is almost as great as that of the blithe turn from F minor into F major towards the end of the finale of op.95. But, to be sure, the later quartet is formally, harmonically and emotionally much more troubled and searching than the 'Harp'. As in the F major 'Razumovsky' the first movement dispenses with an exposition repeat, but its scale is very much more compact, and can be so because the basic material is so briefly and brusquely stated: a flurry around the tonic that is present or implied in most bars of the movement, and which, repeated at the end, makes it clear that none of the problems have yet been solved. An inward adagio after this would seem glib, and so Beethoven provides instead an exploratory allegretto joined to another rough-rhythmed ABABA scherzo. There is then, for the first time in the work, a real slow tempo for the Larghetto espressivo, but this lasts for only seven bars before hastening into the Allegretto agitato of the finale.

These two quartets might be construed as a homage to Haydn, who had died shortly before Beethoven began work on op.74. The key of E flat, common in Beethoven but not used by him before in a quartet, was the one that Haydn had favoured above all others in his quartets, and there was also a precedent in Haydn for a profound A flat slow movement in an E flat quartet: Haydn had done that in op.20 no.1, a work which Beethoven had copied out in the middle 1790s. F minor, too, was a key honoured in quartets by Haydn. But if any tribute was intended, it takes place entirely on Beethoven's terms. The individualizing of the four instruments is his, and so too is the combining of the four movements, which in the F minor quartet is carried to a new pitch of musical and psychological intensity. It is not by chance that the finale reinterprets many of the fundamental motifs and harmonic pulls of the first movement, becoming another tense allegro which can only be brought to an end by a sudden switch into something completely different. And since Beethoven's immediate experience of quartet playing was provided by Schuppanzigh, not Spohr, he could feel some confidence that care and consideration would go into solving the interpretative problem he thus created.

It would require a prose as contrapuntally replete as Beethoven's opp.74 and 95 to give an adequate description of string quartet composition around 1810. While Beethoven was removing himself from history – continuing a historical development, certainly, but treating the medium with a seriousness accorded by none of his contemporaries – Spohr was writing his concerto quartets and the amateur was being served by the similarly abundant publications of Georges Onslow (1784-1853), a well born Auvergnois whose father was the exiled son of an English earl, and who was stimulated to embark on a musical career precisely because of his friendship with a group of amateurs interested in chamber music. There was also the boy Franz Schubert (1797-1828), whose family might well have provided Onslow with custom had they not included one who could himself supplement the household repertory of Haydn and Mozart.

Franz played the viola in the Schubert quartet, with his two brothers as violinists and his father providing a somewhat less than virtuoso cello: hence the caution of the parts he wrote for this instrument in his domestic quartets of c. 1810 to 1814. It has to be admitted, too, that the compositional expertise displayed in these quartets is often limited. The earliest of them to survive is a curious hotch-potch in five movements, of which the first, beginning in C minor, is effectively an introduction to the G minor second, which knows little of sonata form. Then comes a muted minuet in F with a trio in C, a little andante in B flat and a presto in the same key, again much more a patchwork than a sonata. Now any young composer capable of writing parts for four string instruments ought also to have been capable of copying the groundplan of a Haydn or Mozart sonata allegro, particularly when he was in daily contact with their music. That Schubert departed from convention, however gauchely, is therefore to be interpreted not as ignorance but rather as a willingness, even a compulsion to look for other ways of making music work.

Those other ways were necessary because Schubert, like Haydn fifteen years before and Beethoven at the same time, was giving new importance to subsidiary poles other than the dominant. The submediant is the key of the scherzo in Beethoven's op. 74 and of the slow movement and the trio in his op. 95, and similarly third-related keys play important roles in many of Schubert's early quartets, though so can more distant relations. The first movement of the D major quartet D94, for instance, starts to recapitulate in C major. There are also larger structural oddities. In the outer movements of another quartet in D, D74, Schubert essays a kind of sonata form in which there is no development and in which the second half moves back from dominant to tonic just as the first had travelled in the opposite direction (this is roughly the scheme too of the G minor quartet D173 of 1815). Another unorthodox but effective movement is the andante of the B flat quartet D112, which starts in G minor then gradually but effortfully works its way round to F major for a sunny new theme. From that point a 'recapitulation' in D minor is easily achieved, and the movement continues at this level, transplanting the F major music into E flat, and then moving through B flat back to G minor and a final repeat of the opening.

Schubert's early quartets thus show him attacking the interrelated problems of new harmonic relationships and new forms, but as yet there is always some awkwardness or compromise in his solutions, and it is not surprising that the most successful movements are the most conventional ones, including most of the minuets and many of the finales. For the young Schubert was well able to imitate his predecessors when he wanted to (and perhaps to complement them, since it is just possible that the two B flat allegros of D68 were intended to do duty for the missing movements of Haydn's op. 103). In later life he became aware that his youthful quartets were not wholly satisfactory, and in July 1824 he wrote to his brother Ferdinand: 'it would be better if you stuck to other quartets than mine, for there is nothing about them, except that perhaps they please you, who are pleased with anything of mine'. Indeed, by the date of this letter Schubert was well placed to comprehend the deficiencies of his early efforts, since in February and March that year he had written two quartets on an utterly different level, the A minor and the D minor.

Schubert 'Quartettsatz'

The majestic stepping stone to the mature Schubert quartet is the Allegro assai in C minor of 1820 (often known as 'Quartettsatz'), first movement of a quartet that remained, with the B minor symphony of two years later, unfinished. Like many of the opening movements in the early quartets, the C minor allegro is expansive and varied in its choice of material: exposition and recapitulation are very much longer than development, quite against the tendency in Haydn's and Beethoven's quartets. But now the length and the diverseness are balanced by a unity of motif and expression, and Schubert's eccentricities become eccentricities of substance. For instance, the longest melody in the quartet begins at a point when Schubert moves from C minor to A flat (sharing a common secondary key with C minor), and this melody later, in B flat, starts the recapitulation; the home C minor, and with it the initial material, are withheld until the very end of the movement. Schubert thus keeps the argument in the air up to the last bars, and shows himself sharing Beethoven's need to keep the recapitulation from being a pat restatement: Beethoven does so by generally continuing his development in a lengthy coda, Schubert by holding his most pointed reprise until the end.

One reason why the C minor quartet movement seems wholly self-sufficient may be that it opens at the pace of a scherzo, with its rippling semiquavers, and that its content is that of a slow movement, while the delayed recapitulation comes with all the closing force of a finale, so that all the conventional movements are within it represented. Schubert did begin a second movement, an andante in the allegro's main subsidiary key of A flat, but this he abandoned at an early stage, and did not return to quartet composition until the early spring of 1824, when he wrote his first two complete and mature quartets. As with Beethoven, the renewed stimulus came in part from the activities of Schuppanzigh's quartet, who gave the first performance of the A minor soon after it was composed. However, neither work makes any concession at all to the fashion for public quartet recitals, and indeed the A minor quartet has a quality of privacy that anticipates the late group of quartets Beethoven was just on the point of beginning.

One expression of this privacy is self-quotation. The slow movement, in C major, is a musing on the theme from the B flat Act III entr'acte from *Rosamunde*, and the opening of the minuet (so called, though pitifully undance-like) recalls a song of 1819 setting Schiller's 'Die Götter Griechenlands', with its anxious question: 'Fair world, where are you?' But, in other movements too, the privacy of the quartet is also the privacy of song. The texture is full of accompaniment figures and vocal strains, and the work even begins with two bars in the manner of a song accompaniment preparing for the entry of the first violin. However, the privacy of this quartet is of course not just a matter of technical features: its whole expressive nature is intimate and confessional.

To some extent this is connected with the song-like character of the material, which calls up an unusual degree of identification within the listener. Thus when the first movement development begins by transferring the opening to D minor, our sympathies are quickened and even deepened (by the choice of key), so that the feeling is almost unbearably poignant when the theme is not allowed to cadence in A major, as earlier it had in E major, but instead is twisted into F minor:

34 Schubert: Quartet in A minor D804, first movement

Also, in Romantic fashion, the music proclaims its expressive independence by its departure from the norms of structure and taste. Its introduction of the conventional secondary key, C major, comes awkwardly after a caesura, long after it has determined that it is really concerned with the tension between A minor and A major. And the minuet has nothing in common with the dance, whether in its nervy rhythms, its pianissimo dynamic level, the extraordinary fragility of its C major or its intense mood of regret and anxiety. The missing dance then turns up in the finale, which unfolds unusually at a moderate pace, but the medley of vaguely peasant-style dances assembled here is no cleansing of the soul in popular merry-making, for harmonically and expressively the music remains on edge, its A major, as in the first movement, always indecisive.

Schubert D810 in D minor: 'Death and the Maiden'

The D minor quartet is again a personal journey, again taking its bearings from a song, 'Der Tod und das Mädchen', which provides it not only with a theme for its slow movement but also with a nickname. Inevitably this association of song and quartet has influenced interpretation of the quartet, so that, for example, it is difficult not to hear the presto finale, with its pressurized tarantella rhythm and its implacable D minor tonality, as some kind of dance of death. Whether this was part of Schubert's intention or not is an open question, but so too is the matter of whether or not we should be concerned with his intentions. A composition gains meaning during its existence after its creator's death, and whatever his D minor quartet may have meant to Schubert, it has too long been connected with death for this to be forgotten.

Cast in a grim G minor, the 'Death and the Maiden' andante is a set of variations, the only such in Schubert's quartet output, and shows him using the form to great expressive purpose. The quiet opening, with all four instruments tied in chords in the middle register, gives the impression that it is being played by a consort of viols rather than a string quartet, and so seems to track back to legendary times. But then Schubert introduces a twirling virtuoso first violin high above the rest of the ensemble: the effect is that of a ballerina placed within a Breughel engraving. Perhaps this is an ironic image of conventional variation, which Schubert then abandons, notably for a galloping variation in which it is tempting to hear Death riding his horse, carrying off the Maiden. When the first violin again ventures into pre-eminence, it is not to decorate but to give the music an insistent, needling edge, after which it sinks back to the manner of the beginning.

To preface this andante requires an allegro of still greater power and range, which Schubert provides. It is immensely long – nearly five hundred bars, if the repeat of the exposition is taken – and as in the C minor allegro, the main bulk of it is made up by an exposition and a recapitulation that develop much more than does the development proper. Again there are motivic links to carry the thought forward from one idea to the next: a triplet figure has this function in the first half of the exposition, for instance. And such connections are very much needed in an exposition that contains so many distinct ideas outlined within three distinct key areas: the tonic D minor, the normal secondary key F major, and then the 'heightened secondary', as in Mozart's early D minor quartet, of A minor, here mixed with A major once more. The recapitulation grounds all this material in D minor or major, but it leaves out of account the decisive opening music of the movement and its voyaging continuation: the latter then arrives at last in the coda, but not the former, and so, by a development of the structural idea he had introduced in the C minor allegro, Schubert keeps the music open to the end, then closes it with music which itself expects something more.

That something more duly comes in the andante and then in the third movement, which is Schubert's first real quartet scherzo and an astonishingly vigorous one at that. It is in D minor, with a trio of opposed character in D major. Thus three of the movements are centred in the home key of the work, and the fourth, the slow movement, is in the subdominant: this had been Schubert's practice also in the later of his two early quartets in D D74, and it gives a binding tonal unity to the work, within which less usual centres, such as the A of the first movement or the B flat of both outer movements, can be visited without any danger to the feeling of impressive, even oppressive homogeneity this quartet emanates.

Schubert intended his A minor and D minor quartets should be followed by a third to make a volume for publication, but in the event only the A minor was printed, six months after its composition, and indeed no other Schubert quartet was published during his lifetime. This makes it all the more poignant that reviews should have been so uncomprehending. A notice in the Weimar *Musikalische Eilpost* in 1826 considers both Schubert's quartet and a string quintet by Onslow, and is worth quoting in full as, at least, one possible contemporary view:

True to our journal's tendency, which forbids extensive reviews, we may very well combine the announcement of these two works, if we regard them from the point of view of the highest artistic endeavours, which are clearly expressed. Profound feeling, force and charm, significance and vitality and poetic fire characterize both; whoever has any appreciation for this species – and it still survives in many – will certainly enjoy them more than once, and each time with heightened interest.

This is, of course, a scandalously casual assessment (though no one who practises musical criticism can affect too much self-righteousness about such superficial judgments), but what is interesting is the author's assumption that chamber music is a minor and out-of-date genre. That was the background against which Beethoven was, in the same year of 1826, completing his last quartets. And the strength of the background is not much enhanced by the nineteen juvenile quartets composed between 1817 and 1821 as quasi-operatic, quasi-classical *jeux d'esprit* by Gaetano Donizetti (1797-1848), who, like Schubert a little earlier, was writing for domestic quartet parties. Nor even is the continuing vigour of the string quartet particularly indicated by the set of three published in 1824 by Juan Crisóstomo Jacobo Antonio de Arriaga y Balzola (1806-26), whose achievement of grace and melodiousness within a consciously strict and civilized style looks forward to such late quartet writers as Borodin. In the last years of his short life Arriaga was working in the Paris of Luigi Cherubini (1760-1842) and the restored Bourbon monarchy: his quartets are fully representative of the prevailing neo-classicism. There are hints of Haydn and Mozart about them, but the ideas never lead anywhere; they merely come decorously to an end. Arriaga is also capable of the most diminishing prettification, as at the end of the first movement of his E flat quartet:

35 Arriaga: Quartet in E♭, first movement

One further seeming nail in the coffin of the quartet might be lightly hammered into place by Gioacchino Rossini (1792-1868), who in 1809 had produced a set of variations in F for clarinet, string quartet and orchestra, and who in 1825-6 – the very years of Beethoven's last four quartets – published quartet arrangements of his weightless boyhood sonatas for two violins, cello and double bass.

One might wonder why Beethoven ever imagined that the string quartet was still worthy of his interest, were it not that by this stage in his life he had, physically and mentally, left behind all contact with contemporary music – though he still, as we shall see, remained the child of his time. There was, to be sure, an external reason for his return to the quartet, which he had not explored since the F minor work of 1810: towards the end of 1822 Prince Nikolay Golitsïn, another noble Russian amateur of quartets, commissioned one, two or three works in his favourite medium (he was eventually to achieve immortality as the dedicatee of op.127 in E flat, op.132 in A minor and op.130 in B flat). However, some months before this invitation Beethoven had offered a publisher a quartet 'which you could have very soon', and so the impetus towards quartet composition was already there, perhaps assisted by the continuing activities of Schuppanzigh and his ensemble, even though by now, of course, Beethoven would not have been hearing their efforts.

In any event, it is probable that little of the first Golitsïn quartet, op.127, was written before the second half of 1824: essentially, therefore, it dates from after the *Missa solemnis* and the ninth symphony had been completed. It was then given its first performance by Schuppanzigh's quartet on 6 March 1825, in advance of which Beethoven wrote humorously to the players asking each 'to distinguish himself and to vie with his neighbour in excellence'. And indeed a greater independence of the four parts is one of the striking new features brought into the string quartet by op.127, as in the coda to

Beethoven op. 127 in E♭

the first movement, where the leader wheels in a new flight while the others consider aspects of the material they have played:

36 *Beethoven: Quartet in E♭ op. 127, first movement*

A focussing on the instrumentalist as soloist was a feature of the times: this was the age of Spohr and Hummel, Paganini and the boy Liszt. Of course, Beethoven is very, very far from following Spohr along the path of the 'quatuor brillant', and certainly the violin writing in op. 127 is a good deal less extravagant than it is in op. 59. But op. 127 does show, in a much more fundamental and irresistible manner than Spohr came near managing, that the classical concep-tion of the quartet, as a dialogue of four like-minded colleagues, was no longer possible. This was why Arriaga was so intolerably cultivated, Rossini and Donizetti so frothy. Common assumptions could not any more be relied upon, and so the quartet was no longer a convenient model of human discourse (it never had been for Mozart, who had always recognized the scope of individuality, the vast gulf that separates each man or woman from his or her fellows). And though even Beethoven's style of the 1820s could not allow the four members of a quartet to speak wholly different languages – no matter how near this he was to come in the 'Grosse Fuge' at the end of op. 130 – they are much less ready to concur in his late quartets than ever before, much more prone to stake and maintain individual positions.

Inevitably Beethoven's new understanding of the quartet affects form as much as, if not more than, texture. After all, Haydn had developed sonata form and symphonic structure while also developing the string quartet, all three depending on the congruence of dissimilar elements. If the string quartet is now redundant, then so too is sonata form; but if the string quartet is to be retained in its redundancy, then so too may the form with which it was twinned from birth. So it is that op.127 begins a process in which the outlines of sonata form are kept while the musical contents behave in rather different ways. For instance, the first movement of this E flat quartet has the expected sections of exposition (not repeated: there will be repetition only in the first movement of op.130 and the last of op.135), development and recapitulation, but these are curiously undervalued. The recapitulation does not come with the releasing force it had in Haydn or earlier Beethoven, for its key has already for some while been anticipated, and the melody is transposed up an octave, etherealized: the same thing happens again in the last movement of the quartet. Moreover, the movement is differently sectioned by the recurrences of the slow introduction, which is worked into the body of the movement as it will be again in op.132 and op.130. Appearing first in E flat, it comes back in G at the start of the development, here coinciding with a sonata division, and again in C towards the end of the development, where it seems to announce the last bars of the development, the recapitulation and the coda as constituting together some third phase in a new kind of form: the changes of key signature, here as in the other late quartets, draw attention to an understanding of harmony which is exploratory, moving from area to area, not impelled by a single force.

What also weakens the sonata quality of this movement is the absence of dynamism in other respects. The development does not immediately screw up tension but instead waits to luxuriate in G major: the return of the introductory Maestoso even encourages this. And the coda is not a new phase of development but a contemplative apotheosis, as it is again, still more so, in the finale of this quartet. Naturally this weakening of driving force has much to do with a lessening of the tonic–dominant polarity and a new emphasis on harmonic relationships in thirds, which in late Haydn and earlier Beethoven had coloured the principal harmonic qualities but which now come right to the forefront.

The fact that this was also happening in Schubert at the same time is probably not to be attributed to direct influence, more to the common discoveries of two men striving to make music the most that it could be in the 1820s, for while writing op.127 Beethoven could not have been aware of the unpublished and unperformed C minor and D minor quartets Schubert had composed. Yet, extraordinarily enough, the two pivotal keys of the first movement of op.127 are related exactly as are their equivalents in the Schubert quartets, related by having a common secondary key: Beethoven's choice is E flat and G minor, the latter leading neatly into the G major with which the development starts. And the decisive statement of C major later in the movement introduces, of course, another third relation, the submediant, to match the earlier mediant.

Other aspects of op. 127 are equally symptomatic of a new style. The opening allegro is followed by an adagio in A flat, exactly as in Beethoven's previous E flat quartet, op. 74, only here the expressive richness is greatly increased, and music is set on a road towards the 'Heiliger Dankgesang' of op. 132 and the Cavatina of op. 130. After this comes a scherzo which, like all those of Beethoven's late quartets, is not so much joky as possessed – and the gesture with which it starts, four pizzicato chords, reaches far beyond joking to mock the very opening of the work. The central movements thus range across the whole spectrum of musical seriousness, from the profound subjectivity of the slow movement to, immediately following, the brisk deflation at the start of the scherzo (the use of pizzicato will be still more devastatingly ironic in the Andante of op. 130).

Also significant – as a pointer to the newness of op. 127 and as an indicator of what will follow – is the song-like nature of so much of the music, not least in the outer movements. The tradition of the 'singing allegro' belonged very much to Italian composers of quartets and symphonies, and to Mozart, but decidedly not to Haydn, whose expressiveness comes wherever possible from musical action, not evocation. If Haydn is witty, it is because his musical dialogue is witty: the expressive effect is a direct result of what the music is doing. Except in some of the slow movements of his later quartets and symphonies, and in the more dramatic music he wrote around 1770, he avoided placing much emphasis on music's ability to suggest emotional states rather than model emotional patterns, and the string quartet had developed very much as he had wished – which may be one more reason why Mozart, the greatest composer of emotional suggestion, found it an uncongenial medium. Beethoven, the inheritor of both, had been more Haydn-like in his quartets, but now, in op. 127 and its successors, the pressure to make the quartet sing became irresistible. Haydn, the typical classicist, expressed himself through what his music is; Beethoven, now beyond question a Romantic, expresses himself through what his music says.

This is a further reason for the liquidation of sonata form in Beethoven's late quartets. For Haydn, the boundaries of a strict form provided a framework within which he could give his music an inherent intelligibility: his much favoured false reprise was only one way of using formal expectation to gain an expressive effect. But Beethoven, needing the freedom to let his music follow his intention, depends very much less on standard forms – or rather, these can now take on different functions. They can remain as amiable memories of what music used to be like, as in the outer movements of op. 127, or they can be set to war with the new freedom of Beethoven's imagination, as most spectacularly in the 'Grosse Fuge', which the composer described as 'tantôt libre, tantôt recherchée', and which marshals the forces of fugue, sonata, variation and free invention.

But this is still in the future. The work that immediately followed op. 127 was the A minor quartet op. 132, written in the spring and early summer of 1825, and containing within it, as slow movement, a 'Hymn of thanksgiving, to the divinity, from a convalescent, in the Lydian mode', for while working on the quartet Beethoven had suffered a sudden illness. Then came the third Golitsïn quartet, op. 130 in B flat, written between August and November 1825, and in the first half of 1826 yet another, op. 131 in C sharp minor. The Golitsïn commission having been fulfilled, this fourth quartet was composed for the publisher Maurice Schlesinger, to whom Beethoven wrote expressing his satisfaction that 'quartets are now in demand everywhere, and it really seems that our age is taking a step forward'. The equation between civilization and a taste for string quartets one may accept without demur, but Beethoven's view is hardly supported by other evidence, not least the review of Schubert's A minor quartet quoted above. Perhaps he was anxious to maintain his publisher's interest in the promised work, or perhaps, now seeing the world in his own image and having exercised his highest self in the quartet medium for the past two years, the quartet inevitably bulked exceedingly large on his horizons. It would not be unreasonable if this were the case, for the three quartets opp. 130-32 enlarge and extend all that had been achieved in op. 127.

All of them exceed the bounds of four movements, while retaining some hold on the old design. The A minor quartet begins with what might be regarded as a sonata allegro incorporating a slow introduction, but the development is excessively tiny for a movement so large, and again it is more useful to regard the movement as establishing its own three sections, the first contrasting A minor with F major (once more keys with a common secondary key), the second transposing this up a fifth, and the third bringing a return to A minor and also A major. There is then a scherzo, a slow movement (the Lydian 'Heiliger Dankgesang') and an Alla marcia which can be seen as a second scherzo or as an introduction to the A minor finale, which again makes play with E minor and C major, and which is driven into A major by its huge coda.

Beethoven op. 132 in A minor

Beethoven op. 130
in B♭

The B flat quartet takes the expansion a stage further to encompass six movements, but these can be understood as including two attempts at scherzo and slow movement: the first scherzo is in B flat minor and major, followed by an Andante in D flat, but this strangely nonchalant piece is obviously not sufficient to function as a slow movement, and so there is another scherzo, in G and C, marked 'Alla danza tedesca', followed by the Cavatina in E flat and then, in the original version, by the 'Grosse Fuge', which makes all the preceding movements, despite their unusual number and great character, seem a collective preparation for this unparalleled challenge to the resources of chamber musicians and their audiences. Occupying almost as many pages of score as the whole of the rest of the work, it is a fugue in three massive stages, a movement in which Beethoven is at his most uncomfortable, whether in his harmony or his often jagged rhythm, his intensive polyphony or his perpetually striving, stretched sonorities. And as in Beethoven's use of fugue elsewhere, the old structure is in conflict with the more recent sonata principle: indeed, much of its energy comes from the battle of the two, the tendency of fugue to vary a single idea set against the obligation of sonata form to appease two. It is a battle with which Beethoven was much concerned in his late music, whether here in sonata fugue or elsewhere, especially in the slow movements of the last quartets, in sonata variations.

The alternative finale, surveying much of the same harmonic territory as the 'Grosse Fuge' but in a drastically eased style, is no mere concession on Beethoven's part to the anxiety of his publisher, the weakness of his executants and the puzzlement of his public: rather it makes it possible for the work to present a quite different face, the six movements now to be understood as equal planets in the same solar system, not as five satellites around the massive finale.

Beethoven op. 131
in C♯ minor

In the C sharp minor quartet the number of constituent movements is again increased, at least nominally, to seven, but at the same time there is a severe contraction to one single movement, since all seven are to be joined without a break. Moreover, the traditional four-movement structure is once more somewhere in the background. The first movement is a fugal adagio that can be interpreted as an enlargement of the old slow introduction, and it is followed by a sonata allegro (in D, prepared by the emphasis in the adagio on its dominant, A, which is also the submediant of C sharp minor). The third movement is scarcely more than a transition to the A major slow movement in large-scale variation form, after which, quite properly comes the scherzo in E and then the finale, preceded by its own slow introduction, an adagio movement in G sharp minor: the final allegro itself takes up the galloping rhythm of the finale of the E minor 'Razumovsky', also used by Schubert in his D minor quartet.

It has often been observed that there are sub-thematic links among the late quartets, and particularly among the three vaster ones, opp. 130-132. In particular, a set of four notes representing the top half of the minor scale (e.g. E–F–G sharp–A in A minor) is often to be discovered in some form or other, and contributes much to the harmonic colour of these quartets. However, there is a sense in which the trilogy of opp. 130-132 is not only coherent but complete. It will already be evident that these three works all share the preoccupation with third-related keys noted in op. 127. If mediant and submediant relations are interposed into the cycle of fifths, one obtains a cycle of thirds, and it turns out that very nearly the whole of this cycle is explored by these three quartets, each of which is centred on keys from one continuous segment:

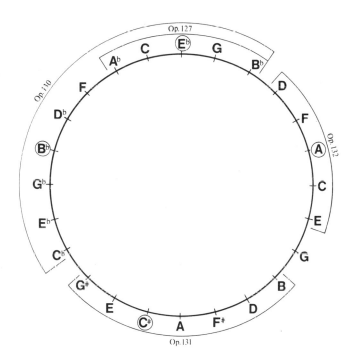

37 Beethoven: Quartets opp. 127, 130, 131, 132

There is, of course, no evidence that Beethoven planned his quartets in such a way, but equally there is no doubt that his awareness of the extent and range of harmonic landscapes was without peer in the whole history of music, and certainly it is not too much to suppose that he instinctively found a way to make opp. 130-32 complementary. It is also suggestive that the breaks occur as they do: one might almost imagine that Beethoven continued clockwise, as it were, from op. 127 to op. 132, then went back to cover a larger span, embracing the whole of that explored in op. 127, and finally continued in an anticlockwise direction to till the ground of op. 131.

Schubert D887 in G   The one note he left out, a G, remained to become the tonic of Schubert's last quartet, D887 in G major, which is dated 20–30 June 1826 and so was written just as Beethoven, elsewhere in the city of Vienna, was coming towards the end of his C sharp minor quartet. If Schubert was aware of what his great contemporary was achieving – and since Schuppanzigh's quartet had performed op. 127 and op. 130 in Vienna he surely must have been – then he chose to amplify the nature of the quartet in a different manner. Superficially the movements are those of convention: an Allegro molto moderato in sonata form, an E minor Andante un poco moto, a fleet D major scherzo with a rustic trio in G major, and an Allegro assai sonata rondo to conclude. But the outwardly standard form holds material of new vastness and scope. The extraordinary opening is a wrenching harmonic twist, as a straightforward G major triad is pulled forward and slips sideways into the minor, and after this comes a Brucknerian spaciousness as violin and then cello sound melodies over soft tremolos in the other instruments:

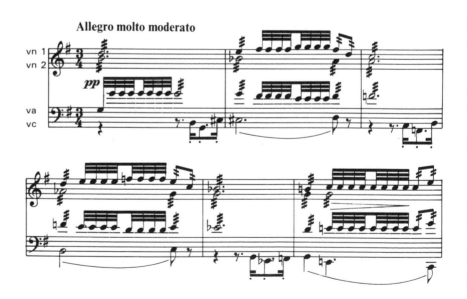

38 *Schubert: Quartet in G* D887, *first movement*

At the end of this passage the cello is wanting to resolve onto a low G a fourth below its bottom note, so that a natural progression is frustrated by nature in a way that Haydn could never have imagined. Nor could Haydn, whose writing for string quartet was always a perfect fit for four instruments, have countenanced Schubert's looser style, in which the particular constitution of the ensemble seems not at all so inevitable.

One symptom of this is the 'orchestral' conception that has sometimes been regarded as a fault in this quartet. Perhaps the above quotation only sounds orchestral because it has been so well and so often orchestrated by Bruckner, but there is no doubt of the unquartet-like breadth of sonority that Schubert obtains at other points, not least near the end of this first movement, where a D major chord vibrates largely across fifteen of the sixteen available strings. Another feature, contrary in substance but equal in effect, is the isolation of different voices within the quartet, even of different voices within one instrument: the second prominent cello solo, for instance, is firmly in the tenor register of the instrument, whereas the first, quoted above, had been in the furthest bass, so that it almost appears two different instruments are involved. The string quartet is ceasing to be music expressly made for four individuals, and becoming instead music that four instruments are able to play: the music was beginning to outgrow the medium. And where much of the tension of Beethoven's late quartets, most especially of the 'Grosse Fuge', comes from his efforts to respect the medium while vastly extending it, Schubert feels no such scruple and is happy for the quartet to sound like a miniature orchestra rather than a group of separate personalities.

It is rather the same, as it has to be, in the arena of form. In the quartets of Haydn the musical ideas execute the form in which they are contained: there is a perfect complicity and interdependence of form and content (with exceedingly rare exceptions such as the finale of op.54 no.2). One effect of this is to make it impossible for one to imagine Haydn's material appearing in any other context. But by the mid-1820s this kind of containment had stopped holding fast, and in the first movement of Schubert's G major quartet the sonata structure is almost arbitrary – as has been remarked also in the case of Beethoven's op.132. In Schubert as in Beethoven at this period the sonata ideal has lost its driving force, and new agencies of continuity and shape have had to be taken on board. Thus the first movement of D887 is much concerned with the uneasy relationship between tonic major and tonic minor, a relationship too unstable to be of much use in sonata building, and also with the crossed functions of tune and transition. The most conspicuous theme in the exposition is heard four times, twice in D, then in B flat and finally in G, so that with so much repetition interest begins to shift to the link material, and it is this link material, not the melody itself, that provides substance for development. Though, again as in Beethoven at this time, there is not very much of that.

One further aspect of the Romantic revolution is a view of the multi-movement work in which the choice and arrangement of movements is not just appropriate but expressively vital. Again Schubert's G major quartet offers a classic instance, for the slow movement, at first peaceable enough, is violently interrupted by a G minor episode which seems like an invasion from the first movement: it is a profoundly disturbing violation of the decencies of four-movement form. And though there is nothing here to compare with the programme of mortality that so readily fits the D minor quartet, the finale is curiously apt, with again a desperate rhythm used to tie together music that looks at various times to Baroque formality and to comic brio.

Beethoven op. 135 in F The month after this Beethoven began his last quartet, in the F major that had been the key also of the last completed quartets of Mozart and Haydn (it was also the key of Beethoven's first quartet, in the order he had chosen for op.18; and the order inherited by posterity is more significant because more lasting than the chronology of actual composition). The work was his op.135, finished in October 1826 and followed only by the lighter finale to op.130 in November, after which Beethoven completed nothing more before his death four months later.

Like Schubert's G major quartet, Beethoven's op.135 is once more in the four usual movements, with a sonata-form allegretto followed by a scherzo, a slow movement in D flat and a finale. But for Beethoven, of course, this was a conscious return, and not without point. On one level there is a parallel with the seventh symphony, and even more so the eighth, coming after a group of more insistently revolutionary works in the same form, for similarly the op.135 quartet is a work of reflection and control, not denying the eccentricities and the battles of its predecessors, but seeing them with a certain detachment. And yet Beethoven had gone much further in his opp.130-132 quartets than ever he had in the symphonies of 1803-8, and so the ironic distance was so much the greater. The tempo of the start, and its nature, suggest something very much in earnest but not quite serious, and if the Lento is a meditation that crowns Beethoven's great series of flat-key quartet slow movements, the finale is at once too good at fulfilling its conventional function – there is even a resuscitation of the old habit of repeating the second half of the movement before the coda – and not good enough. The dialogue which Beethoven famously has his instruments pronouncing – 'Muss es sein? Es muss sein!' (Must it be? It must be!) – has connotations both commonplace and metaphysical: it seems to have had its origins in matters of domestic parsimony (Must I pay? Yes you must!), but critics in search of the cosmic Beethoven have been keener to see it as a profound statement about Choice and Necessity. It is also, however, the self-questioning and the over-emphatic self-assertiveness of music discussing its own progress.

For nearly seventy years the string quartet had been at the centre of instrumental music, and it was still remaining so: Beethoven died with plans for a tenth symphony, a Requiem, a *Faust*, but in fact the only works he finished in the last three years of his life were string quartets. However, this pre-eminence was only being maintained at great cost, at the cost of creating new forms (in opp.130-32) because the old ones were no longer implied by the kind of music that was becoming imaginable, or at the cost of irony (in op.135). Nobody can have the flimsiest notion of the string quartets Beethoven and Schubert might have written – let alone the other works had they not died within a short space of each other in 1827-8. What is certain is that they died having identified a whole array of problems concerned with the composition of Romantic music within the most classical of forms, problems to which no solutions would be discoverable until the Romantic age had reached its twilight.

Part Two

Intermezzo 1827-1870

The forty-five years between Haydn's op.33 and Beethoven's op.135 had seen the first great flowering of the string quartet, the composition of perhaps half the greatest works in the medium, including all the quartets of Beethoven and Schubert, the vast majority of Haydn's great quartets and Mozart's ten masterpieces. By contrast, the harvest of the next forty-five years was meagre indeed, with little more than Mendelssohn's half dozen quartets and Schumann's three to represent the decades of high Romanticism. The development of the string quartet virtually stopped, and even went backwards, for throughout this period, for different reasons, the highest achievements of the 1820s remained little observed. Schubert's G major quartet was not published until 1851, and the late quartets of Beethoven existed only on the fringes of the repertory, rarely played and rarely understood: the extreme case is the 'Grosse Fuge', which apparently lay unheard between its first performance in 1826 and a revival in Paris in 1853.

The causes for the sharp decline in quartet composition are difficult to distinguish from the symptoms. For instance, it is noteworthy that there existed few permanent ensembles who alone might have been able to create a performing tradition for the late Beethoven quartets and to stimulate contemporary composers. Schuppanzigh died in 1830 and had no successor in Vienna until Joseph Hellmesberger (1828-93) formed his quartet in 1849. Meanwhile the only important quartet was that of Karl Müller (1797-1873) and his brothers, who played for the court of Brunswick until 1830 and then for the next twenty-five years toured throughout Europe. They were thus the predecessors of the international quartets of our own day, and like them the Müllers seem to have had little need of new repertory, preferring to play Haydn, Mozart and Beethoven. On the other hand, if composers had shown more interest in the quartet, then perhaps there would have been more regular ensembles.

Another factor was the dominance of the virtuoso performer. When Spohr on his frequent travels was called upon to play quartets, he simply had three local musicians play with him, exactly as he would engage an orchestra to accompany him in a concerto, and so it was no wonder that his quartets were so often conceived as miniature concertos for the leader. Moreover, the great prestige of the pianist–composer brought an inclination towards chamber music involving the piano, again in a solo capacity. Even Mendelssohn and Schumann, despite the great importance they attached to the string quartet, found it easier to write works for piano and strings.

Not unconnected with this vogue of the piano, there was a general blurring of distinctions between genres, a primacy of keyboard thinking. Beethoven in his last years had brought the distinctions to their ultimate, and had created music of exclusively appropriate type for the mass, the symphony, the piano sonata and the string quartet. He had, to be sure, arranged his 'Grosse Fuge' for four hands at a piano, but that arrangement merely provides another outlet for music that strains any medium, whereas when Spohr made similar versions of his less 'brilliant' quartets they were genuine alternatives, made possible by the fact that his music could be transferred quite happily from one medium to another: this was just one respect in which the Romantics joined hands with the masters of the Baroque, and forgot those aspects of textural uniqueness that had made the string quartet not only feasible but perhaps inevitable.

One further point may be relevant. For the Romantics, music was the expression of an individual sensibility, and so it was quite natural that musical performance should be placed in the hands of a single artist, whether singer, instrumentalist or conductor. Music which, by contrast, presupposed collective endeavour, as did most eminently the string quartet, was thus distant from the mood of the time. Of course, this had been so for some time before Beethoven's death: there were already problems at the time of the 'Razumovsky' quartets, more than twenty years before. But as long as Beethoven remained alive, so it seems, the quartet remained a possibility, with however much difficulty, whereas after his death the shutters came down very fast indeed.

One Romantic masterpiece alone slipped through: the quartet in A minor op. 13 of Felix Mendelssohn (1809-47), written in 1827, the very year of Beethoven's death. The young Mendelssohn was evidently impressed by Beethoven's most recent works, including not only the op. 132 quartet in the same key of A minor but the ninth symphony (notably its vehement instrumental recitative and its review

Mendelssohn op. 13 in A minor

113

of earlier movements in the finale) and the late piano sonatas, to whose fugal writing his work perhaps owes more than to Beethoven's quartet fugues. However, these reminiscences of late Beethoven are hardly to Mendelssohn's discredit, given that nobody else, not even his later self, was to enter into a dialogue with that world until Schoenberg eighty years later. And Mendelssohn is here hardly an epigone. Not only does his A minor quartet speak with a quite personal force, it also essays a new form and unprecedented textures.

Yet even in its formal newness it expresses the fact that the possibility of quartet writing was slipping away, for it begins with an A major adagio section which is not so much an introduction as a preparation for the work proper: it is the cover on the volume, and very rightly it reappears at the end of the quartet, a back cover as well as a front, enclosing the music and setting it somewhat in quotation marks, as if the real quartet inside were a narrative relating to some other time, a time when music of this kind could be composed. This is not, of course, to suggest that the narrative is related in anything but the most vivid terms. The A minor Allegro vivace at the start uses E minor as secondary tonality (one may compare Mozart's early D minor quartet), and so its hard-pressed minor feeling is kept up throughout, while the following Adagio non lento, nominally in F major, includes fugal material in which the voices are strained apart as much as in a Beethoven fugue, with the difference that the strain is felt only by the listener and not, as it were, by the voices themselves:

39 Mendelssohn: Quartet in A minor op. 13, second movement

The by now usual scherzo is replaced by an Intermezzo, consisting of a wistful ambling march in A minor with a brilliant trio in the major, the two neatly joined, as Mendelssohn was to do in later quartets, in the coda. The finale, however, is structurally and expressively a very much more extraordinary conception. It begins with dramatic violin recitative which returns after the development as if to protest at the turn the music is taking: the cherished recapitulation of sonata form is thus given a quite new point, so alerting us to the fact that yet another problem for composers of Mendelssohn's generation was that the quartet, like the symphony, had grown up in close association with a structural principle that no longer seemed second nature. So either the outlines of sonata form had to be applied to material which did not call for them – this was Mendelssohn's policy in his later quartets – or else material had to be invented which would justify the form in a new manner: the finale of Mendelssohn's A minor quartet exemplifies this like little else of the period.

But the extremity of the solution has itself to be justified, and Mendelssohn achieves this by having the music alarmingly loaded with recollections of its past (no necessary chain of cause and effect is implied here: the form, the recitative and the memories are all of a piece). The finale has not proceeded far before it starts to remember the slow movement remembering the opening allegro, and then comes a fugal passage on an inversion of the fugue theme from the adagio, followed later by another on the subject turned back the right way up. The eventual outcome is a full quotation of this fugue subject, in the original tempo and metre, after which the first violin is happy to lead the way into the only music with which the work can conceivably end: a repetition of the opening, this now made to seem more substantial than a memory, instead a genuine closure, because it is more fully developed.

In the same year of 1827 Mendelssohn wrote a rather more relaxed work for quartet, the Fugue in E flat that was posthumously published as the fourth number in the op.81 collection of quartet movements. In its even flow it contrasts very much with the quick fugue that the fourteen-year-old Mendelssohn had somewhat self-consciously placed at the end of his 1823 quartet in the same key, a work distinguished only in showing a proficiency in the medium greater than that achieved by anybody else at the same age, decisively not excluding Mozart. It certainly has little to connect it with another E flat quartet Mendelssohn wrote in 1829, his op.12 (both this work and the A minor quartet were published in 1830, the latter confusingly gaining the higher opus number).

115

Mendelssohn op. 12
in Eb
Like the A minor quartet, the E flat op.12 effects a cross-relation between its outer movements, but in a broader and more casual manner, without the depth and intensity of memory that the earlier work gains of itself. It is, more simply, a question of quotation. A little C minor idea, introduced in the development of the first movement, returns in the finale, first briefly and then at greater length, the whole last fifty-five bars of the quartet being an almost exact recapitulation of the first movement's coda. Similarly, the fierce pressure of the A minor quartet's material is not to be found in its successor, where phrases, particularly in the first movement, tend to be regular, song-like and complete in themselves, not asking for extension and change: here was another problem for composers of Mendelssohn's generation, whose very basic musical inventions were not such as would naturally support developing forms, least of all in a medium which lacked orchestral weight and variety of colour, and which could not either, at its purest, offer opportunities for concerto-like display and alternation of forces. Also notable in the comparatively eased E flat quartet is Mendelssohn's altered attitude to Beethoven, whose late quartets are pushed very much into the background if not quite forgotten altogether, while the music turns its sights to op.74, especially at the very beginning.

What remains a distinction of Mendelssohn's op.12, however, is his natural feeling for quartet textures and even his discovery of some new ones. Most characteristically Mendelssohnian is the fleet, light and brilliant movement of the trio section from the Canzonetta (again a miniature character-piece in 2/4 replaces the scherzo), representing a type of music already introduced in the octet for double string quartet of 1825, in the same key of E flat. However, Mendelssohn's ownership of this style was not exclusive, for the trio of yet another E flat Cherubini no. 1
in Eb composition, the first quartet of Luigi Cherubini (1760-1842), is also in this manner, and that Cherubini quartet was written in 1814, though not played until twelve years later, when it might well have been heard by Mendelssohn and incorporated into the background of his own quartet:

40a Cherubini: Quartet no. 1 in Eb, third movement

40b Mendelssohn: Quartet in Eb op. 12, second movement

Some years later, in 1838, this work of Cherubini's was encountered by another composer concerned for the future of the string quartet, though so far only as a critic, not as a contributor to the genre himself: Robert Schumann (1810-56). Like Mendelssohn presumptively, Schumann was particularly impressed by what he called 'the extraordinary trio' and by 'the scherzo with its fanciful Spanish theme', less delighted by what he found 'operatic, overladen' (presumably the slow movement, with its extreme dynamic contrasts and peculiarities of texture, one long passage being taken by the aerial trio of violins and viola) and by what he thought was, on the other hand, 'small-scale, empty and self-willed', here referring perhaps to the cool, calculated approach Cherubini takes to his sonata allegro. But Schumann was aware too that here he was dealing with something outside the quartet tradition as he understood it, the tradition of Haydn, Mozart and Beethoven, and, among the moderns, Mendelssohn (Onslow also he curiously includes among this company). His final comment was a generous extension of sympathy to the Cherubini quartet style: 'the more we learn to understand it, the higher we must esteem it'.

Schumann was, however, perturbed by the orchestral rhetoric of Cherubini's second quartet in C (1829), which was in fact adapted from a Symphony in D, and though he found much to admire in the work, he also considered the movements too various. Now of course many of Schumann's criticisms of Cherubini could also be levelled at Beethoven, whose late quartets certainly contain movement sequences no less diverse, besides being not infrequently 'self-willed', 'operatic' or 'overladen'. And indeed Cherubini obviously admired Beethoven as much as the latter professed to admire him. What really damages his quartets is not drama but the element of artificiality already detected in Arriaga. There is too perfect a balance of one phrase with another, too knowing a use of expressive device in the slow movements, too self-conscious a dexterity and charm even in those scherzos which are most effective in terms of texture. It is a curious paradox that the Romantics, whom normally one imagines to have been quite spontaneous in their musical expression, were in fact beset by inhibitions when they entered the realm of the string quartet, but it does seem that even this most intensely classical form was not distancing enough: there had to be the objectivity of Cherubini, or the deliberate frame of Mendelssohn's A minor quartet which allowed him great scope within. Also significant is the comparative ease with which composers in the late 1820s, 1830s and 1840s wrote their string quartet scherzos, as if this most clearly demarcated form were the easiest to fill with living music.

Mendelssohn op. 44

The difficulties of the quartet got no lighter with the passage of time. In the mid-1830s Cherubini wrote four more quartets, and in 1837-8 Mendelssohn composed a set of three, his op. 44. The Cherubini quartets show a retrenchment in terms of operatic forcefulness, but an extension of those special effects that presumably came from the later Boccherini and that so far had played almost no part in the Austro-German quartet: playing with mutes (scherzo of no. 4), harmonics (same movement), particular use of the violin's G string (first movement of no. 4) and sul ponticello (scherzo of no. 5). However, Cherubini's coldness remains, and his forms are again laid out with expository clarity, even where, in the A minor no. 6 (1837), he experiments with that unification which had obsessed the young Mendelssohn (not least when working in the same key) by bringing back fragments of the initial allegro, slow movement and scherzo in the middle of the finale.

Mendelssohn himself, however, was not attempting such ventures again. His op. 44 quartets are all in four distinct movements, even if they all slightly unusually place the slow movement third. They all include an exposition repeat in the first movement, unlike opp. 12 and 13, and the first of them, in D, even revives the minuet. Moreover, their key schemes are absolutely conventional: the D major's minuet and the scherzo of the E flat quartet no. 3 are in the tonic, the scherzo of the E minor no. 2 being in the tonic major, and the slow movements are in the relative minor (no. 1), the relative major (no. 2) and the subdominant (no. 3). All this suggests how these quartets may justly be termed 'neoclassical', and the music itself shows how elusive a real quartet dynamism had become. The two scherzos are once more brilliant and brilliantly successful, but the slow movements are relaxed songs and the finales often rely on perpetual bustle, while of the so-conscientious first movements, only that of the E flat quartet uses material which sounds perfectly at home scored for quartet and which readily breaks down into small elements for development. More typical is the opening Allegro assai appassionato of the E minor quartet, a pure song inspiration which was to become much more suitably placed when adapted for the Violin Concerto in the same key:

41 Mendelssohn: Quartet in E minor op. 44 no. 2, first movement

Mendelssohn's offering of op. 44 as a set of three quartets was by this date rather anachronistic, and it perhaps deliberately invites comparison of the group with Beethoven's op. 59, especially since here too an E minor work is included as centrepiece. Of course, any such comparison is hardly to the junior composer's advantage, not because Mendelssohn was at all an incompetent or unimaginative musician, but rather because times and the musical language had changed, and a reply to the challenge of the 'Razumovsky' quartets, let alone the late works, had become literally unthinkable, even by a composer who ten years before had been glimpsing some of the essentials of the late Beethoven. The models rather had to be Haydn and Mozart, and it was the time-scale of their quartets that Mendelssohn and also Cherubini came near, not the enlarged span of Beethoven's opp. 59, 130, 131 and 132.

The inferiority feelings that composers felt at the time are well conveyed in the writings of Schumann, who perhaps tactfully refrained from comment on Mendelssohn's op. 44 but at first lavishly praised another set of the same date, the three by Herrmann Hirschbach subsequently published as *Lebensbilder in einem Cyclus von*

Quartetten. Despite their fashionably Romantic title, these works are in standard four-movement form, and one might wonder why there was no one to change the nature of the quartet as radically as Berlioz was changing the nature of the symphony, were it not that the quartet, partly by virtue of its living repertory, partly by virtue of being at once a medium, a genre and a form, had already settled into conservatism. Worse still, the composition of a quartet had become a test of professionalism for a composer, as to some extent it still remains, a test fulfilled in this period by composers otherwise as far apart – from each other and from the string quartet – as Mikhail Glinka (1804-57; F major quartet of 1830) and Richard Wagner (1813-83; D major quartet of 1829, now lost).

In 1842, called upon to review the quartet by Julius Schapler that had won a prize competition, Schumann noted how 'the quartet has come to a serious standstill'. And he went on:

Who does not know the quartets of Haydn, Mozart and Beethoven, and who would wish to say anything against them? In fact it is the most telling testimony to the immortal freshness of their works that yet after a half-century they gladden the hearts of everyone; but it is no good sign that the later generation, after all this time, has not been able to produce anything comparable. Onslow alone met with success, and later Mendelssohn, whose aristocratic–poetic nature is particularly amenable to this genre.

Already, then, the quartets of the great classical masters are beyond reproach: the first, and perhaps the only body of music to be canonized in this manner. And then the key word 'comparable'. New quartets could only be admitted to the repertory if they accepted and attained the standards that had been appropriate, by Schumann's own dating, a half-century earlier. Schumann would never have subscribed to such a conservative doctrine of the symphony, the sonata or the concerto, yet the quartet, for reasons already given, was the natural territory of the status quo. As such, moreover, it showed so much the more clearly the problems of formal instrumental composition in the generation after Beethoven.

Schumann op. 41 And, as we might expect, those problems are nowhere more apparent than in the quartets Schumann himself wrote, his op.41 set of three composed in the early summer of 1842. Again the planning of the group may reveal an attempt to emulate Beethoven's op.59, though equally it may be an extra token of homage to Mendelssohn, to whom Schumann dedicated these, his only quartets. What is certain is that the works were written straight on top of a period of assiduous study of the masters Schumann lauded in his review of the same year, that preparation by itself suggesting the inadequacy felt not by Schumann alone but by his age.

The surprise then is that his quartets are not mere classical pastiche. Instead Schumann's studies would seem to have led him to extract general structural principles and apply them thoroughly within his own music, so that his sonata-form movements, in particular, unfold with a textbook clarity that is scarcely to be found in any 'real' classical music. The first movement of the first of his quartets, for example, has an exposition which is of no great complexity, yet which is repeated exactly in the first fifty-eight bars of the recapitulation, the remainder being no more than a transposition into the tonic with some slight alteration at the very end. Schumann can have found no precedent for such a heroically orthodox procedure in any of the works he studied, and it is surely significant that it was at this same period that theorists were making the first statements of the 'rules' of sonata form: their efforts and Schumann's bespeak an unease that some hefty steering was going to be necessary to keep music on course.

Why that should have been so is also evident from this first quartet of Schumann's op.41. The work begins with an even more venerable historicism, a four-part invention in A minor that serves as slow introduction to the allegro in F major: the third relation has already been noted in Haydn, Beethoven and Schubert, the last of whom also shows the same fondness for keys linked by a common secondary key, as in the C minor quartet movement. However, Schumann's practice leaves the two keys as genuine alternatives, since his first movement has begun very definitely in A minor and ended equally definitely in F (Chopin's Ballade op.38, published only two years earlier with a dedication to Schumann, had taken precisely the opposite route). What happens next is that the centres alternate: the scherzo is in A minor, with an 'Intermezzo' in the relative major as trio, the adagio is in F and the sonata-form finale, which like the first movement asks for a repeat of the exposition, is in A minor moving into A major at the end.

But not even Schumann's hyper-conventional forms can entirely disguise the unsettling alliance of the two underlying tonalities, and it was perhaps in order to work out the relationship more fully that he cast op.41 no.2 in F and the third of the set in A. The F major quartet, with no slow introduction, thus has an opening allegro in the same key as that of its predecessor, and again in watertight form. Then comes an F minor slow movement intriguingly worked as variations on an impalpable, shifting theme, and a C minor scherzo which, like the A minor scherzo of op.41 no.1, is texturally by far the most effective movement in the quartet: Schumann here joins Mendelssohn and Cherubini as a master of the most formalized moment in this formal genre. But the finale shows an even greater lack of confidence than anything in the A minor quartet, for Schumann here revives a practice that had been moribund when Beethoven was a young man: he asks for a repeat not only of the short exposition but also of the whole second part of the movement, incorporating development and recapitulation, before allowing the music to press to its end in a coda.

Schumann's A major quartet, composed after the other two had arrived more or less simultaneously, has customarily been regarded as the greatest of the set, and certainly its first movement is not so patent an imitation of a classical sonata allegro as the Romantics usually contrived. Instead it proceeds at a moderate pace which allows for the wayward unfolding of three elements: music based on the expressive falling fifth of the short slow introduction, a melody in E passing from cello to first violin, and an extraordinary harmonic excursion. As in Beethoven's first 'Razumovsky' and Mendelssohn's A minor quartet, the development begins with a false reprise, though Schumann betrays his worries about formal solidity by asking also for the exposition to be repeated. The case for ignoring this injunction is strong, particularly when the development is very short, and when the recapitulation, though it shortens the primary material, is otherwise literal.

The finale is even more repetitive, since here Schumann is at pains to do justice not only to rondo form but also to scherzo structure, the movement incorporating a trio section in F (again the association of these two tonalities). And a scherzo is needed at this late stage because there has not been one earlier on: its place was taken by an Assai agitato set of variations in F sharp minor, turning the first movement's falling fifth upside down to make a rising fourth, and drawing out the relative minor· flavour that had appeared in its predecessor. The other internal movement is an adagio in D which takes advantage of the medium's sympathy with music of rich inner life, and which, with the similarly challenging but judicious textural inventions of the first and second movements (such as the passage in the allegro's reprise where all four instruments are way above middle C), makes this one of the most fully quartet-like quartets after Beethoven:

42 Schumann: Quartet in A op.41 no.3, third movement

This, though, is exceptional in Schumann. He was, as we have seen, well aware of the difficulties the quartet posed to composers of his generation, and after the summer of 1842, both as critic and as composer, he abandoned the genre.

Not so Mendelssohn. In 1843 he wrote an E minor Capriccio in prelude and fugue form, evidently thinking less of Albrechtsberger than of J. S. Bach, and in 1847 came another full-scale quartet, the F minor op.80, a work of much greater force than any of the op.44 set of the previous decade. Its fierceness has been explained as Mendelssohn's reaction to the death of his sister Fanny, but the quartet is a reaction too to Beethoven's op.95 and to its compact vehemence, though it owes its single-minded power also to its emphasis on a single tonality. The outer movements and the scherzo are all in F minor, which seems to lend itself in Mendelssohn's hands to alarmed forward motion (the scherzo, so different from those of his other quartets, is particularly implacable), and the adagio removes itself only as far as the relative major. Rather disappointingly, the other quartet of Mendelssohn's last year, which like Haydn's last quartet proceeded only as far as a slow movement and a scherzo, shows nothing like the same forcefulness but instead relaxes, like much of op.44, into moulds too well prepared for music of classical purpose. The andante variations in E and scherzo in A minor of this unfinished quartet were published as the first two numbers of op.81, followed by the 1843 Capriccio and the 1827 Fugue.

Mendelssohn op. 80 in F minor

Mendelssohn's death in 1847 did nothing to dislodge him from general acceptance as the greatest, perhaps the only master of the quartet since Beethoven, and indeed for the remainder of the century his works in the genre were revered as without equal. Naturally, therefore, they had a great influence on lesser talents, among them Bernhard Molique (1802-69) and Anton Rubinstein (1829-94), of whom the latter may be regarded as the paradigmatic quartet composer of the middle nineteenth century: academic, conservative and gifted with few ideas of any originality or appeal.

Berwald nos 1 and 2

But this was not always the way. In 1849 the Swedish composer Franz Berwald (1796-1868) wrote two quartets which do not emulate Mendelssohn's classicism but rather the adventurous spirit of his quartets of 1827-9: they are also in the same keys of A minor and E flat. Both works are directed to be played without a break, like Beethoven's C sharp minor quartet, but whereas the A minor quartet falls into the usual sections of adagio introduction, allegro, adagio (in B flat), scherzo (in F: once more this key is closely associated with A minor) and finale (in A major), the E flat quartet is more thoroughly unified by being cast as a palindrome. The first movement has a long expository section in E flat, after which the development is introduced by a new theme in the subdominant and closed by a reprise of that theme in the dominant. The subsequent recapitulation is brief and concerned with peripheral material, and it leads directly into the adagio, also in the subdominant. This in turn gives way to the scherzo, which in its abrupt contrasts and its circling patterns sounds a note of Beethovenian eccentricity:

43 Berwald: Quartet in Eb, scherzo

Then the first part of the adagio returns, to be followed by the expected recapitulation of the E flat exposition of the first movement. Berwald's achievement here of a new formal shape is remarkable enough, even if the single-movement structures of Liszt or Schumann are more tightly bound, but it is remarkable too that it should have been in the quartet, so becalmed a genre at the time, that he should have tried out his experiment.

For between the death of Mendelssohn and the first published quartets of Brahms, twenty-six years later, Schumann's 'serious standstill' became only the more marked. In the 1850s Spohr was still alive and adding to his store of quartets, but otherwise the most individual voice was probably that of Joachim Raff (1822-82), who suffered from a bad conscience in so many directions that it was inevitable he should also feel the need to prove himself in the field of the quartet. Straddling the gap between post-Mendelssohn traditionalism and the 'new German school' around Liszt, he wrote several unexceptional quartets in orthodox if more than a little stilted four-movement form which yet include new gestures, such as the sul ponticello scherzo of his first quartet in D minor op.77 (1855) or the Wagnerian breadth of the melodies of its successor in A major op.90 (1857). But his divided loyalties are most strikingly expressed in a later set of three – perhaps the last to follow the 'Razumovsky' precedent, as had also Rubinstein in his opp.17 and 47 of the 1850s. Raff's triptych, his op.192 of 1874, includes as centrepiece a work famed as the first example of chamber music composed to a definite programme: the piece is entitled *Die schöne Müllerin* (though without explicit reference to the poems set by Schubert), and it comprises an allegretto depiction of 'The Youth', an allegro cleverly suggesting the working of the mill, an andante for 'The Maid', an allegro bringing out the lovers' relationship, an andantino showing 'The Proposal' as a duet between cello and first violin, and finally a march for 'The Eve of the Wedding'. However, in view of the future of music, and not least of the quartet, Raff's pictorialism is less suggestive than the neoclassicism of the other quartets of his op.192, the last a 'suite in canon form' and the first a 'suite in the old style' consisting of march, sarabande, capriccio, aria, gavotte (with musette), minuet and gigue. In terms of conscious Bachism this was obviously going much further than Mendelssohn, and indeed much further than anyone else until Reger a generation later. Even so, Raff's various endeavours in the quartet field hardly look beyond the drawing room.

Part Three

Adagio 1871-1913

Curiously, string quartet composition again became possible towards the end of the third quarter of the nineteenth century. And once more we are confronted by a complex tissue of causes and symptoms. First there was the arrival of a generation of composers for whom four-movement form was natural, among them Johannes Brahms (1833-97), Antonín Dvořák (1841-1904) and Pyotr Ilyich Tchaikovsky (1840-93), all of whom completed their first noteworthy quartets in the 1870s. Then there was the fact that the classical style, represented pre-eminently by the quartets of Haydn, Mozart and Beethoven, was now far enough in the past that a composer could be both academic and artistic. At this time too there was encouragement from quartet leaders : Dvořák wrote his C major quartet op.61 for Hellmesberger and Brahms's op.51 pair were badgered out of him by his friend Joseph Joachim (1813-1907), whose ensemble gave concerts in Berlin and abroad from 1869 onwards. It may also be significant that it was now that Beethoven's late quartets began to be appreciated.

A landmark here is the centenary essay of 1870 by Richard Wagner, who, though not close to chamber music as a creator, draws special attention to the C sharp minor quartet op.131. Admittedly Wagner's interpretation is well within the tradition of Romantic pictorialism: the opening adagio we are asked to understand as a 'penitential prayer', followed by a 'consoling vision' (Allegro molto vivace) before the master settles to work (Allegro moderato) and begins to fashion 'one graceful figure' (Andante), after which he looks to the outer world (Presto) and then prepares himself for a new task (Adagio), which he then fulfils in the final allegro in a manner that has to be quoted complete, in the inimitable translation of Ashton Ellis:

'Tis the dance of the whole world itself: wild joy, the wail of pain, love's transport, utmost bliss, grief, frenzy, riot, suffering, the lightning flickers, thunders growl: and above it the stupendous fiddler who bears and bounds it all, who leads it haughtily from whirlwind into whirlpool, to the brink of the abyss; – he smiles at himself, for to him this sorcery was the merest play. – And night beckons him. His day is done. –

Nevertheless, Wagner was speaking for more than his own fanciful imagination in claiming one of Beethoven's late quartets as among its composer's highest achievements and not the absurd eccentricity of a deaf, sick genius.

For Brahms, however, the great challenge was not these last works but those of Beethoven's thirties, and when he came finally to set his seal of approval on two of his string quartets, in 1873, it was to the 'Razumovsky' quartets that he had them appeal in terms of scale and energy. His delay in publishing a string quartet, like his delay in bringing out a symphony, obviously has much to do with what Charles Rosen has called 'his openly expressed regret that he was born too late', but perhaps too he had to wait for a time when nostalgia could be expressed with maturity and distance. Regret in a twenty-year-old can easily seem trivial; it had to be a man of forty looking back to the sonata ideal. And, furthermore, it had to be the enriched musical language of the 1870s that was used to accomplish so complex a function as reviving classicism and expressing too its irremediable loss. Hence Brahms's dissatisfaction with the twenty quartets he wrote before op. 51, and hence the long period he spent on that opus, perhaps as much as eight years.

The degree of his ambition in the genre is apparent at once at the opening of his C minor quartet op. 51 no. 1, with its broad metre, its lusty main theme quickly counterpoised by more graceful material in F minor which still remembers the dotted pattern that preceded it (typically, this is only one of several subsidiary themes in several subsidiary tonalities in a complex exposition), and its contrast too of 'orchestral' tremolandos inherited from Schubert and Mendelssohn with pure quartet writing:

Brahms op. 51, no. 1 in C minor

44 Brahms: Quartet in C minor op.51 no.1, first movement

One might even see the F minor music here as expressing Brahms's longing for the past, envisioned in a distant sort of subdominant, whereas the C minor music, greatly more vigorous, is the music of the present. However that may be, the elegant convergence of four lines is a rarity in this quartet: it is almost symbolic that Brahms's first striking textural invention in a quartet should involve a double-stopped octave in the viola, for throughout this C minor work the inner parts are strengthened by multiple stopping or other means of suggesting more parts. Of course, this was entirely natural. Brahms's harmony, more than Haydn's or Beethoven's, required the simultaneous sounding quite often of more than four notes, and it is not surprising that the string quartet should have been for him a less congenial medium than the sextet, of which he had published two examples in the 1860s, or the quintet, with added viola or clarinet, which he was to take up after his wrestling with the quartet. By comparison with these works, his quartets exhibit an awkwarder fit of music and medium, and a less personal tone.

One great strength of the op.51 pair is that they turn these difficulties into advantages, in that the strained textures enhance the sense of striving conveyed also by the prominence of the minor in both pieces (one may recall that Brahms owned the autograph manuscript of Haydn's op.20) and by the strenuousness of the motivic development within and between movements. It was in his developments that Brahms showed himself most obviously the heir to the sonata tradition of Haydn and Beethoven, and since the string quartet had become the most prestigious embodiment of that tradition, he must have felt an obligation to be most resourceful and thorough in his quartet developments, or so it would seem from the intensive way in which the themes are disintegrated and weighed in the outer movements of the C minor quartet. The principal motif of the finale is even derived from that of the first movement, and both movements, like most of Brahms's sonata structures, have substantial codas in which the material is further reviewed and, in the case of the finale, the home key definitively re-established at the end of a movement which has been more in flight from C minor than in it.

This quartet also shows in extreme fashion Brahms's efforts to make the internal movements as weighty as their outer companions. Both take a lead from the opening allegro and go deeper into flat territory, the slow Romanze being in A flat and the ensuing Allegretto in F minor. In its anxious restlessness this latter movement has something in common with its equivalent in Mendelssohn's F minor quartet, and more generally Brahms's avoidance of the lighter, squarer music expected of a scherzo has its origins in Mendelssohn and in Schumann, while it was to Schumann again, and to Beethoven, that he inclined in making the Romanze an expressive character piece leading the instruments into a conversation of independent lines. Nor does this slow movement pass without its own clear references to the main idea of the first allegro.

Brahms op. 51, no. 2 in A minor

Such integration is deeper, less conscientiously paraded, in the second quartet of op.51, in A minor, where the first movement is much occupied with material derived from the notes F–A–E, alluding to Joachim's motto 'Frei aber einsam' ('Free but lonely'). Quite unlike its predecessor in op.51 no.1, this opening movement has an expansive exposition looking back more to Schubert than to Beethoven. The first melody unfolds through twenty bars in alla breve time, and the proportions are quite different: where the exposition in the C minor allegro was related in length to the development by the ratio 8:5, in the A minor allegro the ratio is 7:3. But there is compensation in that the recapitulation is itself so extraordinarily developing, as may be seen in two short extracts from the incipits of exposition and reprise:

45 Brahms: Quartet in A minor op. 51 no. 2, first movement

Where in Haydn the recapitulation was a symmetrical return, which could be toyed with because it was going to be so satisfying a completion, in Brahms even more than in Beethoven, especially in this A minor first movement, it has become a new point of arrival, and, by implication, of further departure, not only into the coda but also into the three subsequent movements.

In contrast with the case in the A minor quartets of Beethoven, Schubert, Mendelssohn, Schumann and Berwald, these subsequent movements are all in A, the slow movement being in A major (and again in its later stages replete with four-part polyphony) and the Quasi minuetto in A minor with a trio in A major. Despite its title, this third movement is not an antiquarian dance but rather a light-textured piece almost in Mendelssohn's manner. The dance element, which had been wholly absent from the C minor quartet, is here reserved for the finale, one of Brahms's Hungarian-style rondos.

Brahms op. 67 in Bb

Three years later, in his third and last quartet in B flat op. 67, he took the unusual step of beginning with a dance, the first movement having more the character of a finale in its pace and its material:

46 Brahms: Quartet in Bb op. 67, first movement

What is remarkable here is not only the unbuttoned style but also the naive eccentricity of the quartet textures: in both respects the openings of the C minor and A minor quartets are in complete contrast. Moreover, wildly new textures continue to be a feature of this B flat quartet. The leading by the viola in the third movement is not particularly unusual, especially in Brahms, but its absence is, when the trio is begun by a real trio of violins and cello (perhaps Brahms had crossed his study to refer to Haydn's op.20 no.1), and even more extraordinary is the duet of leader and cello in double octaves at the start of the finale's fourth variation. It is as if here, in his only major-mode quartet, Brahms had simply accepted the impossibility of the medium without trying to make it into something else.

On the other hand, the dancing first movement makes necessary a quite original formal structure. If the 6/8 vigour were all, then the first movement itself would indeed be inadequate to its task, and so the secondary material is conceived as a different dance in 2/4, opening the way to some unprecedented metrical dissonances when the two are overlapped, as happens over the widest span in the coda. The andante, in F, is more in the harmonically rich manner of Brahms's earlier quartet slow movements, and the third movement, in D minor, is again not a scherzo, which would be redundant in any case after the first movement, but an interlude for expressively troubled material to be confined to more symmetrical shapes. Thus the key scheme is a retrograde inversion of that of the C minor quartet, mirrored about the F that appears in both, and the finale is left with the task of providing the weight missing from the first movement and at the same time bringing the work to a decisive end. Brahms's solution is ingenious. The movement is a set of variations which move gradually towards the lively 6/8 music of the opening, recapture it and then move on.

131

Brahms's withdrawal from quartet composition after this movement may in part have been conditioned, like Haydn's three-quarters of a century before, by his encountering a new master of the medium. In 1878, two years after his op.67, he received two quartets from Dvořák, the E major op.80 (1876) and the D minor op.34 (1877), and though he criticized his Czech colleague for carelessness, he also recognized the quality of the music and perhaps silently noted too how Dvořák was possessed of so very natural a quartet style. Partly this was because his harmony was less complex than Brahms's and so could more easily be accommodated by four lines: multiple stopping is comparatively unusual in Dvořák's quartets, except, significantly, when he wants to impress, as in the slow movement of the D minor. There were also other features of Dvořák's style that made the quartet an appropriate medium, notably his liking for presenting a melody first in one instrument then in another with a counter-melody added. But in writing quartets he must have been helped too by his long years of experience as a viola player, experience to which all his mature quartets bear witness in making the viola – not the cello as in Beethoven, Schubert, Mendelssohn and Schumann – the second soloist of the ensemble.

These mature quartets, like those of Brahms, were preceded by several prentice efforts, the difference being that Dvořák allowed his to survive. They are not too impressive. The first three – the A major op.2 (1862), and the B flat and D major from an unnumbered set of three (1869 or 1870) – are all prolix to a degree: the D major plays uncut for around seventy minutes. Savouring their characterless themes over and over again, they are works devised to be enjoyed in the composition more than the performance, which was reasonable enough when Dvořák had no expectation of a public platform. The only one of his first six quartets to be played in concert during his lifetime was the A major, and for that occasion he authorized cuts. He also made no attempt to publish these works, which in fact did not appear in print until after the Second World War. However, there is some growing interest, control and distinctiveness of invention in the later three of them, all in minor keys: the E minor no.4 (1870), F minor no.5 op.9 (1873) and A minor no.6 op.12 (also 1873). The first and last of these were planned as continuous structures of three and five movements respectively, the E minor having two quick movements around an Andante religioso for which Dvořák retained some affection, re-using it in 1875 in his G major string quintet and again some years later adapting it as a nocturne in B major for string orchestra. In the case of the A minor op.12 he changed his mind about the single-movement form and divided the piece into four conventional movements, sadly omitting the most attractive of the original five, an Andante appassionato in F major. Then, as if this had not been sufficient sacrifice to orthodoxy, the next year he wrote another A minor quartet, op.16, that keeps rather severely to the rules of four-movement form and is now, like its two immediate predecessors, more modest, more public in its proportions. It was published almost at once, one of the first of Dvořák's works to appear in print.

The subsequent history of his quartet writing is again one of tension between the conventionality that the genre had come to embody and the spontaneity that was Dvořák's own, a tension between Vienna and a Bohemia that was starting to feel its independence. There had been evidence of this as early as the scherzo of the D major quartet, which is based on a song of Slav patriotism and is also, significantly, the most arresting movement in the first three quartets. But there is much more Slavonic colouring in the E major quartet no.8 op.80 (the high opus *Dvořák op. 80 in E* number was ascribed by the publisher when the work was belatedly printed in 1888: Dvořák had called the work his op.27). The A minor slow movement catches the tone of proud yet yearning melancholy that soon was to become characteristic of Dvořák's understanding of the Ukrainian *dumka*. Also, the first movement is one of his free and original re-interpretations of sonata form, with the relative minor, C sharp minor, acting instead of the dominant as secondary key (it is the key, too, of the scherzo's trio), and with the recapitulation giving place to a second development, more forceful than the first, which makes necessary a second reprise at the end. Equally personal, though absolutely within the great quartet tradition, even if it had been rarely achieved by composers since Beethoven, is the conversational manner that emerges quite naturally, for example, in the first development of this allegro, concerned with a gruppetto figure that runs through the whole movement:

47 Dvořák: Quartet in E op. 80, first movement

By contrast, the D minor quartet was plainly intended to impress Brahms, its dedicatee, by its adherence to the rules. The outer movements are both in straightforward sonata form with a repeat of the exposition (this had been absent from the E major quartet), a correct key scheme and a proper coda. However, the scherzo is marked 'Alla Polka' and brings a new dance flavour to this movement, possibly in emulation of the A major quartet written three years earlier by another Czech, Zdeněk Fibich (1850-1900).

Dvořák op. 51 in Eb Dvořák's next quartet, the E flat no. 10 op. 51 (1878-9), again goes much deeper into national territory, with a second movement in G minor and major that Dvořák now heads 'Dumka' and that now contains a lively 3/8 dance as well as the Slavonic lament:

48 Dvořák: Quartet in Eb op. 51, second movement

This is an even more novel substitute for the scherzo than the polka of the D minor quartet, and it serves to mirror and complement, rather than contrast with, the andante Romanze in B flat. The finale that follows is again folk-inspired, being in the rhythm of the *skočná*, a Czech leaping dance, but the venerable example of Haydn is enough to ensure that such peasant vigour is entirely compatible with rondo form. And in the first movement, which begins with supremely lovely E flat music in the purest quartet style, there is a G major polka episode that chimes perfectly, in terms both of harmony and of folk character, with the rest of the quartet. Moreover, the reprise begins with the secondary material so that the beautiful first invention can return, as in Schubert's unfinished C minor quartet, to close the movement. Once more, in trusting his own wayward imagination rather than what he took to be orthodox procedure, Dvořák produced a quartet that is fresh and authentic in texture and form.

After this, following the zigzag course of the last four quartets, came another mental pilgrimage to Vienna. The E flat quartet had been written for the Quartetto Fiorentino, a German–Italian ensemble led by Jean Becker and active between 1865 and 1880, who had asked for a work of Slavonic feeling, whereas its successor, the C major no.11 op.61 (1881), was composed for the Hellmesberger Quartet, whose invitation Dvořák took to impose a more conventional manner. In complete contrast with the E flat quartet, much in the outer movements of the C major is massive and orchestral in conception, and the slow movement and scherzo behave as slow movements and scherzos are expected to: the scherzo, in particular, is more conventional than any in Dvořák's quartets since the A minor op.16. Nevertheless, the long first movement is Dvořákian – or Schubertian – in the tonal and thematic variety of its material, and the consequent new structural manoeuvres required. For instance, the first theme slips very quickly from C major into C minor, which justifies its recapitulation in A major and minor, the latter being the relative minor of C major. Again, as in the E flat quartet and not at all as in the formally much squarer D minor, the order of events in the first movement reprise is much altered with respect to the exposition, and the first theme has the opportunity to make a gradual descent into its rightful place, appearing a second time in D major and then finally, at the end of the movement, in C major.

Dvořák's quartets from around 1880, particularly those in E major and E flat, are the first completely successful works written in their genre for half a century, but they have tended to be overshadowed by the E minor quartet which another Czech, Bedřich Smetana (1824-84), wrote in 1876 and subtitled 'From my life'. Such is the power of a programme. However, in giving his quartet a narrative outline Smetana was only doing in advance what Wagner had six years earlier done for Beethoven, and nearly all of the work can be understood as abstract music in the usual four movements. The first, preceding Dvořák's E flat quartet in looking to the formal example of

Smetana no. 1 in E minor

135

Schubert's C minor movement, is bounded by questing music in E minor – 'the call of Fate to take up life's struggle' – while within the composer's 'romantic feelings in music, love and life in general' find expression. The second movement takes up the polka rhythm that was occurring to Dvořák at the same time for the same stage of his E major quartet, but Smetana's is a double polka, the peasant kind in F contrasted with the ballroom variety in D flat. After this the A flat largo, in the richly interwoven tradition of quartet slow movements, hardly needs the composer's prompting that it recalls 'the happiness of my first love', and it is evident enough from the zest of the rustic dance finale, in E major, that it conveys his enthusiastic nationalism. The very end, though, is another matter. The dance breaks off and Smetana transcribes into his quartet the whining E that racked his inner ear during his approaching deafness:

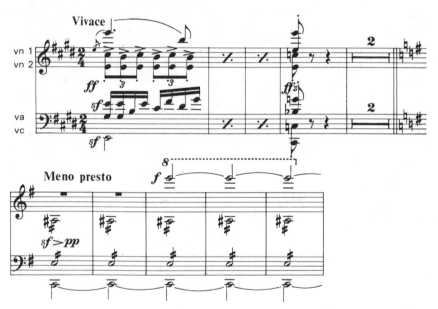

49 Smetana: Quartet no. 1 in E minor, fourth movement

Then the main themes of the first movement and of the finale are heard again as if in recollection, and the work ends uneasily after so poignant an interruption of life into art.

Smetana no. 2 in D minor

Smetana's second quartet, in D minor (1882-3), was his last important work and is, throughout, a still more troubling case of an autobiography created very near the events and states of mind it describes. The first movement leaps wildly from furious energy to deep gloom, and it is hard to be sure whether its lack of control is a conscious creative ploy designed to give the impression of a a mind near breaking point, or whether it is precisely the product of a mind in that state. What follows, in more settled style, is another polka scherzo with contrasting slow music, but then the third movement is again bizarre, beginning with rushing material that may suggest the whirl of ideas in the composer's brain, out of which, with deliberation, he gradually forges a march theme: this is powerful expressive justification for canonic entries, which, in Dvořák and others, had tended to become rather an automatic response at moments of high tension. The quartet's finale, another dance, is in D major, this time without any interruption, but it is too sudden an outburst of lightheartedness, and the work ends, for different reasons, as much in uncertainty as its predecessor.

Both Smetana's quartets are thus intensely personal documents, yet they also exemplify a wider trend in discovering an opera composer turning to the string quartet at a late stage in his career, for in 1873 Verdi wrote his quartet in E minor, his only instrumental work of any consequence. He claimed to have written it merely to pass the time, which it does quite happily, and at first he would not have it published or publicly performed. It is of course an abundantly tuneful piece, but it also reveals, like the quartets of such different composers as Schumann and Dvořák, the insecurity the Romantics felt in this most absolute of forms. In its efforts to be sonata-like, the first movement almost makes a sonata of its exposition, vigorously working at its first idea before the secondary material, properly couched in G major, is introduced and continued to induce a feeling of reprise. The fugal finale might also be taken as a sign of a bad conscience, except that this is a 'Scherzo fuga' in which may be discerned some premonition of the ending of *Falstaff* twenty years later. Nor can Verdi's quartet really be seen as a revival of the tradition of Boccherini: its classicism is so general as to be anonymous (though the material is individual enough), and it had no successors in Italian music. The two quartets by Ferruccio Busoni (1866-1924), the C minor op.19 (1880-81) and the D minor op.26 (1888), are both early, and though Busoni was one composer who might well have found an Italian way into a Germanic form, here he was under the spell of Brahms.

Verdi in E minor

In Russia, though, a quartet tradition was developing every bit as vital as that in Prague. Tchaikovsky wrote his first quartet, his D major op.11, in 1871 for a concert of his works, though it had been preceded by various student exercises in the medium. Like Dvořák at the same stage in his career, Tchaikovsky was torn between the rival claims of Viennese orthodoxy and nationalism. In his case, however,

Tchaikovsky nos 1 – 3

the deference to good quartet manners is positively beneficial. The outer movements are both in clear sonata form, both with exposition repeats, and the invention is lively even if it is also artificial. The slow movement, an Andante cantabile that Tchaikovsky much later adapted for cello and strings, was based on a folksong, though in its melodious warmth it is more characteristic of the composer than are its companions.

Tchaikovsky's uneasiness in the medium becomes much more evident, and much more destructive, in his second quartet, op.22 in F major (1874). This has an arresting start – a major second sounded sforzato by first violin and viola – but the movement to which it gives birth is disintegrated and repetitious, and the finale, though it manages sonata expectations rather more neatly, is one of the worst examples of the unhappy convention, traceable to Haydn, that the development must find issue in fugato. The slow movement is again an andante, but this time with markedly inferior ideas inflated towards the end by an orchestral rhetoric that cannot but sound false from just four players.

In his third quartet, op.30 in E flat minor (1877), Tchaikovsky came no nearer finding authentic quartet textures of his own, but the quality of the material is much higher and the form surer in most respects. The first movement. which has much more to do with B flat than with the supposed home key, is a sonata allegro contained within an expressive andante, and the third, where at last E flat minor comes into its own, is not only the work's tonal centre of gravity but also its emotional heart: it is a funeral march and at the same time an elegiac chant, ending with music in which an obsessive B flat is reviewed in solemn harmony before the movement reaches its dying climax in the extreme high register:

50 Tchaikovsky: Quartet no. 3 in E♭ minor op. 30, third movement

This Andante funebre e doloroso makes explicit the quartet's purpose as a memorial to Tchaikovsky's violinist friend Ferdinand Laub, which only makes it the more disconcerting that a boisterous finale in E flat major should come next to conclude the work.

After this Tchaikovsky wrote no more quartets and precious little further chamber music: his contemporary Nikolay Rimsky-Korsakov (1844-1908) was also to come to the conclusion that the quartet medium was an alien one, though in his case the realization came rather late in the day, after the G major quartet he composed at the age of fifty-four, and after two other complete quartets as well as various single movements. Both composers were perhaps outfaced by the example of Alexander Borodin (1833-87), who also alarmed his close colleagues Mily Balakirev (1837-1910) and Modest Musorgsky (1839-81) by contributing to what they regarded as the outmoded genre of chamber music. In a sense, though, Borodin was not falling in with a tradition. Part of the charm of his quartets lies in their innocence of what had gone before, even though the first of them, in A (1874-9), claims to have been 'suggested by a theme of Beethoven' (from op.130), for the texture is usually quite uncomplicated, dominated by a tune almost from first bar to last, and, corresponding-ly, the forms are normally built from juxtaposed panels, labelling themselves 'first subject', 'second subject', 'development of first subject' and so on. By the 1870s this was certainly not rare, since the string quartet (like other standard forms) was having to struggle for its life against the dictates composers could find in their textbooks, but

Borodin no. 1 in A

Borodin entirely avoids sounding academic because he accepts the rules so unhesitatingly, and because his tunes make no pretence of being earnest quartet material. At a time when almost every other quartet composer was handicapped by debts he supposed he owed to convention, Borodin simply went on his way without worry.

In his first quartet he even gets away with two passages of fugato, one in the development of the long opening moderato, the other in the middle of the slow movement. However, his more harmonically conceived, more lustrous textures are far more typical, whether it is a case of presenting a melody in thirds or sixths – this especially in the radiantly tuneful second quartet in D (1881) – or using special effects. Unlike Tchaikovsky and Rimsky-Korsakov, or indeed Brahms, Borodin was himself a string player, specifically a cellist, and his understanding and enjoyment of the medium are nowhere more striking than in the trio of the first quartet, glistening with harmonics:

Borodin no. 2 in D

51 Borodin: Quartet no. 1 in A, third movement

Apart from these two numbered quartets, Borodin also wrote a short Serenata alla spagnola in D minor to serve as slow movement in a quartet of 1886 which begins with a well behaved sonata allegro by Rimsky-Korsakov, continues with a scherzo by Anatoly Lyadov (1855-1914) and ends with a finale by Alexander Glazunov (1865-1936). Collaborative works were not uncommon in Russia at the time, when rival groupings of composers were concerned to declare their allegiances, but the particular point here was to honour the publisher and patron Mitrofan Belyayev (1836-1904): each movement plays with the motif Bb–A–F, spelling out this Maecenas's name as 'B–La-F'. Belyayev had a special liking for quartets, and in addition to Borodin's pair and the 'B–La–F' compendium he published, for example, the first five quartets of Glazunov (the sixth came much later, under very different circumstances, in 1921), of which the G major third (1888) is splendidly picturesque, with folksong themes in its first movement, a liturgical flavour to its chordal slow movement, a mazurka as scherzo and a finale headed 'Une fête slave' and looking forward to *Petrushka* as a montage of dance episodes.

But Glazunov's is only one of the most highly flavoured of many Slavonic quartets written in Russia at the time. Borodin, like Tchaikovsky, also made use of folk melodies, and those he invented himself, notably the luscious theme of the slow Notturno in the second quartet, belong very much in the melodic world of his nationalist opera *Prince Igor.* Moreover, Rimsky-Korsakov wrote a quartet 'on Russian themes' (1878-9), though only its last movement, a fugue sounding 'At the Monastery', has been published, and he collaborated again with Lyadov and Glazunov on the three-movement 'Jour de fête' quartet, of which he wrote the final 'Choeur dansé russe'. Nor is it surprising that the quartet should have become one of the prime vehicles for musical nationalism, exploited also of course by Dvořák and Smetana at this time, not to mention Edvard Grieg (1843-1907), whose single quartet in G minor op.27 (1877-8) is more Schumannesque than Norwegian, though a distinct folk character is brought into the final 'Presto al saltarello'. For the quartet, in terms of its history and of its discipline, was naturally disposed to embody in their most acute form the fundamental features of the musical language at any particular time. First these had been centred on the dynamic harmony of tonic–dominant polarity, then on the richer, wider understandings of tonality emerging from the 1820s onwards. Now, near the end of the century, the even more complex harmony of Wagner and Brahms was proving difficult to accommodate within the quartet texture: the alternative source of novelty was the variety of inflected tonalities from folk music. There were thus eminently musical reasons, quite apart from the growth of nationalist feeling in the Slav countries in particular, why musical nationalism should have become so prominent in the 1870s and so important to the quartet.

Doubtless, too, Belyayev's encouragement helped as far as Russia was concerned. From 1891 he organized regular quartet recitals in St Petersburg on Friday evenings, whence the volumes later published as *Les vendredis* and incorporating short sonata and dance movements by Borodin, Rimsky-Korsakov, Glazunov, Lyadov and others. But similar lighter music for the string quartet – hitherto the repository almost exclusively of substantial four-movement works – was being written elsewhere, by Giacomo Puccini (1858-1924) in his *Crisantemi* (1890), by Dvořák in his also botanical *Cypřiše* ('Cypresses', 1887) and most notably by Hugo Wolf (1860-1903) in his *Italienische Serenade* (also 1887). Dvořák's *Cypresses* stand as a row of twelve short movements, most of them warm andantes and all arranged from romantic love songs of his youth. Wolf's composition is similarly connected with songs, though with a contemporary project, the Eichendorff settings he was making in the same spring of 1887. It is also, in its delicate playful irony and brittle speed, as far removed from Dvořák's world as Eichendorff is from the soulful verse of the Czech's cypress songs.

Wolf in D minor

Wolf's serenade had been preceded by another character piece, the Intermezzo in E flat (1882-6), and by the large-scale and greatly ambitious quartet in D minor (1878-84), whose first three movements were finished before he was twenty-one. This work carries an epigraph from Goethe's *Faust* – 'Entbehren sollst du, sollst entbehren' ('You must renounce, renounce') – which stands appropriately over music which begins with such dramatic force and passionate intensity:

52 Wolf: Quartet in D minor, first movement

As this slow introduction leads into a sonata allegro, so it becomes clear that a burden of words continues to be borne by instrumental lines that are loaded with expressive wide intervals in a manner that looks sideways to Mahler and back, more directly, to Beethoven's late quartets – particularly, given the fierce energy here, to the 'Grosse Fuge'. The scherzo, marked 'Resolut', is indeed grimly determined, and the slow movement is again richly expressive, starting out from the same kind of triadic purity Wagner had glimpsed in *Tannhäuser* and *Lohengrin*, but continuing with once more a Beethovenian subjectivity. The finale, at 499 bars, has the length to match its predecessors, and an enigmatic liveliness that suggests perhaps renunciation has been achieved.

Though Wolf's emotional intensity is his own, and may even be usefully regarded as self-analytic, his invocation of late Beethoven he shared with others around the time of Wagner's essay. In France the Maurin and Armingaud Quartets, both active from the mid-1850s, helped to make Beethoven's last works known and more generally to draw attention to the serious quartet tradition from Haydn and Mozart to Mendelssohn and Schumann, a tradition whose appreciation had until then been confused by the large and popular outputs of composers from Cambini to Onslow. Naturally French composers of the time were stimulated to essay the genre, one of the first being Edouard Lalo (1823-92), who played viola and second violin in the Armingaud Quartet, and whose single quartet in E flat emerged first as his op.19 in 1859 and then in revised form as his op.45 in 1880. Alexis de Castillon (1838-73) published a quartet in A minor and a movement from an uncompleted second quartet, and among the unpublished works from the still briefer career of Guillaume Lekeu (1870-94) are various compositions for string quartet, among them a startlingly Haydnish title, *Commentaire sur les paroles du Christ* (1887), and a D minor quartet of the same year.

But none of these left anything like the resonance of the D major quartet composed in 1889 by César Franck (1822-90), whose pupils had included both Castillon and Lekeu. This quartet was the last of the great instrumental works composed in the final dozen years of Franck's life, and like its companions it makes no secret of being in cyclic form – re-using themes, that is, from one movement to another. At the start of the finale, for example, the principal materials of the preceding three movements are introduced in turn, in reverse order, and by implication rejected. But if this were all, then Franck's much vaunted cyclic form would be no more than an imitation of Beethoven's practice in his ninth symphony or, to take nearer

Franck in D

143

parallels, Mendelssohn's in his quartets opp.12 and 13. Moreover, recapitulating earlier themes in the finale was very much in the air at the time, to be found in the symphony Bruckner was recomposing while Franck worked at his quartet, no.8, and also in the early G minor quartet (1888) of Carl Nielsen (1865-1931). Franck, of course, goes much further. Not only is his self-quotation more pervasive – for instance, the alien subjects are not, as it turns out, banished from the finale forever – but his themes are all of a piece, with immediately audible connections such as the firm three-note descent in even values that occurs at the start of the first theme of the opening movement (on an arpeggio), similarly at the start of the larghetto melody (on a scale) and again near the beginning of the primary theme of the finale (once more on an arpeggio).

Franck is not, in his quartet, greatly concerned with the development of his themes, for development could easily confuse the identity of themes so closely related. The development section of the first movement is almost alarmingly perfunctory, and always the accent is on the presentation of themes, the reconsideration of them in different harmonic and contrapuntal textures, and, in the finale, their mutual confrontation. This helps to give Franck's themes the self-consciousness for which Beethoven's choral symphony provides a precedent, and one has to be prepared sometimes for an effect of schoolmasterly insistence on elucidation. Something of this can be attributed to the temper of the times. Franck's themes, which seem to proclaim their functions as they arrive, make his music sound more than any other like a practical exercise in the understanding of form that theorists of his time were beginning to achieve. It is also clear that he owed much to Wagner's handling of basic melodies to sustain a large design. Even so, his quartet and other works would not have become the epitome of late nineteenth-century thematicism if he had not been so forceful a didact: a comparison with Arnold Schoenberg (1874-1951) may be revealing here.

And just as it was one of Schoenberg's pupils, Alban Berg (1885-1935), who first laid bare the structure of his master's op.7 quartet, so it was one of Franck's disciples, Vincent d'Indy (1851-1931), who made the definitive analysis of the D major quartet he so revered. His task was hardly as difficult as Berg's, since during the next sixteen years the complexity of the musical language was to grow to a point of saturation, and both champions were helped by dealing with music which, on a rudimentary formal level, virtually analyses itself, as has already been suggested in the case of the Franck. Nevertheless, d'Indy did have to cope with new kinds of form which Franck's emphatic thematicism made possible. The first movement, in particular, enfolds a D minor sonata allegro within a D major Poco lento, the latter giving the movement a slow introduction and a coda, and also a fugal episode after the exposition that makes up for the brevity of the development proper. Beethoven provides some precedents for this, but none that has Franck's authoritative clarity, that decisive purposefulness which makes him start his quartet with massive sonorities, powerfully modelled ideas and a tone of brave, wild triumph:

53 Franck: Quartet in D, first movement

As string quartet writing, of course, this may leave something to be desired, and indeed throughout his quartet Franck tends to regard the ensemble as a harmonic unit except when he is engaging in strict polyphony: he also keeps all four instruments at work almost continuously and, like Brahms, makes the physical strenuousness of his piece even greater by requiring a fair bit of double stopping, especially in the middle voices. But though there might have been better models of quartet texture, and though Franck's symphonic variations and violin sonata are more successful instances of his methods and his expressive ardour, his string quartet gained an immense prestige among his followers, partly because it was his last important composition, partly because it was cast in the loftiest form that music could offer. D'Indy responded at once with a D major quartet of his own, his op.35, and then after adding a second in E major op.45 (1897) waited until he could emulate his teacher by making this medium the vehicle for what were almost his last thoughts, given in his D flat quartet op.96 of 1928-9. It also fell to d'Indy to finish the scherzo of the op.35 C minor quartet left incomplete at his death by Ernest Chausson (1855-99), who in his slow movement embodied lingering echoes of *Parsifal* besides, by choosing the key of A flat, exemplifying the Franck group's liking for Schubertian third relationships: Franck's own quartet had had a scherzo in F sharp minor and a slow movement in B major.

The most productive influence of Franck's quartet is not to be found in the works of either of these pupils, however, but in that of another Frenchman who otherwise took a very different path: Claude Debussy (1862-1918). He composed his only string quartet in 1893, just four years after Franck, and as if acknowledging the gravity of the undertaking he gave this work uniquely an opus number, op. 10. It was also the only one of his published works to lay claim to a key, though 'G minor' is rather an awkward fit for the music: the main harmonic areas in the first movement, for example, are the Phrygian mode on G and the same mode on D. Similarly in this movement, the gestures towards orthodox sonata form – most notably the decisive recapitulation of the first theme – come near impotence, standing as conventional signposts in music which is taking routes of a different kind.

Debussy in G minor

This different variety of motion in Debussy, expressed on a large scale for the first time in his quartet, is intimately linked with a different kind of phrasing. Debussy's ideas are generally short, occupying one or two bars, and often they loosen themselves from the antecedent–consequent logic that Franck's music displays as a paradigm (see, for instance, the quotation above), exactly as his harmony loosens itself from straightforward major–minor tonality. For its furtherance his music has to depend therefore on sequence or literal repetition, on bald contrast or on the happy chances of allusive connection. This last was one chief marker of his genius. Chausson, faced with similar problems in his later quartet, had to indulge instead in a repetitiveness that becomes wearing despite the great beauty of his material, whereas Debussy can always think of some variation, distant or subtle, chosen with indefinable justness. And flexibility of movement naturally goes along with flexibility of speed, the opening Animé et très décidé of this quartet having a proliferation of tempo changes that is remarkable for the period, for although it had become common for the secondary material of a quartet sonata movement to unfold at a different, nearly always slower speed (often achieved simply by longer note values), there is no parallel for the accelerations, decelerations and sudden shifts required here.

In the sphere of the quartet such an innovation bespoke a profound change. Players who have to make up one pliable unit cannot allow themselves so much latitude in matters of individual phrasing, and anyway Debussy's material is not such as to stimulate varieties of approach: there is simply too little of it. The conversational aspects of the medium are thus depressed, and instead of being used as a group of four compatible companions the quartet is seen as an ensemble of different instruments to be joined in different combinations: this new view, extended to bring about the mixed ensembles of Debussy's late sonatas twenty years later, was to be hugely important in the next century. In this quartet it results in a great variety of texture, encompassing merely within the finale, for example, many different ways of joining two or three of the instruments together in octaves and so creating new textures, which, nevertheless, have absolutely nothing to do with the aspiration towards orchestral largeness to be found in most quartets of the period. However novel the sounds, they are judiciously imagined for just four instruments, even when, in his scherzo, Debussy is responding to his recent experience of Indonesian music and conceiving a heterophony of repeating and non-repeating fragments in diverse timbres:

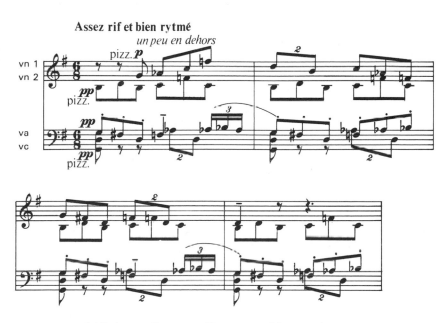

54 Debussy: Quartet in G minor op. 10, second movement

The effect here is perfectly simple and natural, and yet it is worlds away from the classical norms of quartet texture, a model example of Debussy's unfettered inventiveness. At the same time this quotation shows, in the viola part, one of numerous variants Debussy derives from the Phrygian main theme of his first movement. Franck's example was no doubt a stimulus here, but Debussy's practice is quite different, for where Franck is concerned to stamp each of his themes with its own identity – otherwise his cyclic structure would not work – Debussy seems already to be searching instead for fluidity, for constant alteration. When Franck brings back earlier themes in his finale, he does so with very evident reference to earlier movements, whereas Debussy's changes on his basic material introduce new possibilities, repeatedly, and so make the quartet a work that looks constantly forward as the play of variation continues through three of its four movements. The exception also has a point. The slow movement – around D flat, polar opposite of the work's principal G centre – is a withdrawal from the perpetual change around it, a withdrawal into a more conventional kind of Romantic expression though still plentiful-ly endowed with unprecedented sonorities, such as the bare octave fifths sounded by violins and cello. Then, when the finale begins, the fact of the slow movement's digression is made structurally plain, for its successor starts out seduced by the harmony and tempo of what had gone before, and a sudden new beginning is needed before this conclusive movement can properly accelerate towards its finish.

Apart from its influence on the whole future of the string quartet in indicating that new sounds could be achieved by forgetting the old conversational mode, Debussy's quartet was more directly imitated by a few younger composers of his time, notably Maurice Ravel (1875-1937) in his F major quartet of 1902-3 and Ralph Vaughan Williams (1872-1958) in his quartet of 1908-9 – also in Debussy's G minor with modal predilections. Coming from a period when he was particularly close to Debussy musically, Ravel's quartet would almost seem to have been devised as an exaggeration of Debussy's, for though it is more deliberate in its cyclic engineering, it offers a sumptuous exhibition of new quartet textures, to the extent that there is no essential difference in conception between this work and one for a much more varied ensemble, the Introduction and Allegro for harp, flute, clarinet and string quartet. However, there was no need for the lessons of Debussy's quartet to be repeated, for it to be proved again that the four instruments of the ensemble could be removed from all their associations of texture, form and genre (the fact that Debussy keeps to a conventional four-movement outline only helps to demonstrate, of course, how far he is from being symphonic). It is understandable, therefore, that Debussy himself should have quickly abandoned the second quartet he began in the year following the G minor and that he should have completed instead his Prélude à 'L'après-midi d'un faune'.

Meanwhile, in the same year as Debussy wrote his quartet, Dvořák returned to the genre after a gap of a dozen years, and like Debussy looked to the quartet as a testing ground for modal ideas. The result was his twelfth quartet, op.96 in F major, whose original nickname of 'Nigger' has now been replaced by one less offensive but equally misleading: 'American'. In fact the only American thing about the work is that it was written there – though written while Dvořák was spending the summer among a Bohemian colony in Iowa. For the pentatonic scale that gives the work so distinctive a character (the main theme of each movement is in the mode F–G–A–C–D) is not the exclusive property of black American plantation songs or of American Indian music but is to be found all over the world, and not least in Bohemia. Nevertheless, being in the United States may have helped Dvořák forget the rival pulls of Prague and Vienna, and so become, as in the immediately preceding 'New World' Symphony, more purely himself.

Dvořák op. 96 in F: 'American'

Apart from anything else, that meant becoming more purely diatonic. Remarkably in a work of this period, twelve bars of the F major quartet have passed before a single accidental is introduced, and the pentatonic tunes are always heard within an unmistakable context of key, with the same key signature prevailing throughout except in the scherzo's F minor trio (the slow movement is in D minor). However, this return to fundamentals is given a personal touch. The secondary material of the first movement is not in the conventional C but in A minor moving into A major, continuing an association of keys with a common secondary key that has been noted in Schubert (and Chopin). Also, the sunny ease of the music is entirely Dvořák's, undisturbed even by a burst of fugal writing coming all too predictably to wrap up the first movement's development.

As the first great string quartet composed in the New World, Dvořák's F major naturally encouraged efforts from native composers, who until then had regarded the quartet as no more than a necessary student exercise. John Knowles Paine (1839-1906) had written his D major quartet op.5 while studying in Berlin in the late 1850s and never went back to the medium thereafter; Horatio Parker (1863-1919) similarly had written his only quartet, op.11 in F, as a student in Munich. George Whitefield Chadwick (1854-1931), however, proved a hardier quartet composer if not a less academic one, and followed the two quartets of his Leipzig student days with three more written in Boston, two of them soon after Dvořák's F major. His fellow Bostonian Arthur Foote (1853-1937), who unusually did not train in Germany, also wrote two quartets after Dvořák's visit.

These New England Romantic–classicists would seem to have been attracted by the very traditionalism of the string quartet: some doubt is necessary because their works remain obscure, only one of Foote's quartet movements, for instance, having been published. There would then be a parallel with English composers of the time. Hubert Parry (1848-1918), the first Englishman to write quartets since Shield and Charles Wesley around 1780, composed two as a student at Oxford and one a decade later; Charles Villiers Stanford (1852-1924), on the other hand, waited until he was nearly forty before embarking on a series of eight that look back to Mendelssohn and Brahms.

But for a composer totally out of sympathy with tradition, even the string quartet was not to prove sufficient restraint: such a composer was Charles Ives (1874-1954), who wrote his first quartet (1896) while studying with Parker at Yale. Ives's quartet is in four movements, but there its orthodoxy ends. The first movement is not a sonata structure but a mild-mannered fugue which twenty years later was to be orchestrated and placed in the fourth symphony. Like the adagio third movement and the finale it uses hymn tunes – Ives subtitled the quartet at different times 'A Revival Service' and 'From the Salvation Army', and he used some of the movements in church, with two violins on top and himself playing the lower parts on the organ – but the quotations are not ostentatiously paraded in the manner of his later music, though neither are they completely assimilated. There is a misfit, more disconcerting because the genre is so elevated, between the material and its setting, and nowhere is that more so than in the light but robustly down-to-earth second movement.

Dvořák op. 106 in G, op. 105 in A♭ By the time Ives wrote this quartet Dvořák had returned to Prague and composed two more, no.13 in G op.106 and no.14 in A flat op.105 (both 1895). The second of these, begun before the first but completed afterwards, is unproblematic in style and feeling, if not melodically so boldly rudimentary as the F major. Again its harmonic range is neatly restricted: the well developed scherzo is a robust folk dance in F minor with an A flat trio, the slow movement muses on a melody in F major, and this time the secondary material of the first movement is in the proper dominant key of E flat.

The G major quartet is altogether more ambitious, and so perpetuates Dvořák's habit of alternating between works of strong folk inspiration (the quartets in E, E flat, F and A flat) and others conceived with an eye to the Viennese tradition (those in A minor, D minor, C and G). This time, however, the strain of the undertaking is wholly productive. The first movement takes the highly unusual course, needing an extraordinary sudden access of harmonic energy, of moving to B flat for its secondary material: the most decisive proof of the emancipation of the third begun in late Haydn. The importance of the semitone within this secondary material then makes possible, still within the exposition, an expressive momentary shift up to B major. The association with flat keys is continued in the adagio, Dvořák's most inward quartet slow movement, which is a set of variations switching, as in a familiar Haydn pattern, between the major and minor modes on its home E flat. Once more (this had happened too in the first movement of the A flat quartet) Dvořák uses a pentatonic tune harmonized in such a way that there can be no doubt about the tonality:

55 Dvořák: Quartet in G op. 106, second movement

The scherzo, however, takes up the other possibility suggested by the first movement exposition and adopts B minor as its home, with a trio in D major, and so by this stage the quartet has harmonically elaborated two triads, those of E flat and G. Then the finale, with a strength and vigour above mere appropriateness, reaches its emphatic

151

G major ending only after it has substantially reviewed the key of E flat. It is a conclusion of a bigness fitting the rest of the work, which, though not a revelatory adventure to be compared with the last works of Beethoven or Schubert, suitably completes the greatest cycle of quartets written since their deaths.

Inevitably those quartets had still greater influence in Czechoslovakia than in the United States, and particularly among Dvořák's pupils. The first two quartets of Vítězslav Novák (1870-1949), composed within ten years of Dvořák's last two, show this, and so too does the first quartet, op.11 in B flat (1896), by Josef Suk (1874-1935), a work of melodic fluency and, in its slow movement, heavier and more personal expressive charge. Suk was also second violinist in the Bohemian (later Czech) Quartet, which enjoyed an international career from 1892 and 1933, and which had given the first performance of Dvořák's G major quartet: the A flat was played for the first time by what was the other great touring quartet of the time, the Vienna-based ensemble named after its leader Arnold Rosé (1863-1946), active from 1892 onwards and later to give the premières of works by Schoenberg (first and second quartets), Max Reger (1873-1916) and Hans Pfitzner (1869-1949).

By the 1890s, therefore, there was every reason for composers to be writing quartets with a view to public performance first and foremost, as indeed Beethoven had done in 1810, and though quartets continued to be printed in parts for public consumption in private, few amateurs can have been encouraged by the difficulties demanded by, for example, Franck and Debussy. It followed too that quartets were being conceived to be experienced from outside rather than to embody musical dialogue for their performers: again the quartets of Franck and Debussy show this most clearly, Debussy's scherzo being a prime example of a quartet texture that makes no sense for the participants, only for the listener (this might almost be a definition of the distinction between heterophony, instanced here, and polyphony). Another development was the revival, after Spohr and his predecessors, of the quartet with a virtuoso part for the leader, a taste catered for in the E minor work that was the first quartet of Camille Saint-Saëns (1835-1921), though his op.112 and written when he was sixty-four: here the intended soloist was Eugène Ysaÿe (1858-1931).

At the same time, however, the great tradition of quartet writing was not yet dead. Indeed, it meant so much to Schoenberg that it was *Schoenberg in D* in a string quartet, his D major (1897), that he produced his first completely successful composition, though its delightful ingeniousness did not recommend it to the mature composer and it remained unpublished until after his death. Then was revealed a work which owes considerably less to Brahms than to Dvořák, abounding as it does with tuneful melodies and an atmosphere of ease far removed from the later Schoenberg. The outer movements are particularly close to Prague, the birthplace of Schoenberg's mother, and the work as a whole is distinctly more Slavonic than the quartets of Tchaikovsky's trusted pupil Sergey Taneyev (1856-1915).

One thing, however, that Taneyev shared with Schoenberg was a rigorous pursuit of the highest of which he was capable: the six quartets he published, all written within the period 1890-1905, had been preceded by at least four others (another, begun in 1911, remained unfinished). Often his virtues have been taken as faults, and he has been criticized for want of imagination and adherence to classical forms. But the example of his friend and colleague Sergey Rakhmaninov (1873-1943) should be enough to warn us against attaching too much importance to ideas being personal and express-ive: Taneyev's restraint comes not from dim inventive resources but from abnegation, and his clear structures similarly convey a wish to be objective. Such a mode of musical expression is of course particularly suited to the quartet, where, as has already been noted, difficulties can easily arise when a powerful emotional image has to be conveyed by four musicians in dialogue. Here was another reason for the quasi-orchestral treatment of the ensemble by Franck, Wolf, Tchaikovsky and at times Dvořák, whereas the quartets of Taneyev fit much more easily into a medium of musical discourse.

Taneyev achieved his classicism largely through a return to eighteenth-century ideals, and though he was by no means the only Russian composer of his period to do so – Tchaikovsky's veneration of Mozart is well known, and the pieces of Les vendredis include the odd courante and gavotte – he was alone in creating not wistfully picturesque evocations of the past but rather large-scale movements, dependent on motivic working that may suggest Haydn and on a conscientious re-entry into the spirit of sonata form, variations and fugue. Once this had been achieved, his fantasy could take flight. For instance, in the second movement of his third quartet, op.7 in D minor (1886, revised 1896), a highly diverse set of character variations is built on the basis of a classically simple andantino: one is a mazurka played sul tasto, the next a noble adagio for the leader. The other movement of this work, which has the sonata plus variations form of Beethoven's last piano sonata, exemplifies Taneyev's mask of eighteenth-century grace and simplicity:

56 *Taneyev: Quartet no. 3 in D minor op. 7, first movement*

Taneyev's development is not remarkable except for its increasing force, but the balanced phrases elsewhere maintain the movement with authority, even through its expressive use of A minor as secondary tonality (as in other D minor quartets going back to Mozart).

Romantic neoclassicism is not of course restricted to Taneyev's mature quartets: it exists as much in his earlier works, of which the C major quartet of 1882-3 has much that is Haydnesque besides a more than usually purposeful fugal development in the finale, and it exists too in Raff's op. 192 of a few years before. Nowhere, however, is the synthesis of the eighteenth and nineteenth centuries pursued with *Reger op. 54 in G* greater vigour than in the first two published quartets of Reger, the G *minor and A* minor and A major of his op. 54 (1900). These were the first quartets to take note of the great changes music had undergone in the 1890s in the symphonies of Mahler and the tone poems of Strauss, and in Reger, quite by contrast with Taneyev, the contrapuntal impetus only exacerbates the music's instability:

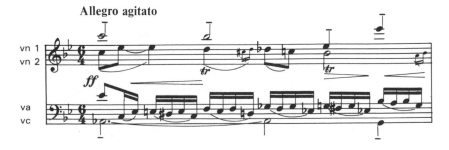

57 Reger: Quartet in G minor op. 54 no. 1, first movement

Here, within a few bars of the opening of the development section
in the first movement of his G minor quartet, Reger has come to one
extreme of the fevered activity and fast harmonic change that operate
throughout the movement. Indeed, keys follow one another so
rapidly, and are often so weakly established, that the listener's tonal
bearings are thoroughly confused, and to an extent greater than in any
of Schoenberg's works until his D minor quartet of five years later.
Reger therefore has to find other ways of keeping his music moving,
since his pressure forever to develop keeps him from taking the
opposite course, to which Debussy was inclining, and abandoning
drive. In this first movement, and more especially in the finale,
progress is assured by contrapuntal imitation taking place at great
speed: the frenetic finale is a double fugue marked Prestissimo assai.

155

Forwards motion is also injected by the speed with which the music moves from one climax to another. The opening Allegro agitato (the latter a favourite term of Reger's) has almost as many tempo changes as occur in Debussy, and a very liberal distribution of dynamic extremes, leading to such moments as the one quoted above, where the high violin line would sound hysterical if the expressive nature of the music were not so obscure. One has the impression of a man gesticulating wildly, trying to make his intentions plain in a language over which even he has lost control.

But that is far from being the whole Reger story. The middle movements of this same quartet are very much clearer in harmony, thematic shape, texture and expression: they are 'verse' counterparts to what Reger (and Schoenberg after him) liked to call his 'musical prose', which is particularly well exemplified in the first movement of the G minor quartet, and which involves an achievement of consistent continuity by means of irregular, often overlapping phrases and exceedingly blurred cadences. The second movement is a scherzo equally typical of Reger in its combination of weight and wit, and the slow movement dwells on elaborate melody in the first violin with warm polyphonically murmuring support.

Reger's other quartets also show how the complication of the G minor's allegro is only one aspect of his style. The companion work in A major is more compact and abrupt in its gestures, with an opening Allegro assai e bizarro that makes its points much more incisively than had the parallel movement in the G minor, followed by a slow movement in variation form and a final rondo so unnervingly spirited that there is no need of a scherzo. Again the D minor quartet op. 74 (1903-4) is comparatively clear in shape and detail, though it differs from the laconic A major in its dimensions: it plays for about fifty minutes, with the opening Allegro agitato e vivace and the slow movement, again an andante with variations, each occupying more than the nineteen minutes of the whole A major.

The reason for this elongation is the same as the reason for great density in the G minor quartet: it is the urgency to develop in Reger, who quickly went far beyond Brahms in this respect. The first movement of his D minor quartet has a very striking first theme announced in octaves (something that could not have been contemplated in the G minor work), and this is subjected to vigorous development, along with various subsidiary ideas, for ninety bars before the main secondary theme arrives as a beautiful melody which departs from the conventional secondary key, F major, rather than lies within it:

58 Reger: Quartet in D minor op. 74, first movement

The speedy modulations which take place even within Reger's basic ideas are very much compatible with his rush to develop, since harmonic instability had always in sonata form been associated with development. But because shifts of key are so very frequent in Reger's expositions, the home tonality is severely compromised, and the reprise only makes sense in thematic, not harmonic terms. It may even be helped towards not making sense at all. In the particular case of the first movement of the D minor quartet, Reger begins his recapitulation quietly, by stealth, and then emphasizes the first theme in its second key of A minor, so projecting a sense of development continuing through the recapitulation which, since it repeats the exposition fairly literally except in choice of keys, readily accepts this interpretation. The movement is not then grounded until its short coda, when at last the first theme appears prominently in D minor, ending a process which – as in the D minor first movement of Mahler's third symphony, introduced only the year before Reger began his quartet – has tended to liquidate the distinctive areas of sonata form in continuous development. Reger even suggests, though by no means as strongly as had Franck or Debussy, that this development goes on right through the work, since near the end of the D major finale there is a reappearance of the theme quoted above from the first movement.

This kind of integration was soon to be pressed to the ultimate by Schoenberg in his D minor quartet op.7 (1905), where the four usual movements are spaced within a seamless whole. It is doubtful whether Schoenberg would have known of Berwald's instance of this in his E flat quartet, but certainly as a keen quartet player he would have been familiar with Mendelssohn's tentatives in the same direction, and of course there were the textbook examples of formal unification: Schubert's 'Wanderer' Fantasia and Liszt's B minor piano sonata. His own quartet, however, works in quite a different way. It is not four movements joined in one but rather a single movement that explores the possibilities of the other three: the scherzo with its trio and the slow movement are presented as development sections within a symphonic allegro, which has its exposition at the start of the work and is not properly concluded until the very end of the rondo finale has brought back once more its opening themes, that finale itself being based on speeded-up versions of ideas from the adagio.

Schoenberg's form is thus not a unification of four movements but an extension, prompted by a deliberately chosen model, of the diversification within a single movement opened up, as in Reger, by the speed of the harmonic movement and the polyphonic freedom of the parts. For here, as in the first movement of Reger's G minor quartet, the four instruments are often able to take quite separate courses: Berg pointed out in his apologia how the bounding melody announced by the leader at the start of the work is accompanied not by mere background material but by themes hardly less characterful:

59 *Schoenberg: Quartet no. 1 in D minor op. 7, opening*

And Berg pointed out too how this three-part invention is texturally redistributed and varied whenever it is called upon to reappear. Nor is it surprising that it should have been in the medium of the string quartet, traditionally the medium of musical discourse, that Schoenberg should have achieved his first instance of omnipresent thematicism, his first work in which the function of harmonic support was tirelessly taken over by thematic lines. Sometimes this could mean, as Schoenberg expressed it, that the 'individual parts . . . moved freely in more remote regions of a tonality and met frequently in vagrant harmonies', that the insistence of each line on being an individual brought the music to places where only contrapuntal energy can keep it going, though Schoenberg's strength of purpose imposes on his music a coherence not found in the Reger parallel.

That, though, hardly makes his quartet any the less expressively intense – rather the reverse – and one of its most appealing features is that, within a world of mood and texture opened up by the first theme, there is room for the work to mock its own seriousness. This it does most particularly in the scherzo section, and most particularly by the use of special effects, including harmonics, pizzicato and *sul ponticello*, which suddenly withdraw the strength of an idea, pull the carpet from under its feet. Reger has nothing like this, though indeed Schoenberg's dominant texture, like Reger's, is one of intimate contrapuntal activity well suited to the quartet while straining it to the utmost: it is significant that Reger and Schoenberg were the first great quartet composers who were not also great symphony composers – Reger wrote no symphonies, and Schoenberg's two were both chamber symphonies – just as Mahler was the first great symphonist, excluding the in every way exceptional Liszt and Berlioz, who wrote no quartets.

The quartet was also at best a marginal activity for the other great symphonists of the early twentieth century, Carl Nielsen (1865-1931), Jean Sibelius (1865-1957) and Edward Elgar (1857-1934). Nielsen's third quartet, his op. 14 in E flat (1898), is a work of great breadth and ambition, but his fourth and last, op. 44 in F (1906), was deliberately intended as a relaxation between symphonic endeavours that had to have their place in the orchestra: it was originally entitled *Piacevolezza* ('Agreeableness'). Elgar's single quartet, op. 83 in E minor (1918), was a late work belonging outside this period. Sibelius's D minor op. 56 (1909), however, followed the just considered quartets of Reger and Schoenberg quite swiftly, and in the same key of D minor, the key also of Wolf's quartet and Smetana's second, not to mention a quartet by the teenage Reger which had the unusual feature of introducing a double bass into the finale. But unlike these works, in

159

which D minor seems specially conducive to an autobiographical intensity of expression, the Sibelius work keeps a cool, aloof disposition: despite its title of *Voces intimae* it is less personal, less engaged than his symphonies of the same period. Nor is it coincidental that this objectivity is achieved in a D minor strongly influenced by the Dorian mode, and in a symmetrical form, where the central adagio is framed on each side by movements in pairs. First comes a short D minor allegro whose development propels it straight into a scherzo in A; then after the F major slow movement comes a more elaborate movement of scherzo type and an energetic finale, both in D minor.

New formal patterns in the quartet were the natural product of new ideas (so they had been in Beethoven): modal harmony, the transferring of themes from one movement to another, the now rapidly growing need, felt especially by Reger and Schoenberg as they progressed from late Beethoven, Schubert, Brahms and Dvořák, to work with a greater variety of themes and keys. Inevitably, therefore, structural innovation was not confined to Schoenberg and Sibelius, *Bartók no. 1* but appears even more strikingly in the first quartet of Béla Bartók (1881-1945), his op. 7 of 1908. As in many of his works, Bartók uses here a two-part structure of slow movement followed by a quicker, clearer piece, a combination that has been plausibly linked with the Hungarian verbunkos dance form but equally shares its basic pattern of expectancy and decisiveness with such well established models as the prelude and fugue. In the first quartet the structure occurs twice. The opening movement begins with an utterly new but absolutely authentic quartet sound:

60 Bartók: Quartet no. 1 op. 7, first movement

This slow, meandering fugue, vaguely remembering Wagner in its chromaticism but already quite individual, gives rise to a more homophonic middle section and then returns, leading directly into the light-textured sonata-form allegretto. Then the whole process is repeated in a more compact, and indeed much more Bartókian manner. There is a slow introduction to the finale that looks back to the first movement, followed by an allegro that uses a motif from the second to create a folk dance.

Since the leading quartet in Budapest at this time was led by Jenő Hubay (1858-1937), a man with little sympathy for Bartók's music, a new and very young quartet was formed to give the first performance of Bartók's work, under the leadership of Imre Waldbauer (1892-1953) and with Jenő Kerpely (1885-1954) as cellist. This group's whole career was shaped by Bartók's quartets: their first concert, on 19 March 1910, included the première of his first quartet: they also introduced the next three; and their last concert, in 1946, was for the Hungarian première of his sixth and last quartet.

Meanwhile in Vienna, on 21 December 1908, the first performance of a new work by the Rosé Quartet had brought a storm of practised indignation: the work was Schoenberg's second quartet in F sharp minor, op. 10 (1907-8), celebrated not only as the first venture into atonality but also as a document of the musical and psychological journey that had that venture as its irresistible outcome. Schoenberg's progress towards atonality is sometimes presented as a straight-line development, an unswerving ride into the abyss, but the truth is a little more complicated. The second quartet is not more complex than the first but in every way simpler. In place of the strenuous polyphony with which the earlier work opens, the F sharp minor quartet has harmonic textures, a moderato pace, triple time and a theme that droops downwards instead of taking an active climb. It does not, of course, stay so straightforward: more themes are introduced – five distinct ones in the exposition – and all the time developed and

Schoenberg no. 2 in F# minor

161

combined even before the development section proper, after which comes a reprise that varies the order and setting of the themes considerably. This is in contrast with Reger's recapitulations, which tend to follow his expositions quite closely, only with transpositions that, given the variety and mutability of his keys, begin to sound arbitrary.

That certainly cannot be said of Schoenberg's structural procedures in the opening movement of his op. 10, but at the same time there is a sense in which sonata form itself was here exposing its arbitrariness. Seventy years had passed since Schumann had perceptively drawn attention to the problems faced by composers in creating abstract forms after Beethoven, seventy years in which the quartet, more than any other medium, had shown up the difficulties (in Schumann, Brahms and Tchaikovsky, for instance) and the extremity of the stratagems needed to avoid them (in Mendelssohn, Franck, Debussy and Reger). Now Schoenberg created a sonata form of deliberate awkwardness, one in which the basic themes come clearly labelled and have to be, or else they could not fulfil their functions, one in which sonata form is no longer the most appropriate way in which to consider the material, as it had been in Haydn, but the only way the composer knows. And as if to keep a tight check on his themes, Schoenberg hurries through the necessary manoeuvres as quickly as possible and this time brings this first movement very soon to an end, at a Haydnesque length quite unusual for the period.

But unlike the only earlier F sharp minor quartet of any note, Haydn's op. 50 no. 4, Schoenberg's does not arrive at the end of its first movement in the major but still in the minor key, and in the depressed uncertainty of its opening. More, then, can yet come: a scherzo in Schoenberg's personal D minor, abundantly developed, frantically busy, with a wild effect in the D major trio of a pizzicato whiplash setting off staccato streams in the first violin, and with a slow interlude after the trio that has the second violin singing the popular song 'O du lieber Augustin' and by implication sounding its message of 'Alles ist hin' ('all is past').

Now started on a programmatic course, which retrospectively colours the emotional feeling of the first movement, the quartet can justifiably draw to itself the resources of the human voice and add a soprano for the last two movements, both setting poems by the writer whom Schoenberg found to be expressing his literary thoughts better than anyone else in these years: Stefan George. The first vocal movement Schoenberg described as being in variation form, chosen lest 'the great dramatic emotionality of the poem might cause me to surpass the borderline of what should be admitted to chamber music', but it is a mobile group of motifs that forms the subject, not a continuous melodic line, and those motifs are chosen from the first two movements. On the structural level, this makes double sure that the addition of the voice will not disrupt the flow of the work. And in expressive terms it makes clear that the sadness of which the soprano sings, her exhausting journey, has been recounted in what has been heard. Her own part, though, moves largely free of the underlying motifs, only at the end touching the most prominent of them, from the first movement, and then with a twist indicative of the desperation in her plea for happiness. The key of E flat minor is also no more than a vague background presence throughout much of the movement, within which the four instruments are freed to indulge in twilight effects of texture beneath the highly nuanced vocal line:

61 Schoenberg: Quartet no. 2 in F# minor op. 10, third movement

The final slow 'Transport' comes as the answer to the prayer that has preceded it, and presents the soul's liberation from earthly ties in music that now dispenses with a key signature and with any more than momentarily definable key, until the final apotheosis for quartet alone leads circuitously round to a chord of F sharp major. Perhaps it needed so decisive and unrepeatable a dissolution for Schoenberg to be able to express the state of becoming 'a roaring of the holy voice', for later in *Die Jakobsleiter* and *Moses und Aron* he was to break off at points where union with God had to be set to music.

Within the context of the string quartet, Schoenberg's introduction of a soprano voice was obviously a quite revolutionary move, for which the symphonic precedents in Beethoven, Liszt and Mahler are hardly any preparation. As a medium with four individual voices of its own, the quartet is greatly compromised when it has to become an accompaniment, and it is not surprising that Schoenberg's innovation should in this respect have had almost no progeny: his pupil Anton Webern (1883-1945) wrote a song for soprano and string quartet, 'Schmerz, immer blick nach oben' (1913), which he originally intended to be the middle movement of a short set with the first and last of the pieces he eventually published as his Six Bagatelles, but this vocal interruption was abandoned. However, the more generally radical move contained in Schoenberg's second quartet, the broach of atonality, has affected music in ways that need no emphasis.

Atonality was a particular problem for the quartet, which had enjoyed greatest favour in those periods when dynamic tonality had been felt most keenly: in the late eighteenth century, when it was new, and in the period of little more than thirty years now drawing to a close in 1908, when tonal forces had to be marshalled with renewed energy in the face of a continuously expanding discovery of non-tonal harmonies. An atonal quartet was unimaginable. Certainly Schoenberg could not imagine it until he had settled firmly into his serial technique nearly two decades later, and even Webern and Berg, both of whom did write quartets in the immediate wake of Schoenberg's second, found that there were problems.

Webern
Five Movements

Webern's Five Movements op.5 (1909) imply as much in their title, a subtle choice which it took the composer some time to find, for the movements are not linked in the way that would justify calling the work 'string quartet', as first he did, yet they are more united than is suggested by another abandoned title, 'five pieces'. The first movement has a certain outward show of sonata form, albeit on a very small scale, with an exposition of only thirteen bars in two contrasted tempos, a similarly compact development and an approximate recapitulation with a coda. However, nothing is really resolved in this keyless universe: the wild minor ninth leap at the start is merely taken up into a more rarefied register and gradually quietened, while in between these limits the music is less concerned with consistency than with sudden shifts of texture, dynamic, pitch range and sonority, as most violently at the opening of the quasi-development:

62 Webern: Five Movements op. 5, first movement

If this movement is a sonata allegro in the process of fracture and disintegration, what follows bends further and further away from the path expected of a quartet. The second movement is indeed an adagio, but on a scale where it becomes meaningless to speak of form: a melodic thread passes up from viola to second violin to first and then back down to second violin, accompanied by faint chords and little ostinatos, always soft and finishing in thirteen bars, experienced as a single breath. After this comes a scherzo bitten off almost before it has begun, another tiny quiet adagio and then a further slow movement as finale, so that what had begun as a string quartet evaporates into a sequence of tremulously expressive fragments.

Berg op. 3   Things did not happen in quite the same way for Berg. His op.3 of the next year, 1910, is genuinely a string quartet, for even though it has only two movements, each is almost as long as all five of Webern's op.5 and together they constitute a single developed form. The first is a sonata structure, but with an unusually short development section, partly, perhaps, because the exposition has already been so full of polyphonic development in a manner suggested by Schoenberg's opp.7 and 10, partly because the movement is due to end with a long retrospective coda, and partly because Berg wants the feeling to be, no less than in his later work for string quartet, lyrical. By contrast with Schoenberg, therefore, there is an unforced quality, almost a casualness about the way the music grows from one idea to a variant, and however different the style, one may be reminded that Berg was much impressed by Debussy. Even the second movement, whose determined pace contrasts with the leisurely progress of its predecessor, is constantly surprising in what it discovers as it takes its rondo path, until near the end it reveals its origin to lie in the same ambling downward motif that dominated the first movement.

Apart from these works of Berg and Webern, few contemporary quartets show any influence of Schoenberg's revolutionary op.10, though it is tempting to imagine that Reger was affected by it in his *Reger op. 121* op.121 quartet (1911), which is in the same key of F sharp minor. The *in F# minor* first movement, as in the Schoenberg, goes in triple time at a moderate pace, and even has something of the same strained harmonic atmosphere. The second movement is once more a scherzo in D, but major not minor, and with the oppressed brilliance and atrophied trio so characteristic of Reger's scherzos. Moreover, the slow movement is no grief-stricken prayer but a full, rich and elevated adagio in a highly chromatic B flat (the work therefore mapping out the wide space of an augmented triad), and the finale is a sonata rondo which has Brahms in a Hungarian restaurant conversing with Mahler in a Viennese café, the latter recalling in mood and harmony a little waltz that figured prominently in the secondary material of the first movement. In sum, this last quartet of Reger's is more an individual parallel to Schoenberg than a direct consequence, and the model from the past to which it appeals most strongly, in terms of variety, obliqueness and profundity, is that of the late Beethoven. This is also the case with Reger's E flat quartet op.109 of two years before, still more hymnic in its adagio and in its first movement integrating strong chordal music in a way probably suggested by Beethoven's op.127 in the same key, though resiliently Regeresque in its concluding fugue, active and unkempt.

For Reger, it would seem, the crisis of atonality had been passed at around the time of his op.54 quartets, and averted: op.109 and op.121 are both in the clearer style of the D minor op.74. But for Schoenberg's pupils the challenge of his F sharp minor quartet was not to be so readily answered, and the tightness of the corner into which they were being pushed is suggested most powerfully by Webern's next quartet work, the Six Bagatelles op.9 (1911-13). Again the title is just. There is now no question that these pieces are movements in a connected design: apart from anything else, they do not move. Rather each minute piece is a separate, distinctive image, a bagatelle not in any frivolous sense but in the tradition of Beethoven: an abstract enigma. Durations are measured in seconds, and as in op.5, only more so, the musical substance is thinned to a fine gauze of little phrases, single notes, individual chords and brief patters of ostinato, all in a generally quiet dynamic and with sonorities varied to the utmost by the use of muting, harmonics, *sul ponticello*, pizzicato and so on. Even eleven years later the extremity of the bagatelles seemed to need an apology, and the opus was published with a preface by Schoenberg calling attention to the magnitude of Webern's achievement in expressing a 'a novel in a single gesture, a joy in a breath', bringing the epoch of Romanticism opened by Beethoven to an end in infinitesimal rapture:

Webern
Six Bagatelles

63 Webern: Six Bagatelles op. 9, no. 5

Part Four

Theme: Stravinsky or Bartók

Something has happened:

64 Stravinsky: Three Pieces, no. 1

Stravinsky wrote his Three Pieces for string quartet in 1914, only a year after Webern had finished his bagatelles: the last breaths, for the moment, of the Austro-German symphonic tradition, committed to the medium which it had created as its own, were so quickly followed by this evidence of the new, erupting unrepentantly in the very same musical arena.

Stravinsky's work, for the first time in the history of the genre, is

Stravinsky Three Pieces

determinedly not a 'string quartet' but a set of pieces to be played by four strings. There is no acknowledgment of a tradition or a form, and the lack of any such acknowledgment only seems iconoclastic because of our own experience of the genre's traditions: subversion is not particularly one of Stravinsky's aims. The slow movement comes last, and is a chant for the four instruments mainly in rhythmic unison, a piece whose only backward glances are to the composer's own *Rite of Spring* (the sage's signal of solo strings in high harmonics, a gesture due to be repeated in, but later deleted from, *The Wedding* – the only such deletion, occurring precisely when strings were omitted from the score). Perhaps too, though, there is some memory of Russian church music, for when the set was arranged for orchestra, to make the first three of the *Quatre études* (1914-18), this piece gained the title 'Cantique'.

As for the first piece, quoted above and eventually named 'Danse', it has absolutely no knowledge of sonata form but is instead a heterophony of utterly simple figures repeated and readjusted over a drone: it is always the same and always different, and the decision to bring it to a finish after forty-eight bars is wholly arbitrary. The second piece too, though given an obvious ABA pattern, is for the most part music of small motifs worked in repetition and review – music also of extraordinary effects, apparently suggested by a performance Stravinsky saw in London given by the clown Little Tich, and including one figure to be played by the second violinist and violist with their instruments reversed, held like cellos: 'Excentrique' is not inaptly the title later vouchsafed.

It is not just such bizarreries, however, that distinguish Stravinsky's Three Pieces, his first quartet composition, from all that had gone before in the genre's extensive literature. Reaching suddenly well beyond Debussy – whose quartet had contained plenty of oddities of its own but had at least approximated to standard four-movement form and feeling – Stravinsky comes to the string quartet as an ensemble without a history. The notion of quartet dialogue has no place here, nor have subtleties of blend: the texture is completely fragmented, with each instrument sounding for itself, as in the first piece (one may compare this with Debussy's scherzo, quoted in ex.54), or else it is part of an anonymous homophony, as in the third. The second piece simply darts from one possibility to the other. And though the orchestration of the work is in terms of value a reduction, making large and obvious those elements of the picturesque that had been pungently cornered in the original, Stravinsky was right to realize that his pieces had no place in the quartet repertory. Indeed they have remained rare visitors there, performed and recorded more frequently within the context of other Stravinsky works than of other quartets.

However, the Three Pieces were taken up by the Swiss–American Flonzaley Quartet (1902-28), one of the outstanding ensembles of the time, and it was to a commission from them that Stravinsky wrote a second work for string quartet in 1920. Again he worked against the accepted nature of the medium, but in a different way: the piece emerged as a concertino, with a long central section where the leader is soloist, though not in any brilliant fashion but rather in clenched double-stopping. Around this comes music that, like the first of the Three Pieces, dances but is frustrated of real movement, and here too the first violin is dominant, sometimes remembering its starring role in the recent *Histoire du soldat*: again history is confined to the history of the composer's own output. Moreover, although Stravinsky described the concertino as being 'in the form of a free sonata allegro', it is nothing of the kind, for the middle andante is a change, not a development, and the end an apotheosis, not a coda. Once more, though a degree more civilized in its bearing (this was the dawn of Stravinsky's neoclassical period), the work has no avenue of connection with the quartet tradition.

At this point, for Stravinsky, the quartet died. We do not meet it again until nearly thirty years later, when it withdraws itself from the orchestra to play the dark prelude to the graveyard scene in *The Rake's Progress* (1947-51), the first part of that opera to be composed. It then participates in *In memoriam Dylan Thomas* (1954), answering a quartet of trombones in the 'dirge canons' and accompanying the tenor voice for the interleaved song. And finally it arrives to unfold a double canon in memory of the painter Raoul Dufy (1959), memorialized in a strict form that permits nothing of the personal involvement in each part that had been the great inheritance of the string quartet, and deprived also of personal involvement to be inferred on the part of the composer: of all the distinguished contemporaries to whom he erected musical monuments, Dufy was the only one Stravinsky did not know.

Now even though Stravinsky's 1959 epitaph for the quartet may be regarded as premature, the fact that the outstanding composer of the twentieth century could treat the ensemble as something totally new or totally dead is one symptom of the revolution in musical composition around the time of the First World War. Hitherto in this book it has been possible to consider the history of the quartet as a continuing tradition, though moving through distinct phases reflected unavoidably in the styles and forms that have been adopted here: progressing through the assimilation of contrast from Haydn and

Mozart to Beethoven and Schubert, hesitant and uncertain of motivation in the period of Schumann and Mendelssohn, dwelling on particular moments with increasing slowness of movement in the span from Brahms to Webern. But the modern age has no such continuity, no confidence about a past or assurance about a future. Its essence is that of variation, as displayed so manifestly in the work of another great composer here introduced as counter-theme: Bartók.

Bartók, quite emphatically, did not believe the quartet to be dead: he wrote six, and was planning a seventh at the time of his death in 1945. His belief in the medium has also been thoroughly justified by the subsequent history of musical performance. Though not widely played during his lifetime, his quartets have since become the only ones since Beethoven to enjoy an undisputed place in the repertory, the only works from a period of more than a century and a half to be performed as a matter of course by every professional quartet. At the same time, they are scarcely any more materially connected with the quartet's traditions than are the works of Stravinsky: Bartók offers new forms, new textures, new playing techniques, and a very definite indication that this is music for virtuosos, having no place in the domestic environment where the quartet had grown, and where to some extent it still lingered even in the challenging works of Reger and Schoenberg.

The one traditional feature of Bartók's quartets is their weight. For Bartók, as only previously for Haydn, the quartet was a creative heartland: he returned to it regularly – in 1908-9, 1915-17, 1927, 1928, 1934, 1939 and again at the end of his life – and he was not much attracted by other chamber combinations, or indeed by any other standard form. Also, and most particularly in the third, fourth and fifth quartets, he used the medium to consider the absolute essentials of his art, with themes reduced to rudimentary motifs in many instances, and structure openly exposed to view. And even though other works of this expository period share the same point of view, it is significant that when Bartók was most constructivist he was most inclined to the quartet, and that some of those other works inhabit the same world: this was the time of the forty-four violin duos (1931), scored for the top half of a quartet, of the Music for Strings, Percussion and Celesta (1936), which is a quartet writ large, and of the Sonata for Two Pianos and Percussion (1937), which Bartók would have called 'quartet' if he had been sure that the percussion parts could always be managed by two players. The sphere of the quartet, for Bartók as for many musicians who would dissociate themselves from Wagner's style of interpretation, is the sphere of absolute music, and even if the quartet was no longer by nature the model conveyance for pure musical thought that it had been for Haydn, it had become so again through tradition. The loss of its natural appositeness was of course the problem for Schumann and his generation, who had no other vehicle for abstract musical thought; the regaining was now coming about through contemporary experience of the quartet's past in the increasing activity of professional ensembles during Bartók's creative life (once more this is not necessarily cause and effect but a case of parallel movements in musical history). Composers of the generation of Bartók and Schoenberg were the first who had learned to match their quartet imaginings against those of the late Beethoven, and the first too who, if temperament allowed, could afford to ignore the amateur. By this time the amateur repertory had petrified around the works of Haydn, Mozart and Beethoven, and if new material was required, it had to be rescued by publishers and editors from among the works of Boccherini, or Dittersdorf, or Charles Wesley.

But if the quartet was made for Bartók, it is not so obvious that Bartók was made for the quartet. Like Schumann and Debussy, neither of them happy for long in the medium, Bartók was a pianist, not a string player as most of the other great quartet composers had been or were (Schoenberg and Webern included). This was, however, for him no disadvantage. It may have been the quartet's tradition that recommended it to Bartók – who even, though by chance, notched up the classical set of six – but it was a tradition he chose to ignore when it came to matters of detail and substance. There is, for instance, no obvious connection with any immediate predecessors, only a generalized hankering after certain tones of conflict and excess characteristic of the late Beethoven. There is also a sense in which, looking at the quartet from the outside, Bartók wrote for the listener and not so much for the performer, and that had a profound effect on his quartet textures. Long solo melodies are very rare, and reserved for quite special occasions: the slow finale of the second quartet, the middle movement of the fourth and the slow music of the sixth. Even more remarkably, Bartók's quartets have little to do with the musical conversation that had been the distinguishing feature of earlier quartet style, even the mark by which a quartet could be judged in the late eighteenth century. Where the four instruments are musing on similar material, as they are right at the beginning of the first quartet (ex. 60) and in other quasi-fugal passages elsewhere, they seem to follow independent trains of thought starting out from the same axiom: there is little question of dialogue or exchange. And similarly, conversation is powerfully suppressed when, as often happens, the four are bound together in octaves, or set on quite different planes (as at the start of the second part of the third quartet, where the second violin has a drone trill, the cello plucked chords and the viola a little glissando figure), or again, most typically, meshed together in imitative textures, such as this from the finale of the fifth quartet:

65 Bartók: Quartet no. 5, fifth movement

Naturally, Bartók's forms are as different from those of tradition as his textures, even though the outline of a sonata or ABA structure may in some respect be followed. Haydn, as a man of the second half of the eighteenth century, created the quartet as the supreme vehicle of development; Bartók, as a man of the first half of the twentieth, recast it for the purposes of variation. Hence his textural and formal innovations: development entails discourse and has as its usual object the resolution of contrasts established both within and among movements, whereas variation implies abrupt change and the erection of incompatibilities (Haydn could not risk using variation form in a finale, though Beethoven could). In gross terms, the one is a subjective mode, appreciated best from inside and drawing the listener into its proceses, whereas the other is objective, to be viewed from without and at a distance.

Quite as much as Stravinsky and Webern, therefore, and indeed before them, Bartók was driven to separate the quartet from the formal principles that had endured since Haydn, to make the quartet non-symphonic. Only in his last quartet did he write a work in four movements, and then in nothing like the conventional pattern. His first quartet had essayed a new kind of arrowed progress, justified and maintained not intrinsically in terms of musical substance but extrinsically in terms of increased speed. Then in the second quartet this form was shuffled to produce the kind of palindromic symmetry that Bartók recognized was suited to his variational mind: first a moderato in sonata form, then a sequence of folkdance episodes worked into an Allegro molto capriccioso, and finally a lento. But at this stage the motivic correspondences that link the outer movements are hidden, and the music lies open to subjective interpretations such as that offered by the composer's great colleague Kodály, who chose to identify the first movement as expressive of a 'quiet life', the second of 'joy' and the third of 'sorrow' (though in fact Bartók's objectivity is already so well entrenched that it is hard to find anything as personal as sorrow in this piece). *Bartók no. 2*

With his third quartet Bartók then found the means to exhibit variation over a long span, within a single movement that abandons the lento to work with the aspects of ambulant-paced song and vigorous dance that had been exposed in its predecessor. The first part of the movement goes at moderato speed and the second at a racing allegro, each of these sections characterized by nothing so much as the incessant variation of tiny units: a motif of rising fourth and falling minor third in the first part, and in the second a scale figure. At the end there is a 'recapitulation' of the first part, in fact more a sort of elliptical memory, and then finally comes a coda to relate similarly to the second part, giving the whole an ABAB form much more intensive, because much more motivically connected, than the vaguely similar pattern in the first quartet. The returning memories also greatly enhance the strength of the slow–fast double that Bartók had favoured in other works, such as the pairs of orchestral *Portraits* and *Pictures*, and that he had found adumbrated in Hungarian folk music as well as, of course, in art forms such as the prelude and fugue. *Bartók no. 3*

The fourth quartet brings symmetrical pairing even more out into the open. There are now five movements in an ABCBA pattern, and each of the movements is also symmetrical in shape. In the case of the first movement this symmetry is achieved within the context – perhaps it should be against the context – of sonata form, requiring the beginning of the development to be as strongly marked as, classically, the beginning of the recapitulation had to be: there is a pause, a call to attention and very soon a new sound, that of glissandos in all four instruments. The finale is a more straightforward ABA structure, using variants of themes from the first movement and ending with exactly the same gesture to anchor the music on its central C (and it goes without saying that Bartók's harmony is shifted against the background of tradition as much as his form: the work is *Bartók no. 4* not 'in C', having no special place for chords in C, for instance, but rather the note C, and most particularly middle C, is at the centre of its universe). This relationship between the first movement and the finale confirms a palindromic relationship that has become inescapable by the time the finale begins, for the second and fourth movements are both fast, both involved with similar themes and both confined to a special timbral world: that of muted strings in the second movement and of pizzicato in the fourth, including the percussive 'Bartók pizzicato', with the string making an explosive crack as it rebounds agains the instrument. This effect appears here for the first time to join a wide range of tone colours in the rest of the work: *col legno* in the finale, *sul ponticello* and *non vibrato* in the third movement, glissandos as already mentioned in the first. Possibly such variety was stimulated by the knowledge Bartók had gained of the quartets of Schoenberg, Berg and Webern, all of whom used special effects much more freely than had been usual in the quartet, and whose common publisher, Universal Edition, Bartók also shared.

Bartók no. 5   It might appear that having found an appropriate structure in his fourth quartet Bartók repeated it in his fifth since the latter is also a quintuple palindrome. It is, however, longer, harmonically simpler (i.e. closer to diatonic normality) and still more obvious in its mirrorings: it is the public counterpart to the secretive fourth. Another difference, not unrelated, is that the heart of the work is turned inside out, with two slow movements in the even-numbered positions around a central scherzo that romps in the complex compound metres Bartók had learned from Bulgarian folk music (4+2+3/8, and for the trio 3+2+2+3/8). In another composer the substitution of two slow movements for one would mark an increase in inwardness, but Bartók is most himself in his excited dances (this is true even in the first and second quartets), whereas the slow movement, in both the fourth and the fifth quartets, has become a genre piece, a 'night music'. The two examples in the fifth quartet are closely related in theme and structure, like the even-numbered scherzos of the fourth, and the centrepiece between them almost makes the symmetry septuple, since, for the first time in a quartet, Bartók here uses the conventional da capo form. Symmetry is, too, more patently paraded in the outer movements, of which the first is a sonata structure with three themes recapitulated in reverse order to preserve the mirroring, and with again a development that clearly marks its departure. Even the most basic materials of this pervasively, almost obsessively symmetrical work are inclined to have a reflecting pattern, whether a miniature arch shape of ascent and descent (outer movements and scherzo) or an immediate answering of motifs by their inversions (slow movements, and throughout).

All that only adds to the impression of incongruity created by the one element that has no mirror image, the grotesque barrel-organ treatment of a theme near the end of the finale. Parody, however, is no more than objectivity exhibited and variation carried to an extreme; and it had always been an option for Bartók, exploited in the finale of the first quartet and again in the middle movements of the sixth, whose Marcia second movement has a middle section more horrible than anything in music before Peter Maxwell Davies (1934-), an appalling burlesqued inversion of the march in the cello (these were the first months of the Second World War) with the viola imitating a banjo and noisome violin tremolandos. Beyond this the sixth quartet, though ostensibly in four movements, is really only in one, a Mesto, which gives rise to three trial efforts before finding its proper shape. Each 'movement' begins with the mesto theme in a different setting: first announced by the viola alone and introducing a vivace, then played by the cello with muted accompaniment from the rest and giving rise to the march, then woven in counterpoint before being interrupted by a Burletta of bizarre happenings, and finally played out for a full movement to create, for the first time since the second quartet, a slow finale.

Bartók no. 6

Now at last, with no dancing to be heard, the slow movement must surely be taken as a personal utterance: we know from his letters that Bartók was very much disturbed by events around the time of the outbreak of war, and his use of the term 'mesto' (sad), rather than the straightforward tempo markings he had normally preferred, cannot be ignored. And yet a marking so historically unusual could be interpreted as a gesture less to expressive intention than to great predecessors: the slow movements of Haydn's op.76 no.5 and of Beethoven's first 'Razumovsky' quartet. Moreover, the caricatures of the middle movements have rendered the emotional ground thoroughly unstable, and Bartók lets his last quartet go with music whose expressiveness is both profound and uncertain. We have come beyond the time of chamber music as amiable conversation, beyond the time of the quartet as 'intimate letters'. But both are remembered.

If more clues are needed to the new direction the quartet was taking, they may be found among Bartók's dedications. The second quartet he inscribed to the ensemble led by Waldbauer, and the fourth and sixth to other leading quartets of the period, the Pro Arte and the Kolisch. The Pro Arte Quartet, a Belgian and later American ensemble, was active with its original membership from 1913 until

1940 and made a particular feature of modern works, giving the first performances of, for example, the single quartet of Albert Roussel (1869-1937), the second and third quartets of Arthur Honegger (1892-1955) and the string quartet with orchestra by Bohuslav Martinů (1890-1959). The Austrian–American Kolisch Quartet, playing between 1922 and 1939, was closely associated with the Schoenberg circle and gave the premières of Schoenberg's third and fourth quartets, Berg's Lyric Suite and Webern's quartet op. 28, as well as the Schoenberg–Handel concerto. Of Bartók's quartets they introduced the last two, and won from him praise for 'their virtuosity, their sonority, their understanding, their style'. With these two ensembles – and with others such as the Amar, in which Paul Hindemith (1895-1963) played the viola, and for which he wrote three of his six quartets – there was ample stimulus for the great upsurge in quartet writing between the wars: the period of Bartók's last four quartets, Schoenberg's last two and a host of others.

But stimulus came too from prizes and patrons. Bartók dedicated his third quartet to the Musical Fund Society of Philadelphia, an ancient chamber music society which had awarded the work a prize jointly with the *Serenata* for five instruments by Alfredo Casella (1883-1953), and his fifth bears the name of Elizabeth Sprague Coolidge (1864-1953), an American lady who provided money for the commissioning not only of this work but also of many others, including Schoenberg's third and fourth quartets and Webern's op. 28, all similarly dedicated to her. Indeed, during the 1930s the paths of the quartet, and the paths of such composers as Bartók, Schoenberg and Hindemith, were leading very much towards the United States, and although so far only one American work, Ives's first quartet, has claimed much attention here, the middle decades of the century were to alter the Atlantic balance very considerably.

Variation 1:
Schoenberg and the serial quartet

Two corners have so far been established in the vast plane of the twentieth-century string quartet: Stravinsky denying its possibility, and Bartók making it in a new way. But two more possibilities remain: continuing to write quartets as if nothing had happened, and endeavouring to extend the tradition with new means. To nominate a representative of the former might perhaps be invidious, but of the latter Schoenberg outstandingly provides the example.

All the conditions were right for Schoenberg to have composed as many quartets as Beethoven. He had a strong attachment to the tradition represented quintessentially by the string quartet, and he thought naturally in quartet terms. According to his own account, the four quartets he published had 'at least five or six predecessors' (four or five, then, in addition to the D major of 1897). Yet for nearly two decades after his second quartet he wrote nothing in the genre, a neglect to be explained only by his relinquishment at the same time of all the other norms of convention: tonality, thematic composition, stability of metre and texture, and so on. Only once these things had been restored, as with the advent of serialism they were (even tonality to some degree), could Schoenberg again turn his mind to string quartets. First there was the wind quintet op.26 (1923-4), an oblique, alien genre to make sure the ground was safe, and then his third quartet op.30 (1927), followed nine years later by his fourth, op.37, and then in June 1949 by brief incipits of a never completed fifth. One might almost see here, in the cycle of quartets as in Schoenberg's creative life more largely, the programme of his piano concerto: 'Life was so easy (D major quartet) but all of a sudden hate broke loose (second quartet); the situation became grave (no quartets) but life has to go on (third and fourth quartets)'.

Argument has continued since the 1920s about just what sort of life Schoenberg's serialism was perpetuating: new, robotic or merely reclothed old. Each of Schoenberg's serial quartets, including the one aborted in 1949, has a four-movement plan of a traditional sort, with the slow movement placed second in op.30 and third in op.37, where it has the form of a short unison recitative followed by a quartet aria, twice over (cf Haydn's op.20 no.2). In both quartets the other internal movement is an intermezzo, as indeed it had been in the early D major quartet, all three of these intermezzos, rather strikingly, giving the main line first to the viola: in this preferential treatment of his own preferred instrument, as in so much else, Schoenberg shows himself the heir above all others of Mozart and Brahms. If one takes into account also the fact that all the movements of the third and fourth quartets are undisguisedly thematic, even if their themes build towards forms only uncertainly to be connected with the normal sonata, variations, ABA or rondo, then it would seem self-evident that Schoenberg was engaged in an exercise in resuscitation. Some might even argue, following Stravinskyan premises, that it is impossible to write a quartet and not create what is no more than a reproduction.

However, to criticize Schoenberg for putting new 'contents' into old 'forms' is absurd, since if one removes the contents from his third and fourth quartets it is difficult to see what 'form' is left: certainly not the sonata model with its clearly distinguished exposition, development and recapitulation. In this respect Schoenberg was much less a prisoner of textbook theory than were Schumann and Brahms in their quartets: it is only an approach to his quartets which expects the old forms that leads to the music sounding square, academically manipulated and uninteresting. Better to have in mind for the first movement of the third quartet Schoenberg's own association of the music with a fairytale image of a ship 'whose captain had been nailed through the head to the topmast by his rebellious crew', for if one tries to follow the music according to the recipe printed in the pocket score, then one is obliged to understand the inversion of the first theme, with a quite changed accompaniment, as a sonata recapitulation. Obviously such a changed form cannot be heard as a reprise in the manner of Haydn or even that of Brahms; rather the effect is one of returning to the same spot and finding only a shadow, and this towards the end of a movement that has no identifiable 'development section' but is, typically, in the manner of Schoenberg's music from before his first quartet, all development.

Serial mechanics essentially gave Schoenberg the means not to revive old forms but instead to find new ones in which aspects of the old are discovered distorted: hence, in part, the nocturnal unease of his serial quartets, the quality they share with his earlier nightscapes, *Pierrot lunaire* and the Serenade. That creepiness also depends more than somewhat on the dance rhythms that flit through all but the slow movements (so much of serial Schoenberg is dance), and that are closely connected with the working of serialism here. For if one is to interpret correctly an inversion as related to its original shape, it will help if the rhythm is preserved, and so Schoenberg's themes are often defined much more by their rhythms than by their pitch contours. This again is something quite alien to the Austro-German tradition of which Schoenberg is often supposed the heir (not least by himself), and it leads to music that connects with that tradition only in order to stress its separateness. The great effort of a Brahms is to suppress any feeling of rhythm as palpable, extractable shape, whereas in Schoenberg's third and fourth quartets rhythm almost leaps off the *Schoenberg no. 3* music's surface:

66 *Schoenberg: Quartet no.3, fourth movement*

Here the changes of contour hardly detract from one's perception of the dit-dit-dit-dit-da-da unit in each bar, and that remains the case no matter how much the idea is subsequently altered in this movement: hence the dance feeling. (It should be noted, however, that rhythm and pitch cannot be separated any more easily than can form and content: the 'rhythm' of the unit depends as much as it does on durational values on there being a wide interval at the start and on its being exactly repeated.) Schoenberg's own analysis of this movement as a rondo is not without its problems, since the repetitions characteristic of the form are disguised in a manner that goes far beyond the finale of Mozart's κ589 quartet. Also, as quite often in Schoenberg (in the Orchestral Variations, for example), the ostensible 'form' is followed by a 'coda' which instead of being a mere tailpiece, or even as in Beethoven a second development, has a quite new thrust and reconsiders the basic materials on a vaster plane. It may even seem that the fixed form is simply the pretext for the freer coda, whose weight is equivalent in many cases to that of the whole of the rest of the movement.

Schoenberg no. 4   Schoenberg's fourth quartet stands in relation to his third somewhat as a Brahms quartet to one by Mozart. It is richer in texture, more continuous in design, less classically pointed in rhythm. It also brings back, albeit modestly, the effects of harmonics, *col legno* and *sul ponticello* that had been inseparable from the substance and the expressive world of the second quartet but rather ostentatiously excluded from the third. Another central difference is in the shaping of themes, which now are all expressions of the twelve-note series, with a particular point made of its constitution from two similar groupings of six notes. The quotation above gives some indication of how the series is not necessarily thematic in the third quartet: here the theme has an immediate repetition of E and D sharp in the second bar, and as yet there is no A. If one can speak of a compositional principle here, it is not so much serialism as a simple tally of all twelve chromatic notes in each bar. And Schoenberg himself was uncertain of the usefulness of discovering the work's series. To Rudolf Kolisch, who had gone to the trouble of working this out some time after giving the first performance, he wrote: 'It must have taken a great deal of effort, and I do not think I would have had the patience. But do you think that knowing it serves any purpose?' In the fourth quartet, however, there is no difficulty in identifying the series and its two halves since these are prominently occupied in every one of the work's gambits. It may be assumed, too, that here knowledge of the series does very definitely serve a purpose in comprehending the structure. The connections that Schoenberg had previously sought to emphasize by rhythmic identities he now believed could be established through serial relationships, which means that the frenetic dancing of the third quartet is somewhat relaxed, though the composer's attention to rhythm is again signalled on occasion by poetic scansion marks over the music. An alert hearing of this quartet therefore presupposes serial awareness, which is not a question of counting by twelves but rather of feeling the harmonic consistency of the six-note units, much as one feels the harmonic consistency of triads in tonal music. And since this is, as Schoenberg insisted, 'twelve-note *music* not *twelve-note* music', the listener is given every help in hearing the music to its fullest, while the fellow composer, as subsequent history has shown, is provided with what is probably Schoenberg's most challenging demonstration of serialism as a self-sufficient method for the articulation of large-scale musical thought.

(There is a footnote. Schoenberg's high seriousness walks unscathed through his original music, but in his arrangements it does not always avoid tottering into the ludicrous. One example is his Concerto for String Quartet and Orchestra (1933), written again for the Kolisch Quartet and following Spohr by the unlikely route of amplifying Handel's Concerto Grosso op.6 no.7. It is here as it is in his Cello Concerto after Monn, of which he wrote: 'I was mainly intent on removing the defects of the Handelian style', among which he enumerated sequences (to be replaced with 'real substance') and the habit of themes to get 'steadily more insignificant and trivial'. In this work at least he had no doubts about the progress inherent in musical tradition.)

If Schoenberg's fourth quartet is still, for all its admirable coherence, a confusing work, that is partly because the fundamental material, the pair of six-note groupings, has to fulfil two functions which were much more clearly separated in tonal music: the thematic and the harmonic. A twelve-note idea in this work can be a theme, but it must also be at the same time a definition of a harmony. And yet this was not without precedent: a similar situation seems to have arisen naturally in the early decades of the classical style, as the frequent arpeggio themes of Haydn's earlier quartets extensively indicate. Schoenberg's practice here may be regarded as typical of a new style in its youth, to be replaced later by ways of presenting the underlying harmony more subtly and giving more freedom in the formation of themes.

That such a replacement has not yet happened may be attributed to the very different, often distinctly un-Schoenbergian ways in which serialism has been understood by other composers, even among Schoenberg's pupils, rather as if Haydn had been followed not by Albrechtsberger, Dittersdorf and Mozart but by Shostakovich and Philip Glass. For example, in Berg's Lyric Suite (1925-6), which predated Schoenberg's op.30 and was the first serial quartet of any

Berg Lyric Suite

consequence, the constructional principles are entirely different from Schoenberg's. Of the six movements, only the first, third (except for its trio) and last are serial, and yet there is no inconsistency of style between these and the others. Berg's serialism is much more willing than Schoenberg's to gather tonal features within its capacious ambit, whether by including triads within the series itself, as here, or by making no pretence of avoiding familiar chords. At the same time, the non-serial movements also resound with fleeting, unstable or longed-for echoes of tonal normality, while containing also some twelve-note ideas in cross-reference to the serial movements. The field is so vast that Berg can even quote in his non-serial fourth movement and serial finale from two chromatic but still decidedly tonal works: respectively the Lyric Symphony of Alexander von Zemlinsky (1872-1942) and *Tristan und Isolde*.

One may guess that serialism appealed to Berg less as a logical system than as a constructive artifice. It was nice to work with, just as it was nice to work with the numbers 23 (Berg's fateful numerical monogram) and 10 in governing movement lengths and metronome markings: for example, the first movement has sixty-nine bars to be played at ♩ =100. Berg's own published notes on the work give evidence of his delight in structural ingenuity, though on the work's expressive meaning he is very much less forthcoming. Adorno's description of it as a 'latent opera' gained widespread agreement, but it was only in 1977 that the composer's detailed programme came to light, revealing that the whole work is concerned with his relationship with Franz Werfel's married sister Hanna Fuchs-Robettin, and giving a new psychological sense to the seemingly arbitrary and extravagant gestures (unlike Schoenberg's third quartet, the Lyric Suite is abundantly coloured with all the playing techniques Schoenberg, Berg and Webern had used in their pre-war quartets) and also to the unusual form, in which the tempo markings, all shaded with an expressive nuance, become progressively more extreme: Allegretto giovale, Andante amoroso, Allegro misterioso, Adagio appassionato, Presto delirando, Largo desolato.

Thus the first movement expresses Berg's smiling pleasure in the person of Hanna Fuchs and in the musical interpretation of her initials (the series runs from F to H, German for B, and the music touches on the keys of B and F major; the number 10, too, turns out to be linked with her). After this the andante pictures Hanna with her children, and then as the tempos become wilder so the tragedy of the lovers becomes ever more doomed and intensely expressed: curiously it had been in his other string quartet, the op.3 of 1910, that Berg had sought to convey the complex raptures of his feelings for the other woman in his life, his wife Helene. But even though the Lyric Suite's programme makes it clear that the dedication to Zemlinsky was a front for a dedication that could not be declared, puzzles still remain. The third movement – an anxious, scurrying tissue of fragments in extreme colours, surrounding an expansive but highly compressed Trio ecstatico – is headed only by a date, '20.5.25', testimony to a private experience that will probably remain forever enigmatic. And the programme's identification of the finale as an unspoken setting of a Baudelaire sonnet in German translation – 'To you, dear and only you, presses my cry from the deepest gorge where my heart lay fallen' – raises as many questions as it answers: questions of performance (did Berg envisage the possibility of a voice singing the poem, with suitable octave displacements in the melodic line that ranges passionately from a low scordatura B in the cello through more than five octaves to a high C in the first violin?) as well as questions of interpretation, for performers now have to decide how much weight to give the Baudelaire, besides having to come to terms with all the other expressive clues in music that can make an emotional outburst of a twelve-note series and provide a companionate framework, highly nuanced in the manner of this quartet, for one of the most potent and individual ideas in musical history, the *Tristan* motif:

67 Berg: Lyric Suite, sixth movement

All quartets face two ways, inwards to the performers and outwards to the audience. The unusual feature of Berg's two is that the directions are reversed: the four players make up the public forum while the music is addressed very specifically to an audience of one, Helene Berg in the case of op.3 and Hanna Fuchs-Robettin in the Lyric Suite. This was not quite, however, without parallel. Leoš Janáček (1854-1928), very much at the same time as the Lyric Suite was being composed, wrote two quartets for Kamila Stösslova, the much younger married woman for whom his *tendresse* was a special encouragement to the extraordinary creative output of his last dozen years. The first (1923) he called 'The Kreutzer Sonata' in reference not to Beethoven but to Tolstoy and his ruthless analysis of the potential destructiveness of marriage, his support for male–female relationships achieved without formal wedlock (a connection, incidentally, with Wagner's thought if not with his musical ideas). The second (1928) bears the name 'Listy důvěrné' ('intimate letters': originally it was to have been 'love letters').

Janáček nos 1 and 2

Intimacy of course is a quality that connoisseurs of chamber music like to find in the genre generally and in quartets most particularly, but perhaps not the embarrassing intimacy that Janáček confesses: embarrassing because it is so evidently private, and evidently private because there is so much in the music that must appear merely odd unless one supposes a personal significance. The case is again that of the Lyric Suite: both the quartets are further 'latent operas', though unlike Hanna Fuchs-Robettin, Kamila Stösslova would seem not to have reciprocated the composer's feeling, and even to have been uninterested in his attentions. (Hanna lived in Prague, Kamila sixty miles away in Písek: one wonders if their paths ever crossed.)

Both Janáček's quartets are in the expected four movements, but in neither case is there the usual separation of functions. Life is not cleanly divided into scherzos and slow movements, and so here the elements of dancing vivacity and passionate song are present all through: the only important bow to convention is that the outer movements tend to be progressive whereas the inner ones are reflective. In some movements the opening material returns at the end (this happens with the sad Slavonic barcarolle in the third movement of the second quartet), but more often the arbitrariness of the form is emphasized by endings which are too sudden (the very end of the second quartet) or else hang in mid-air (much of the first).

There is no less eccentricity, and therefore no less encouragement to emotional interpretation, in the small-scale detail of Janáček's quartets, the way ideas succeed one another with no obvious motivation, as at the start of the second quartet, where the violins sound straight away the work's most prominent theme, followed by a viola solo:

68 *Janáček: Quartet no. 2, first movement*

It may be that by having the viola play *sul ponticello* here, and in other passages, Janáček was hoping to suggest the tone of the viola d'amore, which he had first envisaged for this quartet and which he had revived for two operas closely associated with Stösslova, *Katya Kabanova* and *The Makropulos Case*. Apparently he was attracted as much by the obsolete instrument's name as by its sound, but even so, his willingness to alter even the hallowed constitution of the string quartet is evidence of his placing his own creative drive above the dictates of tradition. This was not entirely new. Quite apart from Schoenberg's addition of a soprano in his second quartet (and, practicably, Berg's similar extension of the ensemble in his Lyric Suite), Reger had brought in a double bass for the finale of his juvenile D minor quartet. But Janáček's quartets show most acutely the conflict between an individual and independent temperament and the proprieties of a tradition: the problem, as Schoenberg might have seen it, of conveying musical truth through means that the composer had not himself chosen. A Haydn or a Brahms could not have recognized the possibility of music outside a certain circle of genres, but with the dissolution of almost all received ideas in the first decade of the twentieth century, the string quartet, as the most prescriptive of musical forms, was set on a difficult road.

We have already seen how Schoenberg attempted to give it a new firm route, along which Berg (and parenthetically the decidedly tonal, non-serial Janáček) was not persuaded to go. However, his serial method was welcomed with ardour by the other great pupil of his early years, Webern. Webern's quartet op. 28 (1937-8) is one of several late instrumental works in which the series is, with extraordinary starkness, presented as both thematic and harmonic entity, always eschewing as far as possible any traffic with triads or other aspects of tonality (a Wagner quotation in a Webern quartet is wholly unimaginable). Webern's series is thematic in the sense that statements of it are constantly in the foreground, and harmonic in the sense that the make-up of the series influences the directions and the goals the music takes. For instance the series of the string quartet, not untypically, is full of internal symmetries: every other interval is a semitone, the remainder being all major or minor thirds, and the twelve-note succession can be divided into similar halves or thirds. All this gives a predisposition towards larger structures based on symmetry and likeness, and it is no accident that the first of the quartet's three movements should be a theme and six variations couched altogether in ABA form, that the second should be a pizzicato scherzo with trio, and that the last should be in Webern's terms a fugue also of scherzo form and character, all three movements being very largely canonic at the same time.

The appreciation of these larger forms and structures is, however, quite severely compromised by the density of question–answer incident on the tiniest scale, since the symmetries within the series produce also a tendency to surface repetitions which Webern does nothing to hide: on the contrary, he rejoices in them, even freezing pitches in the same registers for a while so that similarities are absolutely as obvious as possible:

Webern op. 28

69 *Webern: Quartet op. 28, first movement*

According to Webern's own commentary, this opening passage of his quartet is a theme in two phrases, but only the tempo changes allow one to perceive the music that way. Otherwise it might seem that the theme is nothing more than the interval of a semitone, perpetually reinterpreted within a closed system, like an object in a box of mirrors.

This extremely close-knit, watertight construction is something unknown in western music since the Renaissance, and Webern was rather naively fond of pointing out to his friends and pupils the new ingenuity that serialism made possible, even feeling that the technique allowed him to surpass his earlier music. 'It almost seems to me that this is altogether my first work', he wrote to Kolisch after finishing the quartet, and certainly it gained the unequivocal denomination of 'string quartet' that had been denied the earlier movements and bagatelles. It was also a fresh start in what it offered to later composers: to John Cage (1912-) an extreme reduction in the kinds of sounds and rhythms that can appear, and to later serial composers a mode of thinking in which twelve-note statements are subsumed into subsections and those subsections into sections and those sections into the whole work, relationships at each level operating by analogous principles, among which in Webern's op. 28 tripartite symmetry is the most important.

The string quartet also had a natural attraction for serial composers of the twenties, thirties and forties because of Schoenberg's respect for the medium, and the serial quartet tends to come at a point of some importance in a composer's output: Schoenberg himself wrote his third quartet at a time when the genre could confirm the worthiness of the technique, and his fourth when new confirmation was needed for the changes he had brought about in his serial usage in America, while Berg's Lyric Suite was his first substantial essay in serialism. Ernst Krenek (1900-), one of the few outside the Schoenberg school to use the serial method before the Second World War, crowned his first efforts in the new technique with his sixth quartet op.78 (1936), where Schoenberg's driving thematic polyphony is fractured in the mirrors of Webern's motivic working. There are five movements, but in fact the gross form is traditional, since the first can be seen as a slow introduction to the allegro that follows (there are no breaks between movements), after which come a scherzo, an adagio and a decisive 'Fuga a quattro soggetti'. This title may suggest a homage to Haydn's op.20 no.2, though the fact that the movement resolves onto a loud unison A flat, 'As' in German, is perhaps a tribute rather to the founder of serialism.

Among later composers too – Milton Babbitt (1916-), George Perle (1915-), Alexander Goehr (1932-) – an inclination towards a well-ordered twelve-note technique would seem to go along with an inclination towards the string quartet. Nor is it hard to see why this should be so. By the standards which the twentieth century has set for itself, serialism is an orthodox technique: it implies the primacy of pitch, the importance of structure on the minutest scale, the use of the equal-tempered semitone system, the existence of counterpoint. Naturally it allies itself readily with the pre-eminently orthodox genre in the western tradition, and the alliance is backed too by other considerations. As a polyphonic medium the quartet adapts itself well to the kinds of texture Schoenberg enjoyed and encouraged others to emulate (though Webern's perpetual canoning is not so close to the medium's traditions). It also accommodates the claim made by many serial composers, though very definitely not by Berg, to abstract thought.

A case in point is Schoenberg's Spanish pupil Roberto Gerhard (1896-1970). Significantly, he wrote his first quartet (1955-6) soon after he had belatedly entered the twelve-note field long after the period of his studies: like Stravinsky, he came properly to serialism only after its originator was dead. But straight away his serial method was far from conventional (again like Stravinsky's). Instead of trusting to a serial logic that remained vaguely assumed, or else guiding the ear with tonal harmonies as Berg had done, or else hoping like some other serialists for extraordinary powers of attentiveness and retentiveness on the part of his audience, Gerhard asks of his serial technique that it make itself directly understood in its own terms, and for him that means relinquishing much of the detailed order of the series, as Schoenberg himself, Berg and Krenek (though not Webern) had all done, though never with such devastating clarity. The quartet opens simply with two chords giving the two halves of the series, and the whole work develops as a weighing of their harmonic pulls, and of the smaller harmonic pulls they may be said to contain, particularly in their three-note groupings. Within all these six-note and three-note units the order does not matter, any more than the order of notes in an arpeggio changes its general harmonic implication in a piece of tonal music.

Gerhard's understanding of the series as a source of harmonic quantities, and hardly at all of themes, is similar in his second quartet (1961), but now his interest in raw sound is deeper and much less bound by tradition. Nothing must be permitted to interrupt the sonic adventures set in train by the first bars, which again bring into earshot the basic six-note segments, and so the four movements of the first quartet — a sonata-like allegro, a muted scherzo, a spare slow movement and a vigorous finale — are replaced by a continuous design of seven sections in a compact twelve-and-a-half minutes. Moreover, the development is ruthlessly simplified to make it strong and sure, so that it can cope with the dynamic repetitions and ostinatos that had appeared only in the finale of the first quartet, as well as with the noises that had been brought into string writing only very recently by composers a full generation and more younger than Gerhard, notably Iannis Xenakis (1922-) and Krzysztof Penderecki (1933-). An extreme case of this noise invasion occurs early on, at the start of the second section, but it is worth noting that the onslaught is not unprovoked, that it is stirred by Gerhard's arrangement of his chords to emphasize grating semitones after the more euphonious minor thirds and stretched minor ninths:

Gerhard no. 2

70 *Gerhard: Quartet no. 2*

This is distant indeed from Webern, whose op.28 quartet, in its juggling with what are primarily pitch ideas, uses pizzicato, muting and *sul ponticello* in a severely formal way, without any of the impalpable effects of his opp.5 and 9. It is distant too from the contemporary quartets of Babbitt, heir to both Schoenberg and Webern, and the composer who has most actively and coherently pursued the sort of serialism implied in particular by Schoenberg's fourth quartet and much of Webern: a serialism dependent, that is, on its own functions and contained in its own forms. His second quartet (1954) is one of his most Webernian works in the sense that much of it works with patterns of two or three notes that answer each other in regular fashion, and in the sense too that the whole structure springs from a simple serial conceit. The work's beginning is based on just the first two notes of the series (Webern's tight semitones replaced by open, confident major thirds and minor sixths), then the third is added, and so on until all twelve have been assembled. It is perhaps unfortunate though that, as with Webern, exposed artifice and the composer's own theoretical writings may distract attention from other qualities of the composition: in Webern's op.28 the preservation of his nightmare wit, his sensitivity to sound and his romantic yearning packed into the smallest sighs of tone, and in Babbitt a mobile jazzy feel, good humour and an enjoyment of the smaller ensembles of two or three instruments the quartet can provide.

The rhythmic bounce is general: Babbitt's serial music dances quite as much as Schoenberg's for the reason again that rhythmic patterns are audibly marshalled as entities additional to pitch patterns. However, Babbitt's later quartets offer much less small-scale pattern-making in the manner of his second, and yet the composer explicitly challenges his audience, in the case of his third quartet (1969-70), to comprehend his structure, to go beyond 'those local coherences and immediate modes of progression and association which are instantly apparent' to a perception of 'the total foreground as a totality'. In his hands the quartet fully attains one of its most characteristic goals, that of high structural sophistication, but quite divorced, or so it would seem, from the expressive intimacy and depth so readily associated with similar complexity of form in tonal music: a classic example would be the last quartets of Beethoven. Schoenberg's quartets set him squarely in the Beethovenian tradition; Babbitt, though he has expressed a greater liking for Schoenberg than for his influential pupil, owes his prodigious cool to Webern's mastery, displayed most particularly in his op.28 quartet, of a kind of music in which everything is form, in which every line, every chord, every rhythm is justified within a strongly determined polyphony. That is, on one level, serialism's highest achievement.

Babbitt no. 3

Variation 2: Cage or Carter

If this were one of the double variation forms cherished by Haydn, then now would be the point for a return to the matter of the opening theme. And in fact, though it might seem that Stravinsky's effective pronouncement of the death of the quartet needed no echo, there have been many who have rushed to drive home the message in various ways, and with an enthusiasm that of course implies that the medium is not so firmly ensconced in its grave. There have been those who have wholly ignored it, though ever since the early nineteenth century there have been musical styles in which a quartet is unimaginable: those of Carl Maria von Weber (1786-1826) and Hector Berlioz (1803-69) in the earlier age, those of Edgard Varèse (1883-1965) and Harrison Birtwistle (1934-) in our own. And more interesting than absent quartets must be those which exist, like Stravinsky's, to spite all the medium's prejudices.

Yet the full title of Cage's one work in the genre would seem to affirm a basic truth about it: 'String Quartet in Four Parts'. The very essence of the work, however, is that it is not in four horizontal parts at all, that it wholly ignores this precept of proper quartet style. Written in 1949-50, the quartet comes from a period when Cage was working with fixed 'gamuts' of notes and chords, to be sounded one at a time. In an article of the time he quotes Meister Eckhart's thoroughly unquartettish thought that: 'The soul itself is so simple that it cannot have more than one idea at a time of anything.' The four parts of the title, then, are not voices but movements, arranged in a seasonal cycle. Cage has said that the first is concerned with summer in France and the second with autumn in America (though with a use of the open fifth that suggests rather spring in Appalachia). The winter movement is the most extreme, both in its repetitions of the same few chords and its rhythmic evenness:

71 Cage: String Quartet in Four Parts, third movement.
Copyright 1960 by Henmar Press Inc.

while the short spring finale, marked 'Quodlibet', expresses renewal in homespun dance figures while still keeping to this unique view of the string quartet as a homophonic instrument.

However, a composer's indifference to the quartet tradition can emerge in other ways, even in diametrically opposed ways, as in some of the quartets of Cage's teacher Henry Cowell (1897-1965). In his later quartets Cowell tended to use the medium as a repository for musical impressions picked up from around the world, but the earlier ones convey an unencumbered spirit of enquiry, a willingness to experiment with independent rhythmic layers (the unnumbered *Quartet Euphometric* of 1916-19), with atonal counterpoint (second quartet, 1934) or with sections to be arranged at will (third 'Mosaic' quartet, 1935).

Alternatively, the whole nature of the string quartet can be called into question by an extreme use of what in Webern or Bartók were special string effects, but which in the 1960s became common currency. Gerhard's second quartet has already given an example, but there the unconventional timbres were well determined and quite precisely functional. It is not so obvious that this is the case in   *Xenakis ST/4* Xenakis's *ST/4-1, 080262*:

72 Xenakis: ST/4, 1080262

Nothing could be more different from the Cage, and yet nothing so similar in departing far from anything like a normal quartet texture – and similar too in destroying any feeling of the quartet as a group of four distinct instruments. The rapidity of change is so great, and the difficulty of performance so enormous, that the main impression is likely to be one of hectic activity over the widest possible spectra of pitch and sonority. This, however, is the intention. The first part of the title indicates that this is 'stochastic music', as Xenakis calls it, music in which the composer is concerned with global effects and not so much with detail: there are analogies with such phenomena as a rainstorm or the noise of a crowd, where again one is aware of a mass impression, not of separate, individual events. It still remains open, of course, to the composer to alter the degree of randomness at any moment, from the maximum of the opening quoted above to the minimum of a single note reiterated by one instrument. However, to achieve such calculated randomnesses as Xenakis wants requires a great deal of arithmetic, which can safely be consigned to a computer: the numerical part of the title, apart from being poetically apt for a work elaborated with the aid of digital technology, serves to inform us that this is a piece for four instruments, the first of its kind, computed on 8 February 1962. And here is the only link between stochastic and serial music: both appear to invite us to consider pre-compositional conditions, to switch attention from the finished work to the processes that made it, to replace the enigma of inspiration by method.

Xenakis's use of the computer to fill in random details has to be distinguished from the approach of Lejaren Hiller (1924-), who, almost at the same time in collaboration with Leonard Isaacson, was facilitating the composition by an Illiac computer of the first piece of music dictated by an artificial intelligence, the *Illiac Suite* for string quartet (1957). Even so, Xenakis's quartet excites curious problems of appreciation. The general shapes, densities and speeds are the composer's, but it would seem useless to look for any kind of meaning in the detail. Xenakis has argued that this is merely realism, that the most complex serial music is in fact perceived only in terms of its large features, but even if one accepts such a simplistic view, it is perhaps not so easy to tell one's perceiving mind that confusion is of no account, and it may be that the hard tension of Xenakis's music comes not only from its high virtuosity (in performance) but also from its frustration of order, from its almost unthinking denial of everything that two centuries had imagined the string quartet to be about.

Holliger　　A decade later, when Heinz Holliger (1939-) composed his quartet (1973), the range of new playing techniques had become much greater, which may be why Holliger, as a performer himself, was stimulated to write a work for four human beings rather than four instruments. It is a piece that contains within itself the physical and mental exhaustion that its virtuoso demands entail, a piece concerned only peripherally with purely musical issues, centrally with the physiology of performance, which new techniques test to an extreme. For instance, each player has to read two staves, one for each hand, which itself suggests Holliger's emphasis on the bodily problems of sound production rather than on the sound produced. At the end of half an hour of this one might well expect the players to be exhausted, but Holliger adds an artificial exhaustion as well, giving detailed instructions as to how the musicians are to breathe. And this is not a joke. 'Fatigue from unaccustomed lengths of respiration should,' he notes, 'manifest itself in the tone (shaky bow; tense, halting bowing, etc).' So the work descends, without ever leaving the realms of noise or at best marginal pitch, from manic activity to tremulous grey pianissimos and silence.

Within the framework of a normal quartet recital, a work like Holliger's or Xenakis's or Cage's must appear as an interruption. All these works have as little place there as Stravinsky's Three Pieces, and yet, certainly in the case of the Holliger quartet, the dislocation would appear to be intentional: the piece would make less effect within a recital exclusively of modern quartets – as indeed would any modern quartet, since whether he follows tradition or ignores it, no composer can be unaware that a tradition exists. (One wonders what a string quartet might be like written by a historically illiterate composer who just happened to think of the combination of two violins, viola and cello.) Mauricio Kagel (1931-) insists that his quartet (1965-7) must *Kagel* be played on a normal programme where it is most certainly not part of the normal course of events.

There are two movements, which Kagel advises should be separated by an interval or another work: the rupture his composition brings to the programme is therefore not to be confined to a corner and explained away as the excusable, ignorable outrageousness of a contemporary novelty. As so often with him, the score is more a playscript than a piece of musical notation, particularly in the first movement, where much is made of the players' normal seating arrangements and of various eccentric alternatives. Near the start, for instance, the cellist is playing in his usual seat while the violist walks across the hall playing, then sits in a corner, and the two violins are heard from offstage. What they perform is equally strange. The instruments are prepared (in the sense of Cage's prepared piano) with matches, a knitting needle, paperclips and pieces of paper inserted between the strings. In the second movement the preparations are fewer but the range of effects no less wild, including bowing with notched pieces of wood, drumming with fingers on the strings, attempting to play with a thick leather glove on the left hand, and using every variety of more customary technique.

All this is scrupulously notated, but any quotation here would not only need an undue amount of explanation but could only illustrate a particular moment in a work that has no stable characteristics except absurdity. It is the most anti-traditional of quartets and yet also the most traditional, for a similar piece of music theatre engaging some other ensemble could not be so outrageous. Indeed, Kagel's quartet is one of his most striking inventions precisely because the string quartet of all media provides him with the most elevated history and repertory to hold in low esteem. And one shudders for the fate of any work played between its two movements.

Kagel, Holliger, Xenakis, Cage: all are attempts to make the quartet something quite different, once, to imitate Stravinsky's innocence. Successors to Bartók – composers who have created a whole series redesigning the quartet according to their own lights – are less easy to find, though many have been influenced by him. Naturally, since one of his aims was to create the conditions for a specifically Hungarian kind of music, his influence has been felt keenly in his native country, not only by Kodály but also by later composers with styles differing markedly from his, by György Kurtág (1926-) in his quartet op.1 (1959), which also looks to Webern's clean fracturings, and by György Ligeti (1923-).

Ligeti nos 1 and 2 Most of Ligeti's published music dates from after his emigration to western Europe in 1956; his first quartet (1953-4) is one of the few works he has allowed to reveal what he calls the 'prehistoric' Ligeti, and, as with any artist strong enough to create his own personality, it turns out that that personality is implicit even in what must regarded as juvenilia, despite the great gulf in experience, stylistic awareness and aim that separates the first quartet from its successor of 1968. Both works set up a game of variations, with clear acknowledgment of Bartók, in which a simple basic element is paraded in a bewildering variety of textures and moods, and in which the textures are so artfully contrived that their expressive import is held in mid-air: it may be deliberately framed, or taken to a ludicrous extreme, or treated objectively. There is a connection here not only with Bartók but with Ravel, though Bartók is the predecessor called to mind by Ligeti's enjoyment of creative and re-creative virtuosity, with its guarantee of precision in effect, and by his willingness to let objectivity spill over into parody.

The first quartet, subtitled *Métamorphoses nocturnes*, is a continuous succession of images as various as a syrupy waltz, a mad clockwork prestissimo, a crystallization into the stasis of sustained chords and, at the beginning and the end, a moment of Slavonic heart-searching. The difference in the second quartet is that the images are less easy to name, less easy to associate with any original, and yet they are just as exact, attractive and grotesque. There is nothing here that is not odd. The virtuosity is such that even a simple descending chromatic scale can become – through choice of register, the use of harmonics, the absence of vibrato and the octave doublings – an unearthly melody that finds a quite new voice in the string quartet while using it in a wholly orthodox manner:

73 Ligeti: Quartet no. 2, first movement

This comes as the entirely unexpected ending to the first movement, pulled out of the hat after an Allegro nervoso of scratchy high harmonics and a Prestissimo sfrenato in streams of vain motion: the markings ostentatiously recall Berg's Lyric Suite in stipulating both speed and character, but in doing so they call attention to the gap between Berg's authentic expressiveness and Ligeti's carnival. Nobody could ever suppose that Ligeti's quartet followed an intimate programme or that it was a 'latent opera', or if they did, the opera and the programme would have to be as surreal and puppet-like as the composer's own later *Le grand macabre*.

The second and third movements dwell on quite opposite and distinct kinds of music, first a protracted unison from which the instruments eventually and severally waver, then an automatic ticking which is also disrupted as the instruments get out of alignment with each other (another hint of Ligeti's objectivity is that one thinks of them as instruments and not as Holliger's people). The fourth movement, in its heading a piece far beyond the Berg model, is a Presto furioso, brutale, tumultoso in which heavy, awkward multiple-stoppings are so thrown on top of one another that they dance with their own kind of galumphing elegance, and the finale is an Allegro con delicatezza, mostly whispering, fast and tremulous. This is certainly not a symmetrical return to the start as in Bartók's five-movement quartets, but rather the abandonment of a process in which, as Ligeti has said, 'the same musical idea receives five quite different musical realisations'. The game of disguise could easily continue.

Outside Hungary, Bartók's influence has been felt most especially by British and American composers of quartets, for example by Alan Bush (1900-) in his remarkably strenuous single-movement *Dialectic* op.15 (1929), which strives through musical argument to hold a Marxist position, and strives too to counter the strain of nostalgic pastoralism that had become a cliché of English chamber music. That there was much English chamber music can be attributed in good measure to the activities of Walter Wilson Cobbett (1847-1937), the English equivalent of Coolidge, who instituted prizes for chamber works that had, rather significantly, to pretend allegiance to some native tradition by taking the form of 'phantasies', or single-movement structures analogous to the viol fancies of the Elizabethans and Jacobeans. Two generations of British composers grew into chamber music under the influence of this curious nationalist doctrine: Frank Bridge (1879-1941) received the accolade for a piano trio of 1907, and Benjamin Britten (1913-76) entered the competition with his oboe quartet of 1932.

Bridge nos 3 and 4   Bush, however, was not of this school, and nor was Bridge in his last two quartets, no.3 (1926) and no.4 (1937), which were also influenced by Bartók as well as by the quartets of Berg. It was to Berg

that Bridge owed the enlarged euphoniousness of his atonal counterpoint, and to both his continental contemporaries that he looked for
models of incisive phrasing, especially in his trenchant third quartet;
the fourth is more refined and elusive in tone. Both also have
something of Bartókian symmetry in their three-movement forms with
an intermezzo-like centrepiece that detaches itself from the surrounding argument, though in neither work does Bridge quite screen out the
wandering Englishness that he had espoused in his earlier quartets as
much as any other British composer of his time.

Britten, a boy pupil of Bridge at the time of the latter's third
quartet, must have been impressed by his teacher's achievement, and
perhaps even oppressed by it as much as he was, self-confessedly, by
the sonata expectations of the quartet medium. An early quartet in D
major (1931) remained unpublished until after he had revised it near
the end of his life, and his official first quartet, his op.25, also in D, *Britten no. 1 in D*
emerged just six months after Bridge's death, by which time he was in *(op. 25)*
America and responding to a commission from Coolidge. The piece is
not at all like Bridge. It is not so very much like Britten. It is a
particular Britten of the quartet we encounter here, freed from all the
mannerisms of his operas and song cycles, and the influence of Bartók
is sublimated into a concern with fundamentals, fundamentals in
particular of harmonic tension. The first movement starts with the
major third D–F sharp plucked by the cello and played high in the
treble by viola and first violin, with the second violin adding an
intrusive E:

74 *Britten: Quartet no. 1, first movement*

As at the opening of Bartók's first quartet, a completely new and
thoroughly authentic quartet sound is introduced, and one that
provides fuel for more than one work: Britten's third quartet op.94
(1975) will again begin with clashing major seconds in an environment of the gentlest concord. In the first quartet, in a first movement
that owes little to Beethoven's integration of introduction and allegro,

the initial andante music is, as if acted upon by the ensuing allegro, taken up a minor third to F and then brought back down again. The step is just: F is the key of the scherzo that follows, and the B flat of the slow movement – again a texturally and expressively original conception in 5/4 – will be remembered in the finale.

Britten no. 2 in C   If there is little hint in this work of Britten's Englishness, his second quartet op.36, written only four years later, is a different matter. It was composed back in England, and its final movement is explicitly a homage, on the occasion of his 250th anniversary, to the fellow-countryman Britten most admired: Purcell. The form is a little like that of Bartók's second quartet, with a moderately paced sonata movement followed by an energetic scherzo and then a slow finale, but in this case the slow movement – given the Purcellian title of 'Chacony' (Britten also arranged for quartet Purcell's Chacony in G minor) – is longer than the other two put together. Effectively the quartet incorporates the composer's return home, from the cosmopolitanism of his first movement, which is remarkable for a recapitulation so compacted that it barely functions as a return, through to the true return of the finale, which within itself weaves a wayward course as it moves towards its ending in the quartet's home key of C major.

It is tempting to see more than coincidence in the fact that C major is also the tonality presented most directly, without subterfuge, doubt or compromise, in the other two of Britten's numbered quartets: in the slow movement of the first, and at the very end of the slow movement of the third. The effect in both works is of a glimpse into peaceful, luminous territory from which the remainder of the music is excluded: in psychological terms, perhaps, it is the image of childhood innocence that was of inescapable significance to Britten in his vocal works, a state of grace achieved in the second quartet after an emphatic identification with Purcell, but lost in the other two works.

Britten no. 3   Britten's third quartet, indeed, is concerned with a very different journey. Again the groundplan looks like a borrowing from Bartók: there are five movements after the pattern of the latter's fourth quartet, in which, interestingly, C had functioned as main pivot. Also as in the Bartók, the movements outline a clear symmetry, the central 'Solo' having passages of high violin calm separated by a section of more character-stamped, even parodic figures for the leader accompanied by loose textures, the scherzos 'Ostinato' and 'Burlesque' having the link of ABA form and an obsessive four-note pattern, rising in sevenths in the first and seconds in its companion, and the outer movements both beginning with those exquisitely discordant major seconds remembered from the first quartet.

However, the urge of the Britten quartet is not circular and self-contained as in the Bartók, but questing and directed always onward, no matter how uncertain the direction for most of the time. Its uncertainty, indeed, brings problems of interpretation even for those most closely associated with the work. According to Colin Matthews, who was working as Britten's musical assistant at the time of the quartet's composition, the first movement, with its title of 'Duets' preparing one for music in which all six possible pairings of the instruments are used, 'is an elegiac Andante, with an agitated central section, recalled briefly before the coda', whereas Hans Keller, the quartet's dedicatee, would see this same movement as a sonata structure in which the material of maximum tension (the development's) is, in the coda, used to achieve a maximum relaxation so that the same motivic substance is employed to opposite purposes.

Formally and expressively the last movement, 'Recitative and Passacaglia (La serenissima)', is less of a conundrum. This time the homecoming is not to Purcell, to the chaconne and to C major but instead to Venice, to the passacaglia (international equivalent of the chaconne) and a begrudged E major, though a firm close in that key would be a sham such as this work disclaims. By using themes from his opera *Death in Venice* – if not as well the psychological theme of that work – this last of Britten's compositions seems to redeem the entire operatic output that had occupied him during the thirty years since his previous quartets, and after its vision of C major tranquillity, after its sadly, sweetly corrupt E major, so very Venetian, it has the perseverance and the honesty to go on without more illusions or wish-fulfilment, to end, as Britten wanted it to end, with a question.

Meanwhile Britten's striving to accommodate himself to the string quartet – to find some discourse between England and the Austro-German-Hungarian heartland of the genre – had been paralleled in the work of other English composers, who similarly had reached back into their own history for a ground bass. What Purcell was for Britten, medieval English music was for Peter Maxwell Davies in his fiercely meditative single-movement quartet of 1961, and madrigals were for Michael Tippett (1905-). Tippett has been acutely conscious of the problem of reconciling personal imagination with given form: he writes of his first three quartets, dating from 1934-46, as 'concerned with my almost total preoccupation then with matters of form' and notes that the second is 'the closest to a "standard" four-movement piece'. Originally, though, the first quartet (1934-5) was also in four movements, if in an unconventional slow–fast–slow–fast pattern that owes less to Bartók's third quartet than to Tippett's predisposition

Tippett no. 1

towards thinking in terms of balancing pairs, towards a kind of dynamic equipoise he would have found in the pavane–galliard coupling of the English Renaissance (his alternative to the *lassú-friss* model from Hungarian folk music that served for Bartók). Indeed, the third movement he calls a pavane, and the finale, though fugal, is the first instance of that aerial dancing typical of the composer, most especially in his writing for strings. The first two movements, however, were replaced in 1943 by a single new opening, in a rather more definite and personal kind of sonata form than Tippett had earlier managed in his original second movement: its characteristic features include an extreme contrast between the two kinds of music used as primary and secondary subjects (again the conscious balancing of opposites) and a resolution of conflict through the almost operatic agency of a soloist, here the cellist.

Tippett no. 2   By the time Tippett wrote this movement he had completed his second quartet (1941-2), where the four-movement form is respected but reversed. The heavy sonata allegro comes at the end, and the first movement, also in Tippettian sonata form, is much more light and graceful, sped on its way by extreme sharp tonalities (the quartet is in F sharp), by treble textures and most of all by lines kept airborne by the athletic pacing of rival metres, somewhat in madrigalian fashion:

75 Tippett: Quartet no.2 in F#, first movement.
Copyright 1944 by Schott & Co. Ltd.

The same kind of sprung rhythm occurs in the finale, and also in the scherzo, a dance more precisely figured than the first movement and answering the slow fugue that came between.

Tippett no. 3   In Tippett's third quartet (1945-6) there is at last no sonata movement, and earlier attempts to reinterpret the old pattern give way to a form dependent on the composer's own established styles of brilliant dance and slow lyrical calm, three fast fugues being interleaved with two meditations: once more the Bartók model, that of his fifth quartet, seems distinctly less important than the composer's

Jungian analysis of complementary musical archetypes to be found equally within the great tradition (in Beethoven, for example) and outside it. Apparently Tippett intended to follow this quartet with a fourth (Eliot too was important to him at this time), but the successor was not in fact written for more than thirty years, 1977-9, by which time Tippett was identifying not with any general norms of musical tradition so much as with a very specific moment in it, the late Beethoven.

The great interruption in the quartets of both Britten and Tippett, from the mid-forties to the mid-seventies, can neatly be filled by the three quartets of their American contemporary Elliott Carter (1908-), who may be accounted the truest of Bartók's heirs: not noticeably influenced by his musical substance, but challenged to emulate him in creating a quartet cycle that charts its own strong course. His first *Carter no. 1* quartet (1950-51) was written at almost exactly the same time as Cage's, but it is startlingly opposite in its need for an ensemble with the string quartet's powers of polyphonic enterprise and divergent grouping. In its span of almost forty minutes it seems to run through every possibility of textural arrangement, beginning with an unaccompanied cello solo that is completed at the end by the first violin alone, and in between including everything from the simple Cageian open fifth to the extreme separation in the slow movement of high, becalmed, muted violins above the effortful recitative of the lower instruments, or from the interlocking of two or three instruments in the same melodic line to the hectic independence of much of the first movement:

76 Carter: Quartet no. 1, first movement

On occasion the complexity of the counterpoint even requires the composer to add a fifth and even a sixth stave, sometimes for practical reasons to notate a wide chord, sometimes in order to make clear his intentions as to the combined effect of two or three voices. But this is not a sign that the quartet is unequal to the task imposed upon it. The very difficulty of the work, for performers and no less for audiences, is part of its meaning. With it, as the composer has said, he abandoned any idea of writing 'for' his audience, since the music the quartet was bringing to his mind had no obvious connections with the tastes of any known public. He withdrew to the Arizona desert and wrote only for himself, in what had become by convention the most private of genres. Yet – and this is a fact of the quartet in general – the exploration in depth of a private world proved to be of more public significance than works written with the intention of appealing, and for Carter, in his early forties, this was the first work to realize his potentialities. (Another example might be the justly titled *Quartetto intimo* written in 1931-2 by John Foulds (1880-1939) – intimate in that it explores a private imaginative world, though big and various in doing so, and carrying a mediocre composer way beyond the level of anything else he wrote.)

What Carter discovered in the desert, or rather within himself, was not only a newly dense mode of thought but a newly fluid form. Indeed, the one entails the other, is simply the vertical result of a fluctuating overlap of musical materials which, on the largest scale, runs the four traditional movements together and then chops them apart almost at random to produce the three sections into which the work is divided. This *trouvaille,* that a 'movement' need not be coextensive with a segment of music isolated in time, is a hallmark of Carter's mature style appearing for the first time in this quartet, whose opening Fantasia leads from the initial cadenza into the combative allegro and then into the moto perpetuo scherzo, which is continued in the second section as introduction to the adagio, after which come the Variations so fantastically spawning of change that they have already begun before their marked beginning.

In Carter's second quartet (1959), and also in his third (1971), the interpenetration of differently characterized musical units, different 'movements', is carried further but exposed more schematically. The second quartet, too, shares with the first a concern with 'motion, change, progression in which literal or mechanical repetition finds little place', but it also owes much to the publication and performance in the interim of a work half a century old, namely the second quartet of Ives.

Ives began his second quartet some time around 1905, by which time he had given up any notion of adapting himself to convention as he dutifully had in his first. The work was in several short movements 'related only by contrasts', and while calling it a quartet Ives happily added other instruments, as he did also in his 'Concord' sonata for piano: a double bass, a flute, a piano. 'In short,' as he wrote, 'this string quartet was not a string quartet at all – perhaps maybe because of the fact that the Kneisel Quartet played so exquisitely "nice" that I lost some respect for those four instruments. A whole evening of mellifluous sounds, perfect cadences, perfect ladies, perfect programs, and not a dissonant cuss word to stop the anemia and the beauty during the whole evening.' *Ives no. 1*

His irritation is easy to understand. It is the irritation of an adventurous composer confronted by a medium of unimpeachable propriety; it is the other side of the quartet's orthodoxy. But it is the irritation too of one who wanted music to stir the soul, who violently resisted the idea that it should be painless and pleasant, and who no doubt found the atmosphere at quartet recitals too often one of snobbery and smugness rather than interest and passion. Eventually, however, Ives decided to fight his battles from within the medium. The quartet with added obbligatos was abandoned, its movements left to stand as separate pieces or else reworked as songs, while a new second quartet was written between 1911 and 1913 in order to 'have some fun with making those men fiddlers get up and do something like men'. *Ives no. 2*

If that meant energizing the quartet, then Ives succeeded in his aim, partly by giving free rein to his atonal polyphony in long and angular melodic lines, and partly by dramatizing the element of conversation that had been perhaps more discreetly managed in the namby-pamby quartets he heard at evenings with the Kneisel. His first movement is subtitled 'Discussions' and his second 'Arguments', the music conveying all the difference in pacing, force of idea and sympathy of response that one might expect from these headings. In 'Arguments' the second violin, so often overlooked in quartet textures, is allowed to assert itself as Ives's imaginary Rollo, the custodian of tradition and musical safety. Rollo tries to anchor the ranging talk of the others, sometimes by insisting on ostinatos, sometimes by taking the centre of the stage, as he does in a short cadenza marked 'Andante emasculata' and the brief, irreverently dispatched 'Largo sweetota' that follows. But in the last part of the movement the second violin loses track of Rollo as all four instruments join in a racing babble of quotations and counter-ideas:

77 Ives: Quartet no.2, second movement

The paucity of phrasing and dynamic markings here is in accord with Ives's distrust of everything but the essential: the quartet also eschews colour effects, having not a note of pizzicato. Thanks to Ives's characterful dialogue, however, it hardly seems to lack incident, and the first two movements do not need the composer's marginal notes about how the discussions and arguments are going: certainly they go so far that no cosy resolution is going to do, even if Ives had been capable of such a thing. Instead he provides music which is wholly appeased but still lean and strenuous, an adagio subtitled 'The Call of the Mountains' in which double-stopping is the rule as the instruments move equably within a largely homophonic texture, the complex chords conveying a stasis tugged in several different directions at the same time (and so slightly analogous to the closing movement of Stravinsky's Three Pieces). It is as Ives describes the work on the first page of his manuscript: 'S.Q for 4 men – who converse, discuss, argue (in re 'politick'), fight, shake hands, shut up – then walk up the mountain-side to view the firmament'.

Since this work just antedates the Stravinsky pieces, it ought perhaps to have been taken as the prime champion of twentieth-century iconoclasm, but whereas Stravinsky's set was known, published and played from the time of its composition, Ives's work did not emerge from the scrawled obscurity of its manuscript until 1954, in time to affect the course of Carter's second quartet. This is also a *Carter no. 2* work of discussions and arguments, and it also projects the second violin as a stabilizing force, though now a more beneficent one. As in the first quartet, but here without interruption, the usual four movement types are welded into one, and in the same sequence of allegro, scherzo, slow movement and finale, all enclosed within an introduction and a conclusion. But this time the form is more compact (the duration is halved) and the cadenzas, including one for viola as well as for cello and first violin again, are brought inside to occupy the spaces between movement types and so clarify the structure. The work is also made much sharper in outline by the association of each instrument with a particular group of musical characteristics, which makes the conversation of the quartet something more than a metaphor and brings an evocation of the Ives quartet as the players variously lead, imitate, argue and scoff.

Carter's third quartet has a more complicated assemblage of *Carter no. 3* movements – four for the duo of first violin and cello, and six for that of the middle instruments, both collections being cut and scattered through the continuous work – but again, perhaps even more so, the differences between movement types are well defined, the roles of the musicians decisively assigned. Relationships and transitions are left to be formed by the listener's understanding instead of being engineered within the music, as had happened in the first quartet. And yet that first quartet was in other ways a prototype, certainly in terms of density, of considering each instrument as a distinct individual, and even in such details as the isolated duos of the slow movement, due to be taken up again in the third quartet. The first quartet was a discovery; its successors are rationalizations, attempts to comprehend and order.

Variation 3:
Shostakovich and the multiple quartet

Historically quartets came in sixes, and though since Beethoven's time they have been published singly, the idea persists that a quartet is naturally part of a larger whole: part of the entire quartet tradition in the widest view, and more narrowly part of a 'cycle'. Of course, composers who want to dissociate themselves from the quartet tradition will also want to dissociate themselves from the notion of a cycle: indeed the whole meaning of a work like Cage's quartet would be drastically altered if it were one of a sequence in the composer's output. There are also others, like Gabriel Fauré (1845-1924), who reserved the quartet for their last thoughts, taking Beethoven as their model and, in the particular case of Fauré's E minor quartet op.121 (1923-4), producing a rarefied distillation of the whole miniature musical culture he had brought into being in his songs and piano music. Britten's third quartet, too, though part of a small cycle, shows this prestige of the medium as a vehicle for the elevated swansong.

But there are other composers who have viewed the genre in a more workaday fashion, and regularly dispatched quartets as if to keep a diary of their creative lives. Heitor Villa-Lobos (1887-1959) wrote seventeen between 1915 and 1957, and there are comparably lengthy series by, for instance, Vagn Holmboe (1909-), Elizabeth Maconchy (1907-) and Darius Milhaud (1892-1974). In 1920, the year of what was already his fifth quartet. Milhaud rather charmingly announced: 'I want to write eighteen quartets'. And so he did. The last arrived in 1950, and after that he stopped, drawing out his quartet pen again only to write an epitaph for Stravinsky twenty-one years later. One might ask why he picked the figure of eighteen: perhaps with the prescient intention of capping Villa-Lobos's output, or to complete the equivalent of three Haydn sets. But why not eighteen? With Milhaud the number had only to be large yet gainable.

Two of his quartets, nos. 14 and 15 (1949), he wrote so that they could be performed either separately or simultaneously as an octet – an economy of time that might tempt one to imagine the whole eighteeen being played at once by a rather ill balanced string orchestra. Nor is that so very implausible, since a sort of loose-linked simultaneity is all of a piece with Milhaud's style, where an easeful polytonality lends itself to the converse of distinct lines:

78 Milhaud: Quartet no. 8, op. 121, first movement

No doubt that helped dispose Milhaud to the medium in the first place, the quartet being so much a genre of dialogue; though it is hard to imagine he needed much of a push towards any medium when he wrote so copiously and fluently in all.

It would not be correct, however, to suppose that Milhaud's quartets are indistinguishable. Some are in four movements and some in three. Some are marked by the Latin American music he so much enjoyed: an example is the 'Mexicana' finale to no. 13. And though the general pattern is fast–slow–fast, with an added scherzo if there is a fourth movement, Milhaud remained capable of such novel forms as he introduced in his very last quartet, inscribed to the memory of his parents and interposing two quick hymns between a pair of slow movements. Even here, though, the multiple approach was at work, the piece coming at the end of a family triptych in which the quartets are dedicated to the composer's wife and his son.

211

The cycle of fifteen quartets by Dmitry Shostakovich (1906-75) is a different matter, the weightiest long sequence in the genre since Beethoven. They cover a period of more than thirty years, and yet their chronological order is relatively unimportant – less so even than in the case of the symphonies, since the quartet, as a medium for rather small and specialized audiences, invited less political prescription than the mass forum of the symphony (there is no 'Leningrad' quartet, no 'The Year 1917', no 'Soviet Artist's Reply to Just Criticism'). The first quartet op.49 (1938) is a slender work, but then so too are the seventh op.108 (1960) and the eleventh op.122 (1966). The last four quartets, with the last two symphonies, belong to what has widely been identified as a distinctive late period, but the intensity of personal utterance is scarcely less in the eighth quartet op.110 (1960), or in the third op.73 (1946), or in anything else Shostakovich wrote. Nevertheless, one feature of timing does seem significant: his late and, on one level, gradual entry into the medium. Nineteen at the première of his first symphony, he waited until he was thirty-one before he wrote his first quartet.

Partly this may be explained by political doubts about the function of chamber music in a socialist state. As we have seen, the string quartet flourished best in imperial Russia when it was fostered by connoisseurs and appreciated within small circles. It was not very obviously an apt vehicle for the music of the people, and nor did it appeal, because of its traditional associations, to those composers who were actively pursuing revolution and experiment in music. This latter party, however, had been vigorously diverted or eliminated by the late 1930s; and with the dominance in Soviet music of a view that the traditional moulds were the only ones safe, writing quartets again became possible. It was even encouraged if the music could be based on some folk tradition within the USSR, as if that could ensure an art that was both popular and national.

Prokofiev did this in his second quartet, his op.92 in F (1942), written when he was a wartime evacuee in the Caucasian city of Nalchik, and composed on Kabardinian themes (his first quartet, the B minor op.50, had been a more personal work composed twelve years earlier, before he had become definitively a Soviet composer). But of course, the string quartet was no stranger to folk accents: it had known them since Haydn, and within Prokofiev's own musical world since Borodin and Tchaikovsky (not to mention the earlier history of the 'thème russe'). It was also at this same period gaining a new lease of life from the rude shock of Hungarian folk music, though perspicaciously analysed and scrutinized by Bartók. Prokofiev's borrowing is a lot more direct, sometimes amounting to no more than transcription (e.g. the melody of its romantic adagio), but it is quite within the quartet tradition and certainly breaks no ground in finding a new social position for the medium, if that were possible: the quartet is, after all, about small groupings, not classes and nations.

It is also about personal sensibility, and it was here that Prokofiev's colleague Shostakovich was working, even if his first quartet appears to ignore all the medium's pretensions in being brief (its four movements are all over within a quarter of an hour), in not excluding the trivial and in allowing a quite astonishing thinness of texture. Of course, effective quartet textures were never dependent on all four instruments playing at once, which is why an authentic quartet sound can be evoked by a string trio or even, in Mozart's duos, by just a violin and a viola. But Shostakovich throughout his cycle takes the quartet into regions of bareness only otherwise approached, rather differently, by Cage: the second movement of his first quartet begins with a ten-bar viola solo, preparing for those long solo or duo passages that occur in each succeeding work.

His second quartet op.68 (1944), however, seems almost excessive- *Shostakovich no. 2*
ly determined to redeem its predecessor's 'faults' of aim and play the game according to the rules. It is the only one of the fifteen in the correct form, beginning with a sonata allegro that even sports an exposition repeat (the fifth quartet op.92 of 1952 will bow to this pressure as well), and then continuing with a slow movement, a scherzo and a finale in variation form which powerfully insists on turning the A major of the first movement into A minor. Shostakovich slightly mars the regularity of his scheme by choosing odd keys for the internal movements, B flat major and E flat minor, though of course this is in keeping with the general trend throughout the tonal tradition for increasingly distant keys to become structurally important, and the instability of Shostakovich's tonality – of any realistic tonality by the 1940s – makes it perfectly possible for the finale, for instance, to begin with a step down from E flat to B flat and end up emphatically in A minor. A more individual touch comes in the cheapening subtitles for the middle movements, 'Recitative and Romance' for the adagio and 'Valse' for the scherzo. These are perfectly exact, since the slow movement does indeed surround a song with solo declamation and since the scherzo is indisputably a waltz, however sardonic, but at the same time they imply, as the music itself implies, a mistrust of the confident, archetypical structures that are being re-embodied.

Already, with these two first quartets, there are difficulties of interpretation. Shostakovich's musical tragedy, not unconnected with his personal and public tragedies, was to be possessed of a style which is immediately recognizable and extremely adaptable but which could not gain from him complete belief. The very elements of that style, particularly as it is encountered in the quartets – the wandering melodic lines, the insufficient harmonies, the widespread textures, the banal rhythms, the extreme timbres – all carry with them a sense of hollowness, alienation or irony, and so a certain disconcerting shadow inevitably hangs over anything he composed. That makes it hard to be sure of his intentions, as perhaps he intended. Is the first quartet simply a divertissement in the Russian tradition, its disturbing flavour merely an unintended gift of Shostakovich's creative mind? (One might want to see significance in the fact that this work was first presented by the Glazunov Quartet, whereas all the rest were introduced by the Beethoven.) Moreover, the naivety of Shostakovich's invention raises other difficulties. Should one regard the first quartet as a deliberate attempt not to be profound, or as a piece whose simplicity is that of a novice effort, or as straightforward music made out of naive ideas? Is the second quartet a failure because it boasts too much or a success because its over-emphasis is satirically intended?

The problems are only more acute in these early works because the first writing of a string quartet is for any post-Beethoven composer a crucial experience. As by now must be clear, the quartet was only a natural mode of expression during the period when it was most feverishly practised, a period limited roughly to the last two decades of the eighteenth century. Then there were specific needs for it: as exercise for the playing amateur, as object of study and delight for the connoisseur, as saleable item for the publisher, and possibly for the composer as a medium for the particular kind of music to be made with one player to a part, a kind which the orchestra had relinquished in its recent growth. The very nature of the quartet as amicable conversation is evidence of the agreement it celebrated. Yet even during this favoured period the impediments to the quartet's further progress were becoming evident: the gain in density of harmony and sonority that stretched the capacities of four string instruments (Haydn's opp. 76 and 77 are already less natural than opp. 33 and 50 in matching medium and idea), and the parallel growth in the view of music as a composer's individual expression, not always easy to square with quartet dialogue (the first quartet composers, Haydn, Boccherini and Mozart, were also the first to keep catalogues of their compositions). Shostakovich's delay in venturing on a quartet, like Brahms's or Fauré's, indicates he was aware of the factors that made it a forbidding medium, and his particular approach to it may suggest he did not want to conceal but rather to expose the difficulties.

About his control of the medium, however, any doubts disappear with the third quartet. The standard four-movement form remains powerfully felt as a background presence, as it will to the end, but it is not again to be directly interpreted as it was in the second quartet. Instead the third has a separate fifth movement to begin – not an enlarged slow introduction as in Krenek's sixth or a way to symmetry as in Bartók's fourth and fifth, but a jaunty piece very typical of Shostakovich's irony in its self-deprecating manner, bouncing along at the diminutive, frivolous tempo of allegretto. How often that marking will reappear: for all but one of the fourth quartet's four movements, for the first movements of the sixth and seventh quartets, the central movements of the eighth and ninth, the finales of the tenth and twelfth, both outer movements of the fourteenth. How often, too, Shostakovich will repeat his third quartet's claim to be understood as a single experience, the movements conjoined or referring to one another. Here the slow movement leads directly into the finale; in nos. 5, 7, 8, 9, 11, 13, 14 and 15 all the movements are joined together. And the third quartet's thrust of weight into the finale, as a summing-up which looks back on the movements played earlier, is to recur in all the quartets from the fifth to the ninth and again in the twelfth.

Of course the creation of wholeness has a notable history in quartet writing, going back to Bartók, to Schoenberg, to Franck and, most decisive of origins, to Beethoven. For even if Shostakovich's tiny F sharp quartet (no. 7) conveys a hint of Haydn, it was clearly Beethoven who was the weightier influence on his quartets, felt in the symphonic spaciousness of his forms, the importance of solo recitative and song, the preferring of the quartet medium in what in Shostakovich's case would seem to have been a consciously articulated late style (four of his last fifteen works are quartets) and the new patterns of movements. The great central quartets of the fifties and early sixties ring changes on the four-movement model of tradition, but later Shostakovich – and above all late Shostakovich – goes a long way from the norm. The eleventh quartet is a chain of seven genre pieces, an insolent gloss perhaps on Beethoven's C sharp minor quartet. The thirteenth op. 138 (1970) is an adagio with a middle section at double speed, a pattern which its immediate successor, op. 142, reverses by placing an adagio between its two allegrettos. And, strangest of all, the last quartet, op. 144 (1974), is a linked sequence of six adagios.

Shostakovich no. 3

215

Such idiosyncrasies of structure are, again as in Beethoven, merely the most outward show of an incapacity simply to repeat established practice. In that respect Shostakovich, though finding use in the major–minor system to the end, can hardly be described as a traditional composer: he was too much himself. And indeed it no longer seems so very surprising that, for example, his fifth quartet should have been contemporary with Carter's first or his twelfth with Ligeti's second. Nor can one call conventional a style which questions the conventions as it adopts them, for the doublethink which Shostakovich was obliged to employ in his dealings with politicians has its highly productive musical counterpart, giving rise in, say, the finale of the ninth quartet op.117 (1964), or even more so that of the twelfth, to emphatic allegro music that is positive only on the surface while underneath it is clear that the exultation is compelled, even hysterical. However one understands this – and the problems have already been outlined – the duality is inescapable.

It would be wrong, therefore, to suppose that the quartets are Shostakovich's 'private' music in contrast with the 'public' symphonies. Any composer since late Haydn has known that the quartet is a public as well as a private genre; any composer since early Schoenberg has been aware that its private life is practically non-existent as far as new works are concerned. Shostakovich knew that he was writing for an audience, and the private and public voices, often divergent to the extent of being antagonistic, sound together in his quartets as much as in his symphonies. Nevertheless, the eighth quartet op.110 (1960) may owe its relative popularity to the fact that it is ostensibly a public expression of privacy, and so seems to hold more the proper character of a quartet. It is filled with quotations from other works by the composer, and yet these are framed and distanced, partly by the context, partly by the use too of the musical monogram D–E flat–C–B (in German spelling D–Es–C–H, hence 'D. Schostakowitsch'). The effect of this is to announce the self-quotation (in this case from the first symphony) with a certain objectivity, like a music example in a book:

Shostakovich no. 8

79 Shostakovich: Quartet no. 8, first movement

Much more puzzling is the sixth quartet op. 101 (1956), often taken as a light piece, though more probably the strolling inconsequentiality of its first movement is to be heard as whistling in the dark, the sudden determination of its scherzo as intrusion, or as a violent recall from escapism and fantasy. Puzzling too is the first movement of the fifth quartet, the last big sonata first movement in Shostakovich's quartets, but with its pretensions made to seem excessively exaggerated by repetition and wildness of gesture. And even more hard to reckon is the middle movement of the ninth quartet, which presages the more explicit use of the gallop from Rossini's *William Tell* overture in the fifteenth symphony: in both works the private meaning has retreated into secrecy, enigma.

Variation 4: Boulez or Haydn

Boulez Livre

Denial or continuation: various sorts of the former have already been encountered, but perhaps none as striking as that of Pierre Boulez (1925-), who wrote one of the great postwar quartets, his *Livre pour quatuor* (1948-9), and then disowned it. Coming immediately after his tumultuous piano sonata, this venture into the very different medium of the string quartet entailed, as Boulez has remarked, 'a certain restraint', but even so the *Livre* flashes with variously fashioned rhythms and with all the possibilities of string timbre that had been introduced in the quartets of Debussy, Webern and Bartók. The weightless strangeness of its world is further compounded by the fact that the instruments rarely play distinguishable lines: as in Webern's bagatelles (see ex.63) they may all be in very much the same register, crossing each other, contributing together to what is heard as a simple unity rather than an allied quaternity. In the Webern pieces one is not troubled by an inability to sort out the parts, since the music is over so quickly. But Boulez's work is much lengthier: there are six movements, of which the four that were published (I, II, III and V) play for half an hour, giving ample time for the textures to establish themselves as quite distinct from· traditional quartet discourse: the element of character present in conversational parts is attenuated, the medium purified in a way foreshadowed by Bartók as well as Webern, though taken to this extreme only by Boulez. The forms, too, are new. Boulez had destroyed the old four-movement pattern in his second piano sonata and it could not reappear. Instead the *Livre* proceeds by tight motivic interplay (especially in the second movement), by unexpected contrast and by a free-wheeling perpetual variation, which in the first movement leads, at first with gentle continuity and then by abrupt shock, back to the high C sharp with which the music had begun.

The *Livre pour quatuor* was in every respect of form and style a radically new departure, traditional only in its length and density of thought, challenging the accumulated conventions of nearly two centuries in the most orthodox medium music knows. Naturally the medium put up some resistance. Nothing of the work was heard until 1955, when the first two movements were performed for the first time, and then over the next few years the remainder followed (though not the fourth movement). This piecemeal presentation was not against the nature of the work as Boulez saw it, since, like one of Couperin's *ordres*, the *Livre* was offered as a volume from which performers could make their own selections. Nevertheless, the slowness with which the work was making its way in the quartet world eventually persuaded Boulez to rewrite it for string orchestra; he had come to feel too that 'writing for the quartet is . . . a thing of the past'.

Hence in 1968 the *Livre pour quatuor* began to become a *Livre pour cordes*, with the original quartet music teased out vertically to create what the composer has called 'effects of sound on sound – more precise lines being inscribed on hazily contoured backgrounds', requiring a full symphonic ensemble of sixty strings. There were plenty of precedents for this withdrawal into a less hostile and exposed environment. Pfitzner had converted his C sharp minor quartet (1925) into a symphony seven years later, and the same direction had been taken by Schoenberg's *Verklärte Nacht* and his second quartet, Berg's Lyric Suite and Webern's op.5. Of course, in none of those earlier cases had the adaptation been so extreme: Webern was amazed at himself that in arranging his five movements he took the music on to ten staves, but this was only to aquatint the original with solo–ensemble effects and doublings, not to add the profusion of quite new lines that Boulez draws from and around the substance of his quartet. Moreover, whereas Boulez has deemed that the *Livre pour cordes* makes its predecessor obsolete, Schoenberg, Berg and Webern all considered their orchestral versions as alternatives, not replacements. Berg, indeed, created only a suite from the suite, arranging just three of the original six movements.

Nonetheless, it is noteworthy that these adaptations all went the same way. In Haydn's time publishers were eager to have symphonies made available for chamber combinations, whether string quartet or piano trio, so that works that had been created for special and unusual occasions (which orchestral concerts were) could enter the common-wealth of normal music making, represented by the drawing-room chamber music party. In the twentieth century the situation is almost exactly reversed. The orchestral concert is the principal forum, replaced latterly by the record of orchestral music; chamber music in the home has virtually disappeared except among professional musicians. Schoenberg, Berg and Webern, therefore, were all encouraged by their common publisher to render their quartets suitable for the major outlet of orchestral performance, and by the way to draw attention to an orchestral tendency in the quartet that had erupted first in Beethoven's *Grosse Fuge*. Certainly if judged by any reasonable criterion of musical sociology – the wishes of performers, needs of publishers, receptiveness of audiences – writing for the quartet had become a thing of the past long before Boulez decided so.

This has not, however, prevented several composers who share many of Boulez's assumptions from composing string quartets: an outstanding example is provided by Brian Ferneyhough (1943-), who turned to the medium near the outset of his composing life for his

Ferneyhough Sonatas

Sonatas (1967). Here the choice of the quartet seems to have been determined partly by the great virtuosity both in individual perform-ance and in ensemble that could be expected of performing teams in the second half of the twentieth century (though the work was not played in its entirety until 1975), partly by the abundance of colour effects available from four string instruments (different kinds and combinations of glissando, pizzicato, harmonic, *sul tasto* and *sul ponticello* are all used freely), and partly as an affirmation of high ambition, a claim of affiliation to the rarefied, speculative world of late Beethoven in particular.

Boulez's *Livre*, which by now had been withdrawn, was probably less of an influence than his later 'total serialism', whose importance here Ferneyhough has admitted. He has also placed among his Sonatas' ancestors the atonal, pre-serial music of Webern, particularly the quartet bagatelles, which have the same liberty of colour and the same tendency to move in a thin, tense treble atmosphere. However, in neither of these repertories, the Boulez and the Webern, could he have found a model for a structure lasting without a break for forty-two minutes, a structure for which the only parallels are to be found in the works of Jean Barraqué (1928-73), with whom Ferneyhough shares also the intensity, the completeness and the resolution of his imaginings, conveying the sense of living always in heightened extremes but absolutely without rhetoric: one might even understand his Sonatas as a substitute for the *Hymnes à Plotia* Barraqué projected for his *La mort de Virgile*.

Any poetic interpretation, however, is unnecessary when this formidable and, for the performers, formidably difficult work is so stocked with images executed only in sound. Much of the music is ceaselessly active when it is not fast, and the few stiller passages contrive to remain at a distance, a chill and beautiful distance, from anything previously understood as quartet texture. One example is the very ending of the work, which repeats the cello harmonic in regular rhythm from the strained, expectant opening, and places above it a chime of tiny bell sounds from the two violins:

Note: The violins are rhythmically independent from the viola and cello: vertical correspondents are approximate.

80 Ferneyhough: Sonatas, ending.
Copyright 1968 by Hinrichsen Edition, Peters Edition Ltd., London

The use of unusual timbres, here and throughout the score, helps give the music its air of strangeness and is far from being merely decorative. Following an idea that had become general in the late forties and fifties, and already left its mark on the quartets of Boulez and Babbitt for example, colour becomes an instrument of order, and material associated with a particular playing technique may well have a logic of development that is partly hidden by the intercutting of different materials, one emphasizing multiple-stopping, another the instant repetition of notes, or harmonics, or glissandos. The length of the composition appears a natural result of this tangle of developments, and even though the whole is divided into twenty-four Greek-lettered sections, its growth is continuous, a model of how impulse can be retained and transmuted through a succession of blocks different in length, texture and speed.

Ferneyhough no. 2   Ferneyhough's second quartet (1980), which he calls thus and so implicitly styles the Sonatas his first, is again a work of rapid, even frenetic musical imagination, seeming the more so because of the composer's characteristic choice of small note values: there is something a bit condescending about this, as if the composed score were too difficult for the general ear and had to be slowed down in performance in an attempt at patient explanation. The composer himself speaks of 'dense webs of organisation . . . becoming deliberately absorbed into a flickering interplay of surface gestures', but holds that these still 'remain permeable to other areas of insight'. Whatever those other areas may be, it is clear that in this quartet evēn more than in the Sonatas, and despite the fact that it lasts only half as long, a moment-to-moment understanding such as a Haydn quartet supposes is not to be imagined. Indeed, the fascination of Ferneyhough's music lies partly in its incomprehensibility, which is not vain incomprehensibility like that of a chance-composed score, since we know it to have been the labour of a human mind. We may therefore think it reasonable to struggle to understand, and while we make that struggle, while we try but fail to find a safe ground for our attention in the music's processes, we have little power against its expressive potency.

In Ferneyhough that potency is conveyed to the performer purely in terms of the extraordinarily intricate musical notation, which poetic
Nono Fragmente-   markings merely challenge or confirm. But in *Fragmente-Ştille, an*
Stille   *Diotima* (1979-80), the first string quartet of Luigi Nono (1924-), the whole score is threaded with phrases from Hölderlin, which the players are not to speak but instead to '"sing" . . . inwardly in their self-sufficiency, the self-sufficiency of sounds striving for a "delicate harmony of the inner life"' (again the quotation is from Hölderlin). And so, in the way of more usual markings like the 'very tender' and 'extremely calm' of Webern's op.5, the performers' responses to the words will colour their sounds, and perhaps will colour most intensely the fermatas in which this music of fragments and stillnesses abounds: these, again to quote the composer's foreword, 'should always sound different from each other, with free imagination – of dreaming spaces, – of sudden ecstasies, – of unutterable thoughts, – of tranquil respiration, – of silences "sung" "timelessly"'. This is, then, though

the post-serial style is simpler, as much music of fine expressive extremes as that of Ferneyhough, whose second quartet the composer has also confessed to be concerned essentially with silence.

In Nono it is the silence of the word that is most important. Most of his works have in some way or another departed from the conventions of normal concert life, but here in his string quartet he abides by them zealously. And it is part of the ritual that performers do not speak, only appear and play, for speech is a property of human beings whereas the members of a quartet, above all other musicians, are only instruments: the figments of a leader's emotional world are the gracious trickery of a Haydn minuet, the exertion of a Schoenberg allegro or the turning profundity of a Beethoven adagio, not any details of his private life. To mix words with the music of a quartet is therefore almost indecent. In Schoenberg's second quartet the soprano makes the meaning manifest, but she also effectively jams the quartet: while she sings they disappear and become an accompaniment, to emerge again only when she stops, which is why a substantial quartet coda to the finale is needed if the work is to regain its status as a string quartet. In Kagel's quartet or in the *Black Angels* (1970) of George Crumb (1929-) the case is less ambiguous, for vocalization is deliberately introduced because it makes an absurd effect in the former and a bizarre one in the latter. Nono's stance is quite different. In a complete reversal of what happens in a song, even the songs of Schoenberg's quartet, it is the text that aids the performers towards a proper interpretation of the music: the silent folksong of Schoenberg's scherzo is a nearer parallel.

There is also a curious coincidence from Nono's own time. The third string quartet (1976-8) of Hugh Wood (1932-) has a similar skein of poetic superscriptions, and is unlikely to have been known to Nono (the score was not published until 1980, the year in which he finished *Fragmente-Stille*). In Wood's piece the words come from Donne and Herbert, and they are not tiny snippets but complete phrases and sentences, speaking of spiritual negation and rebirth as the music makes its continuous way through a balanced abutting of short sections – as in the Nono, and as in Wood's own more rudely adventurous, Gerhard-like second quartet (1970). But though a clearer verbal meaning is suggested, and though Wood unlike Nono remains silent about his intentions, it must be that here too the words are no more than a path to the primary experience, which is that of the music alone.

One common feature linking Wood not only with Nono but also with Ferneyhough and Boulez is that all these composers were importantly touched by the new serialism of the 1950s. So too was George Rochberg (1918-). The first of his quartets (1952), like many American quartets of its time (though certainly not those of Cage, Carter and Babbitt), belongs with the league of Bartók. But then he became a Schoenbergian, not only in adopting serialism but also in accepting the emphatic doctrine of progress that Schoenberg had done much to power, perhaps in defence against the awareness that in broaching atonality he had destroyed the clocks, put an end to the natural progress that was inherent in the diatonic system (as revealed, for instance, in the growing harmonic variety of music from Haydn to Beethoven to Brahms to Shostakovich). Rochberg's second quartet (1959-61) is accordingly a serial work, and also a rare visitor to the timbral world of Schoenberg's second, since it adds a soprano singing Rilke.

Soon after this Rochberg, in common with many other composers at the time, decided that serialism was not enough, and eventually that, in his own words, 'the music of the "old masters" was a living presence, that its spiritual values had not been displaced or destroyed by the new music'. This is unexceptionable, and perhaps also unexceptional, but the lesson that Rochberg drew from it was rather extraordinary. Instead of making history, as he had felt himself to be doing before, he determined to let history make him. In his third quartet (1972-3) he set out quite consciously to reproduce the past, sometimes a quite specific past, as in the central slow meditations which imitate late Beethoven, sometimes a more general past, or a parade of fragments from several pasts, near and far. And indeed by these means Rochberg found a way to continue the great tradition in its most characteristic genres, not least the string quartet, of which he

Rochberg 'Concord' wrote three more in 1977-8 and gave them the collective title 'Concord', in homage, one may imagine, not only to Ives's sonata, and not only to the Concord Quartet which gave the triptych its first performance, but also to an aspect of harmony he had been able to rediscover with relief.

These 'Concord' quartets include some of the same kinds of movement as had been ventured in the third. Again the most simply tonal are the slow movements: a fugue in no.4 ending maestoso in C major, an E flat minor mesto in no.5, and in no.6 a set of variations in D on the theme of Pachelbel's ubiquitous canon, though the subject may be obscured from view by a more recent, characteristically Mahlerian kind of expressiveness:

81 Rochberg: Quartet no. 6, third movement

Mahler is also called to mind in some of the more long, formally complex and materially various movements, such as the Serenade of the fourth quartet and the Scherzo–Humoresque of the sixth, but of course there is no consistent attempt on Rochberg's part to supply the quartet literature with the works Mahler himself never wrote. Rather Mahler would seem to represent for him, as also for Berio in his *Sinfonia*, a great crossroads, with routes back to the Baroque and forward to Schoenberg and Bartók, the death of progress being graphically portrayed as the music conducts itself freely within this network.

If Rochberg's brand of historicism were merely his own, then it would be eccentric to a degree, but in fact it corresponds with a general feeling of regression in contemporary musical culture, to be recognized not only in the huge revival of interest in 'early' music but also – of more particular consequence here – in a wish to examine again the period of the turn of the century, the period of harmonic collapse, the period when it all went wrong. Profitting from this, within the world of the quartet, have been the works of Reger, Pfitzner, Franz Schmidt (1874-1939) and Zemlinsky, which are almost as much products of the 1970s as are the quartets of Britten and Carter, Wood and Rochberg.

The intervening neglect is particularly striking in the case of Zemlinsky's second quartet op. 15 (1914), which once gained the *Zemlinsky no. 2* admiration of Schoenberg and Berg, but which only began to be heard again after the celebration of the composer's centenary in 1971 (it was recorded in 1978). Like Schoenberg's first quartet, but in a much less intensively propelled and developed manner, it welds the four standard movements into one forty-minute span. It also concerns itself with a very few motifs that can be varied endlessly, and sometimes

225

most surprisingly, as when the scherzo suddenly gives way to a slow passage recalling the very opening of the work:

82 Zemlinsky: Quartet no. 2 op. 15

The coexistence here of the barbarously mechanical and the fulsomely expressive is characteristic of Zemlinsky, and is one feature to give this quartet an independent atmosphere despite the many reminiscences of Mahler, of Reger and most particularly of Schoenberg, Zemlinsky's brother-in-law and sometime pupil.

But if Zemlinsky's quartet has come to seem in its readoption a child of the 1970s, it also holds true that, in Rochberg's words, the music of the 'old masters' is a 'living presence', for music is marked not only by its date of composition but also by the history of its performance and by the conditions of its experience now: a Haydn quartet in the 1980s is not what it was in the 1780s, since in the two centuries between its meaning has worked through, and been worked upon by, the quartets of Mozart, Beethoven and a hundred others, and since people who play and hear it have the style and understanding of the present (the recorded legacy is now long enough to show that even 'authentic' styles change in time, as they must). Only music which has stayed sealed can properly speak of its age, and so a true history of the string quartet ought perhaps to begin with the works of Asplmayr and F. X. Dušek, for as long as these remain untainted by contemporary performance and experience, and work its way through finally to Mozart and Carter, Bartók and Haydn as our contemporaries.

Nor is there any conflict here with Boulez's view of the composition of a quartet as 'a thing of the past'. All great quartets belong in the present, because all are being played now, but they all too cast back to a time when the quartet was invented as a natural compositional activity – natural at least for its presumed inventor Haydn (for Mozart it was not so easy). The constitution of the ensemble, uniquely in the history of music, has not changed: it would be possible to imagine the Haydn–Dittersdorf–Mozart–Vanhal quartet sitting down to tackle Carter or Xenakis. Naturally the 'old masters' would note that the original purpose of the quartet had been modified in these works, that the possibilities of communicative music-making were compromised by a certain public address and even more so by the difficulty of the parts, which leaves little room for an individual moulding of statement or response. They might feel that the old ideals were more easily to be discovered in other genres now: perhaps in such works of live electronic music as the *Kurzwellen* (1968) of Karlheinz Stockhausen (1928-), wherein the composer even increases collective responsibility by providing not musical material but a process of change in which the musicians 'call out to each other, issue invitations, so that together they can observe a single event passing amongst them for a stretch of time, letting it shrink and grow, bundling it up and spreading it out, darkening it and brightening it, condensing it and losing it in embellishments'. But Haydn and his colleagues might well remark too on the continuity of the quartet, the permanence of its two most distinctive modes so suited to this medium – the socially witty and the personally profound – and the way any new quartet looks not only to its performers and audience but also in a third direction, to the world of musical intelligence that reached its fulfilment in the late eighteenth century and above all in the string quartet.

Appendix One
References

PART ONE

Introduction

The essential, comprehensive source for information about Haydn and his music is H. C. Robbins Landon's *Haydn: Chronicle and Works* in five volumes (London, 1976-81). See especially pp.228-32 and 251-7 in the first volume for opp.1 and 2, and pp.315-24 in the second volume for opp.9 and 17.

A detailed study of Haydn's earlier quartets, and also of the whole history of the string quartet up to Haydn's op.33, is contained in Ludwig Finscher's *Studien zur Geschichte des Streichquartetts*, volume I (Kassel, 1974). Reginald Barrett-Ayres's *Joseph Haydn and the String Quartet* (London, 1974) covers a longer period, up to Haydn's last works and Beethoven's op.18, but it similarly considers some of the lesser figures with the greater: Gassmann, Ordonez, Vanhal, etc. Rosemary Hughes's BBC Music Guide *Haydn String Quartets* (London, 1966) is a brief companion.

The argument that Haydn's opp.1 and 2 were intended for solo string quartet is maintained by James Webster in three important articles: 'Towards a History of Viennese Chamber Music in the Early Classical Period', *Journal of the American Musicological Society*, xxvii (1974), 212-47; 'Violoncello and Double Bass in the Chamber Music of Haydn and his Viennese Contemporaries, 1750-1780', *JAMS*, xxix (1976), 413-38; and 'The Bass Part in Haydn's Early String Quartets', *Musical Quarterly*, lxiii (1977), 390-424. Roger Hickman argues on the contrary that the change from orchestral to quartet conception did not take place until the late 1760s: see his 'The Nascent Viennese String Quartet', *MQ*, lxvii (1981), 193-212.

The probability of Hoffstetter's authorship of 'Haydn's op.3' was raised by Alan Tyson and H. C. Robbins Landon in their article 'Who Composed Haydn's op.3?' *Musical Times*, cv (1964), 506-7. Other Haydn apocrypha are considered in Robbins Landon's 'Doubtful and Spurious Quartets and Quintets Attributed to Haydn', *Music Review*, xviii (1957), 213-21, and in Georg Feder's 'Apokryphe "Haydn"-Streichquartette', *Haydn-Studien*, iii (1974), 125-50.

Sammartini's late concertinos are discussed by Henry G. Mishkin in his 'Five Autograph String Quartets by Giovanni Battista Sammartini', *JAMS*, vi (1953), 136-47.

There are standard thematic catalogues of Boccherini by Yves Gérard (London, 1969), of Haydn by Anthony van Hoboken (Mainz, 1957-71) and of Mozart by Ludwig Köchel (Leipzig, 1862, sixth edition 1964).

EDITIONS AND RECORDINGS

Modern editions of scores [s] and parts [p] are listed below, together with recordings that claim attention for their rarity or completeness (□).

Albrechtsberger: Divertimento in A, ed. Franz Brodsky, Diletto musicale no.291, Doblinger [p].

Boccherini: op.8 no.6 (as op.6 no.6), op.9 no.2 (op.10 no.2), op.9 no.6 (op.10 no.6) and op.15 no.1 (op.8 no.5), with four other quartets, ed. Richard Hofmann, Peters [p].

——: op.2 no.1, with six other quartets, ed. Walter Upmeyer, Bärenreiter [p].

——: op.2 no.1 (op.1 no.1), op.2 no.6 (op.1 no.6), op.8 (op.6), op.9 no.1 (op.10 no.1), op.9 no.4 (op.10 no.4), ed. Enrico Polo, Ricordi [s].

Haydn: opp. '0', 1, 2, 9 and 17, ed. H. C. Robbins Landon and Reginald Barrett-Ayres, Doblinger [sp]. These works can also be found in volumes xii/1-2 of the complete edition [s]; among other editions, that by Eulenburg includes 'op.3' [s]. □ Aeolian, Argo HDNM 52-6 (opp. '0', 1, 2), HDNV 82-4 ('op.3'), HDNQ 61-6 (opp.9, 17).

Mozart: K80, various editions, including those by Dover [s], Eulenburg [s] and Peters [p], and volume VIII/20/1/i of the *Neue Mozart Ausgabe*. □ Amadeus, DG 2740 165.

Richter: set of six printed in London in 1768, *Denkmäler der Tonkunst in Bayern*, xxvii, 1914 [s]; a further set of five, *Musica Antiqua Bohemica*, lxxi, 1969 [s].

EXPOSITION

Robbins Landon's five-volume *Haydn* remains of central importance. The second volume covers op.20 (pp.315-34), op.33 (pp.454-6 and 576-82), op.42 (pp.624-5), op.50 (pp.625-9), opp.54-5 (pp.635-41) and op.64 (pp.655-9); opp.71 and 74 are considered on pp.455-82 of the third volume, op.76 on pp.284-310 of the fourth, op.77 on pp.501-23 of the fourth, and op.103 on pp.275-8 of the fifth. Also useful are the books above-mentioned by Finscher, Barrett-Ayres and Hughes.

The standard critical study of Mozart is that by Alfred Einstein (New York, 1945; London, 1946; much reprinted). There is also a strikingly illuminating essay on the quartets by Hans Keller in *The Mozart Companion*, ed. H. C. Robbins Landon and Donald Mitchell (London, 1956). A more particular matter, the dating of Mozart's last three quartets, is considered by Alan Tyson in his 'New Light on Mozart's "Prussian" Quartets', *Musical Times*, cxvi (1975), 126-30.

On a more specialist level, *The String Quartets of Haydn, Mozart and Beethoven: Studies of the Autograph Manuscripts*, ed. Christoph Wolff (Cambridge, Mass., 1980), includes essays by James Webster on performing indications in Haydn, by Georg Feder on corrections in Haydn's opp.64, 71 and 74, by Ludwig Finscher on Mozart's compositional process and by the editor on Mozart's quartet fragments. Warren Kirkendale's *Fugue and Fugato in Rococo and Classical Chamber Music* (Durham, N.C., 1979) includes valuable

documentation in addition to its learned commentary.

Charles Rosen's *The Classical Style* (New York and London, 1971, second edition 1972) is full of stimulus.

EDITIONS AND RECORDINGS

Albrechtsberger: op.1 no.2 and op.1 no.5, Kistner & Siegel [p].
——: op.2 no.6, ed. Franz Brodsky, Diletto musicale no.337, Doblinger [p].
——: op.7 nos. 1-3 and op.10 no.6, *Denkmäler der Tonkunst in Österreich*, xxxiii, 1909 [s].
——: op.20 no.1, ed. Franz Brodsky, Diletto musicale no.288, Doblinger [p].

Boccherini: op.24 no.6 (op.27 no.2), op.26 no.4 (op.32 no.4), op.32 no.5 (op.33 no.5) and op.32 no.6 (op.33 no.6), with four other quartets, ed. Richard Hofmann, Peters [p].
——: op.24 no.1 (op.24 no.5), op.39, op.41 no.1, op.41 no.2, op.44 no.4 and op.48 no.3 (op.48 no.2), with one other quartet, ed. Walter Upmeyer, Bärenreiter [p].
——: op.24 no.2 (op.27 no.4), op.24 no.4 (op.27 no.3) and op.32 no.6 (op.33 no.6), ed. Enrico Polo, Ricordi [s].
——: op.33 and op.53 no.6 (op.40 no.5), ed. W. Höckner and H. Mlynarczyk, Simrock [p].
——: op.22 no.4 (no.8), ed. H. Sitt, International [p].

Dittersdorf: E flat, Peters [p]; E flat and G, Philharmonia [s].

Förster: op.16 nos.4 and 5, *Denkmäler der Tonkunst in Österreich*, lxvii, 1928 [s].

Haydn: opp.20, 33, 42, 50, 54, 55, 64, 71, 74, 76, 77 and 103, ed. H. C. Robbins Landon and Reginald Barrett-Ayres, Doblinger [sp]. These works can also be found in volumes xii/3-6 of the complete edition; among other editions, that by Eulenburg includes op.51.

Haydn, Michael: P124, 118, 122, 120, 119 and 116, Diletto musicale nos.331-6, Doblinger [sp].

Mozart: K136-8, 155-60, 168-73, 387, 421, 428, 458, 464, 465, 499, 546, 575, 589 and 590, various editions, including those by Dover ([s], except K136-8 and 546), Eulenburg [s] and Peters [p], and volumes IV:11/x (K546), IV:12/vi (K136-8) and

VIII:20/1/i-iii of the *Neue Mozart Ausgabe*. □ Amadeus, DG2740 165 (K136-8, 155-60 and 168-73); the later quartets have been often recorded.

Vanhal: six miscellaneous quartets, ed. David Wyn Jones, Cardiff, 1980 [s].

Development and Recapitulation

Among several books devoted to Beethoven's string quartets the outstanding study is Joseph Kerman's *The Beethoven Quartets* (New York, 1967; London, 1967), though Basil Lam's shorter *Beethoven String Quartets* (London, 1975) is also full of information and insights. The Harvard symposium edited by Christoph Wolff, mentioned above, includes an important study and documentation of Beethoven's quartet fugues by Richard Kramer, as well as an essay on op.132 by Sieghard Brandenburg. For the later period in general, Martin Cooper's *Beethoven: the Last Decade 1817-1827* (London, 1970) is without peer.

The literature on Schubert's quartets is very much less extensive, and indeed the most useful material is contained in more general works, notably Otto Erich Deutsch's classic *Schubert: a Documentary Biography* (London, 1946) and Alfred Einstein's *Schubert* (London, 1951).

Spohr's *Autobiography* (London, 1865, reprinted 1969) includes glimpses into the conditions of quartet performance in the first half of the nineteenth century, but otherwise his quartets have been little considered. Nor, understandably, has much been written on the quartets of Arriaga, Donizetti and Rossini.

EDITIONS AND RECORDINGS

Arriaga: three quartets, Union Musical Española [p]. □ Chilingirian, CRD 1012-3.

Beethoven: opp.18, 59, 74, 95, 127, 130, 131, 132, 133 and 135, various editions, including the Dover [s], Eulenburg [s] and Peters [p], and volumes vi/3 (op.18 and the arrangement of op.14 no.1) and vi/4 (opp.59, 74 and 95) of the new collected edition.

Donizetti: eighteen quartets, Istituto Italiana per la Storia della Musica, Rome and Buenos Aires, ?1948.

Schubert: D18, 32, 36, 46, 68, 74, 87, 94, 112, 173, 353, 703, 804, 810 and 887,

various editions, including those by Dover [s], Eulenburg [s], Lea Pocket Scores [s] and Peters [p].

Spohr: double quartets opp.65, 77, 87 and 136, Eulenburg [s].

PART TWO

Intermezzo

Leon Plantinga's *Schumann as Critic* (New Haven, 1967, reprinted 1977) includes useful material on his writings about quartets, while his own chamber music is considered by John Gardner in *Robert Schumann*, ed. Alan Walker (London, 1972, second edition 1976), and by A. E. F. Dickinson in *Schumann: a Symposium*, ed. Gerald Abraham (London, 1952). John Horton's *Mendelssohn Chamber Music* (London, 1972) is a good short survey. Serious studies of the quartets of Cherubini, Onslow and Raff are awaited.

EDITIONS AND RECORDINGS

Berwald: nos.1-3, volume xi of the complete edition [s].

Cherubini: nos.1-6, Eulenburg [s]. □ Melos, DG 2723 044.

Mendelssohn: opp.12, 13, 44, 80 and 81, various editions, including those by Dover [s], Eulenburg [s], Lea Pocket Scores [s] and Peters [p], and volumes iii/1 (opp.12-13) and · iii/2 (op.44) of the new complete edition. □ Melos, DG 2740 267; Bartholdy, Acanta HA 21.815 and 21.966.

Schumann: op.41, various editions, including those by Dover [s], Eulenburg [s] and Peters [p].

PART THREE

Adagio

Wagner's 1870 essay on Beethoven is contained in volume v of the Ashton Ellis translation of his *Prose Works* (London, 1892-9): see especially pp.96-8. As for the major quartet composers of this period, general studies are much more plentiful than books or articles concentrated on chamber music, and Walter Wilson Cobbett's *Cyclopaedia of Chamber Music* (London, 1929, revised edition by Colin Mason, 1963) becomes a useful source of information and opinion. Valuable for the end of the period is *Schoenberg, Berg, Webern: The String Quartets*, ed. Ursula von Rauchhaupt (Hamburg, 1971), which contains essays and relevant quotations from letters by all three composers, and which was published with a complete recording of their quartet outputs.

EDITIONS AND RECORDINGS

Berg: op.3, Universal [sp]. □ LaSalle, DG 2720 029.
Borodin: nos.1-2, Eulenburg [s].
Brahms: opp.51 and 67, various editions, including those by Eulenburg [s], Lea Pocket Scores [s] and Peters [p].
Debussy: Durand [sp].
Dvořák: most of the first six quartets were not published until their appearance as volume iv/5 of the complete edition, of which volume iv/6 includes nos.7-11 and iv/7 nos.12-14; the last seven quartets are also published by Eulenburg [s] and Simrock [p]. □ Prague, DG 2740 177.
Franck: Hamelle [sp]. □ Fitzwilliam, L'Oiseau-Lyre DSLO 46.
Reger: op.54, Universal [sp], Philharmonia [s]; op.74, Bote & Bock [sp], Eulenburg [s]; op.109, Bote & Bock [sp]; op.121, Peters [sp], Eulenburg [s]. □ Reger, Vox Box SVBX 587.
Schoenberg: D, Faber [sp]; opp.7 and 10, Universal [sp], Philharmonia [s]. □ LaSalle, DG 2720 029.
Sibelius: Eulenburg [s], Lienau [p].
Smetana: nos.1-2, Eulenburg [s].
Taneyev: op.7, Belwin-Mills [p]. □ C major of 1882-3, Taneyev, Melodiya C 10–12411–12.
Tchaikovsky: nos.1-3, Eulenburg [s].
Webern: 1905 quartet, Boosey & Hawkes [s]; opp.5 and 9, Universal [sp], Philharmonia [s]. □ LaSalle, DG 2720 029.
Wolf: D minor quartet, Intermezzo, *Italienische Serenade*, volumes xv/1-3 of the collected edition [s].

PART FOUR

Theme and variations

Bartók's quartets inevitably loom large in the monographs on him by Halsey Stevens (New York, 1953, second edition 1964) and József Ujfalussy (Budapest, 1971, in English). More particular studies include Milton Babbitt's 'The String Quartets of Bartók', MQ, xxxv (1949), 377, János Kárpáti's *Bartók's Chamber Music* (Budapest, 1975, in English) and Stephen Walsh's *Bartók Chamber Music* (London, 1982).

For most other composers of the twentieth century reference may be made to the standard studies: see bibliographies in *The New Grove*. Invaluable for Foulds is Calum MacDonald's 'John Foulds and the String Quartet', *Tempo*, no.132 (1980), 16-25.

EDITIONS AND RECORDINGS

Babbitt: no.2, Associated [s]; nos.3-4, Peters [s]. □ no.2, Composers, Nonesuch H 71280; no.3, Fine Arts, Turnabout TV 34515s.
Bartók: nos.1 and 6, Boosey & Hawkes [sp]; nos.2-5, Philharmonia [s], Universal [p].
Berg: Lyric Suite, Philharmonia [s], Universal [p]. □ in complete Schoenberg–Berg–Webern set, LaSalle, DG 2720 029.
Berio: String Quartet, Suvini Zerboni [s]; *Sincronie*, Universal [s].
Boulez: *Livre pour quatuor* I-III and V, Heugel [s, withdrawn]. □ I, III and V, Parrenin, Erato STU 70580; I and II, Parrenin, V, Hamann, Mainstream MS 5009; *Livre pour cordes* I, Boulez, CBS 73191.
Bridge: nos.3-4, Augener, reprinted Galliard [sp]. □ nos.3-4, Allegri, Argo ZRG 714.
Britten: 1931 and no.3, Faber [sp]; nos.1-2, Boosey & Hawkes [sp].
Bussotti: *I semi di Gramsci, Quartetto Gramsci*, Ricordi [s].
Cage: Peters [s]. □ LaSalle, DG 2530 735.
Carter: nos.1-3, Associated [s]. □ nos.1-2, Composers, Nonesuch H 71249; nos.2-3, Juilliard, Columbia.
Crawford Seeger: New Music [s]. □ Composers, Nonesuch H 71280.
Dutilleux: *Ainsi la nuit*, Heugel [s].
Elgar: Novello [sp].
Fauré: Durand [sp].
Foulds: no.9. □ Endellion, Pearl SHE 564.
Gerhard: no.1, Keith Prowse [s]; no.2, OUP [sp].
Goehr: nos.2-3, Schott [s]. □ no.2, Allegri, Argo ZRG 748.
Hindemith: nos.1-6, Schott [sp].
Holliger: Schott [s]. □ Bern, Wergo 60084.

Ives: no.2, Peer [s]. □ with no.1, Concord, Nonesuch H 71306.
Janáček: nos.1-2, Hudební Matice [sp].
Kagel: Universal [s].
Krenek: nos.1, 3, 5, 6 and 7, Philharmonia [s].
Ligeti: nos.1-2, Schott [s]. □ nos.1-2, Arditti, Wergo 60079.
Lutosławski: Chester, Polski Wydawnictwo Mzyczne [p]. □ LaSalle, DG 2530 735.
Milhaud: nos.1-2, Durand; nos.4-5, Salabert; nos.6-7, Philharmonia [s]; nos.8-9, Editions Sociales Internationales [s]; nos.10-13, Salabert [s]; nos.14-18, Heugel [s].
Nono: *Fragmente-Stille, an Diotima*, Ricordi [s].
Perle: no.5, Presser [s]. □ no.5, Composers, Nonesuch H 71280; no.7, New York, CRI SD 387.
Prokofiev: no.1, Editions Russes de Musique; no.2, International [sp].
Rochberg: nos.1-6, Presser [s]. □ no.3, Concord, Nonesuch H 71283.
Schoenberg: no.3, Philharmonia [s], Univer-

sal [p]; no.4, Schirmer [sp]; concerto, Schirmer [s]. □ nos.3-4 in complete Schoenberg–Berg–Webern set, LaSalle, DG 2720 029.
Shostakovich: nos.1-15, Anglo-Soviet Music Press [sp]. □ nos.1-15, Fitzwilliam, Decca D 188 D 7.
Stravinsky: Three Pieces, Boosey & Hawkes [sp]; Concertino, Chester [sp]; *In memoriam Dylan Thomas* and Double Canon, Boosey & Hawkes [s].
Tippett: nos.1-4, Schott [sp]. □ nos.1-3, Lindsay, L'Oiseau-Lyre DSLO 10.
Webern: op.28, Philharmonia [s], Universal [p]. □ in complete Schoenberg–Berg–Webern set, LaSalle, DG 2720 029.
Weill: op.8, Philharmonia [s], Universal [p].
Wellesz: nos.1-2, Ahn & Sim; no.4, Universal; no.5, Schott; no.8, Sikorski; no.9, Doblinger.
Xenakis: *ST/4, 1080262*, Boosey & Hawkes [s].
Zemlinsky: nos.2-3, Universal [p]. □ no.2, LaSalle, DG 2530 982.

Appendix Two
Chronology

This is only a rough guide. Works composed during the course of more than one year are listed against the year of completion; a doubtful dating is indicated by a prefixed ~. Particular importance is suggested by the use of **bold** type.

1759 ~ **Haydn op.1** (Bb, Eb, D, G, *, C), 'op.0' (Eb)
1760 Albrechtsberger (D, Bb, F), ~ Albrechtsberger (A)
1761 Boccherini op.2 (c, Bb, D, Eb, E, C), F. X. Dušek (A)
1762 ~ **Haydn op.2** (A, E, *, F, *, Bb)
1763
1764 Albrechtsberger (E), F. X. Dušek (G)
1765 ~ Asplmayr op.6 (F, A, Bb, Eb, F, D), F. X. Dušek (Bb), ~ Hoffstetter (F, F), ~ Ordonez op.1 (A, F, c, Eb, Bb, G)
1766

1767 Sammartini (Eb, G, Eb)
1768 ~ Gassmann op.1 (C, F, A, c, F, Bb), ~ Richter (six+five)
1769 ~ Abel op.8 (six), ~ Asplmayr op.2 (G, D, F, E, C, Eb), Boccherini op.8 (D, c, Eb, g, F, A), ~ Gossec op.14 (six), ~ Vanhal op.1 (six), op.2 (Eb, F, Bb, Eb, G, E)
1770 Boccherini op.9 (c, d, F, Eb, D, E), ~ **Haydn op.9** (C, Eb, G, d, Bb, A), ~ Hoffstetter op.1 (D, G, C, F, Bb, Eb), Mozart K80 (G)
1771 **Haydn op.17** (E, F, Eb, c, G, D)
1772 Boccherini op.15 (D, F, E, F, Eb, c), **Haydn op.20** (Eb, C, g, D, f, A), Mozart K136-8 (D, Bb, F), ~ Saint-Georges op.1 (four), ~ Vanhal op.6 (six), op.9 (Eb, G, F, Bb, F, Eb)
1773 ~ Davaux op.6 (six), ~ Grétry op.3 (G, Eb, F, D, G, Eb), **Mozart K155-60**

(D, G, C, F, Bb, Eb), κ168-73 (F, A, C, Eb, Bb, d), ~ Vachon op.6 (six), op.7 (six), Vanhal op.13 (six)

1774 C. Stamitz (six)

1775 ~ Abel op.12 (C, A, F, D, Bb, G), Boccherini op.22 (C, D, Eb, Bb, a, C), ~ Starzer (C, a), ~ Vachon op.5 (six), ~ Vanhal op.21 (Eb, G, E, F, Eb, D)

1776 ~ J. C. Bach (D, C, A), ~ M. Haydn (F), ~ Vachon op.6 (six), ~ C. Wesley

1777 ~ M. Haydn P124 (Bb), ~ Hoffstetter: 'Haydn's op.3' (E, C, G, Bb, F, A), ~ Saint-Georges (six).

1778 Boccherini op.24 (D, A, Eb, C, c, g), op.26 (Bb, g, Eb, A, F, f).

1779 ~ Davaux, op.9 (six), ~ Vanhal op.4 (six), op.24 (six)

1780 ~ Abel op.15 (six), Albrechtsberger op.1 (G, A, Bb, f, a, Eb), Boccherini op.32, (Eb, e, D, C, g, A), ~ Davaux op.10 (six), ~ Hoffstetter op.2 (F, Bb, D, G, C, Eb), ~ Mysliveček op. 1 (Eb, C, D, F, Bb, G)

1781 Boccherini op.33 (E, C, G, Bb, e, Eb), Haydn op. 33 (b, Eb, C, Bb, G, D), ~ M. Haydn P116 (C), P118 (Eb)

1782 Albrechtsberger op.2 (D, G, E, c, f, D), ~ op.7 (D, A, F, ?, ?, ?), Mozart κ387 (G), arrangements of five Bach fugues κ405 (c, Eb, E, d, D), ~ Mysliveček op.2 (six), Shield op.3 (six), ~ Vachon op.11 (six), ~ Vanhal op.11 (six)

1783 ~ M. Haydn P119-20 (F, g), Mozart κ421 (d), κ428 (Eb), ~ Pleyel op.1 (C, E, A, Bb, G, D), ~ Vanhal op.28 (six)

1784 Mozart κ458 (Bb), ~ Pleyel (A, C, g, Eb, Bb, D)

1785 Haydn op. 42 (d), Mozart κ464-5 (A, C), ~ Pleyel (Bb, A, e, C, Eb, D), ~ Saint-Georges op.14 (six), ~ Vanhal op.33 (six), ~ Viotti op.1 (six), op.3 (six)

1786 Albrechtsberger op.5 (Bb, g, d, F, A, e), Mozart κ499 (D), ~ Pleyel (Bb, G, d; C, A, Eb; D, F, g; G, c, D), (C, G, F, A, Bb, D), (Eb, Bb, A, C, G, F)

1787 Boccherini op.39 (A), Gyrowetz op.1 (C, G, Bb, A, Eb, D), Haydn op.50 (Bb, C, Eb, f#, F, D), ~ Haydn: *Seven Last Words* op.51, ~ Vanhal (six)·, Wranitzky op.4 (six)

1788 Boccherini op.41 (c, C), Dittersdorf (six), ~ Haydn op.54 (G, C, E), op.55 (A, f, Bb), Mozart: Adagio and Fugue κ546 (c), ~ Pleyel (F, A, F), (C, F, Eb, G, Bb, A), ~ Wranitzky op.1 (three), op.2 (three)

1789 Boccherini op.42 (A, C), ~ Gyrowetz op.2 (C, G, D, Bb, F, A), Mozart κ575 (D), Pleyel (D, F, A, G, Bb, C)

1790 Boccherini op.43 (A, A), ~ Danzi opp.5-7 (three each), Davaux op.14 (four), ~ Gyrowetz op.3 (D, A, F, G, C, Eb), Haydn op.64 (C, b, Bb, G, D, Eb), ~ Kozeluch (Bb, G, Eb), Mozart κ589-90 (Bb, F)

1791 ~ Gyrowetz (D, Eb, C), ~ Kozeluch (C, A, F), ~ Pleyel (C, Bb, e, G, A, f), ~ Wranitzky op.15 (six).

1792 Albrechtsberger op.10 (d, F, a, e, C, Ab), Boccherini op.44 (Bb, e, F, G, D, Eb), ~ Pleyel (F, Bb, D, Eb, G, E), ~ Wranitzky op.9 (six)

1793 ~ Gyrowetz op.5 (C, D, A), Haydn op.71 (Bb, D, Eb), op.74 (C, F, g), ~ Krommer op.1 (Bb, G, Eb), op.3 (C, A, D), ~ Wranitzky op.15 (three), op.16 (six), op.23 (six)

1794 Boccherini op.48 (F, A, b, Eb, G, C), Eybler op.1 (three), ~ Förster op.7 (A, F, D, Bb, G, Eb), ~ Gyrowetz op.9 (F, g, G), M. Haydn (F, G), ~ Krommer op.4 (G, Eb, Bb), ~ Wranitzky op.30 (six.)

1795 Boccherini op.52 (C, D, G, f), op.53 (Eb, D, C, A, C, Eb), ~ Wranitzky op.16 (three)

1796 ~ Gyrowetz op.13 (D, C, Eb), op.16 (Bb, G, A), ~ M. Haydn P122 (A), Krommer op.5 (Eb, F, Bb)

1797 Albrechtsberger op.16 (A, d, G, c, F, Bb), ~ Haydn op.76 (G, d, C, Bb, D, Eb), Krommer op.7 (C, e, A)

1798 Albrechtsberger op.14 (G, Eb, C, F, D, Bb), op.18 (D, G, C, F, d, Bb), op.19 (A, A), ~ Gyrowetz op.21 (A, F, D), ~ Krommer op.10 (F, Bb, G), op.16 (Eb, F, C), ~ Wranitzky op.32 (six).

1799 Boccherini op.58 (C, Eb, Bb, b, D, Eb), ~ Gyrowetz op.29 (Eb, G, Bb), Haydn op. 77 (G, F)

1800 Albrechtsberger op.20 (G, Bb, Eb, F, C, d), Beethoven op.18 (F, G, D, c, A, Bb), ~ Danzi op.16, ~ Krommer op.18 (D, A, Eb), op.26 (C, F, A)

1801 ~ Förster op.16 (D, Bb, Eb, C, f, A),

others (D, g, E♭, b, G, B♭, B♭, b, G, d, C, A♭, C), ~ Krommer op.19 (C, F, B♭)

1802 Beethoven arrangement of Piano Sonata op.14 no.1 (F), ~ Gyrowetz op.42 (F, D, E♭,), ~ M. Haydn (D), ~ Krommer op.23 (G), op.24 (D, E♭, B♭).

1803 ~ Förster op.21 (C, d, A, E♭, B♭, e), ~ **Haydn op.103** (d, unfinished), ~ Krommer op.34 (G, d, E♭), ~ Pleyel (C, B♭, f), ~ Wranitzky op.40 (three).

1804 Boccherini (F, D, latter unfinished), ~ Gyrowetz op.44 (G, B, A♭), ~ Krommer op.48 (E♭, C, D), op.50 (F, B♭, A), op.53 (E♭, A, C), ~ Reicha op.48 (C, G, E♭), ~ Rossini Sonatas (G, A, C, B♭, E♭, D), ~ Wranitzky opp.41, 45, 49 (one each)

1805 Albrechtsberger op.23 (C, E♭, A♭, F, d, A), ~ Danzi op.29 (three), ~ Förster (D, A, c, F, B♭, G, f, B♭, a, E♭, d, C, g, E♭, F, e, C, D), ~ Krommer op.54 (F, D, B♭), op.56 (B♭, D, G), ~ Reicha op.49 (c, D, B), op.52 (C), op.58 (A)

1806 **Beethoven op.59** (F, e, C), Dussek op.60 (G, B♭, E♭), Reicha *La pantomime*, ~ *Quatuor scientifique*

1807 Albrechtsberger op.24 (C, E♭, B♭, G, b, A), Spohr op.4 (C, g), op.11 (d).

1808 Albrechtsberger op.26 (E♭, c, B♭, D, e, C), ~ Krommer op.68 (f, C, A), op.72 (C, E, A♭), op.74 (B♭, G, d), ~ Reicha op.90 (E♭, G, C, e, F, D), op.94 (three), op.95 (three), Spohr op.15 (E♭, D)

1809 **Beethoven op.74** (E♭), Eybler op.10 (three), Krommer op.85 (F, B♭, D), op.90 (c, C, B♭)

1810 **Beethoven op.95** (f), ~ Onslow op.4 (B♭, D, a), op.8 (c, F, A), op.9 (g, C, F), op.10 (b, d, E♭), ~ Schubert D18 (g-B♭)

1811 Schubert D94 (D)

1812 Schubert D32 (C), Spohr op.27 (g)

1813 ~ Danzi op.44 (three), Schubert D36 (B♭), D46 (C), D68 (B♭), D74 (D), D87 (E♭)

1814 Cherubini no.1 (E♭), **Schubert D112** (B♭), Spohr op.30 (A)

1815 Alyabyev (E♭), Schubert D173 (g), Spohr op.29 (E♭, C, f)

1816 ~ Krommer op.92 (D, B♭, G), Reicha

Ouverture, **Schubert D353** (E)

1817 Donizetti no.1 (E♭), Spohr op.43 (E), ~ Viotti (three)

1818 Berwald no.1 (g), Donizetti nos.2-4 (A, c, D), Spohr op.45 (C, e, f)

1819 Donizetti nos.5-8 (e, g, f, B♭), Spohr op.61 (b)

1820 ~ Onslow op.21 (B♭, e, E♭), **Schubert D703** (c)

1821 ~ Danzi op.55 (three), Donizetti nos.9-19 (d, g, C, C, A, D, e, D, F, b, C), ~ Krommer op.103 (e, C, a), Mendelssohn 15 Fugues

1822 Spohr op.58 (E♭, a, G)

1823 Mendelssohn (E♭), Spohr op.68 (A), Double Quartet op.65 (d)

1824 ~ Arriaga (d, A, E♭), **Beethoven op.127** (E♭), **Schubert D804** (a), **D810** (d)

1825 Alyabyev (G), **Beethoven op.132** (a)

1826 **Beethoven op.130** (B♭), *Grosse Fuge* **op.133** (B♭), **op.131** (c♯), **op.135** (F), ~ Rossini *Sei sonate a quattro* arranged (G, A, C, B♭, E♭, D), **Schubert D887** (G), Spohr op.74 (a, B♭, d)

1827 **Mendelssohn op.13** (a), Fugue op.81 no.4 (E♭), Spohr Double Quartet op.77 (E♭)

1828

1829 Cherubini no.2 (C), **Mendelssohn op.12** (E♭), Spohr op.82 (E, G, a), op.83 (E♭)

1830 Glinka (F), ~ Onslow op.36 (e, E♭, D), op.46 (f♯, F, g), op.47 (c), op.48 (A), op.49 (e), op.50 (B♭)

1831

1832 Spohr op.84 (d, A♭, b)

1833 Spohr Double Quartet op.87 (e)

1834 Cherubini no.3 (d)

1835 Cherubini nos.4-5 (E, F), Spohr op.93 (A)

1836

1837 Cherubini no.6 (a)

1838 Hirschbach (e, B♭, D), **Mendelssohn op.44** (D, e, E♭)

1839

1840 ~ Onslow op.52 (C), op.53 (d), op.54 (E♭), op.55 (d), op.56 (E♭), op.62 (B♭), op.63 (b), op.64 (C), op.65 (g), op.66 (D)

1841 ~ Molique op.16 (G), op.17 (c), Schapler (one)

1842 **Schumann op.41** (a, F, A)

1843 Mendelssohn Capriccio op.81 no.3 (e), ~ Molique op.18 (F, a, E♭)

1844
1845 Spohr Concerto op.131 (a)
1846 Spohr op.132 (A)
1847 **Mendelssohn op.80** (f), Andante op.81 no.1 (E), Scherzo op.81 no.2 (a), ~ Molique op.28 (f), Spohr Double Quartet, op.136 (g)
1848
1849 **Berwald no.2** (a), **no.3** (Eb), Spohr op.141 (C)
1850
1851 Spohr op.146 (G)
1852
1853 ~ Molique op.44 (A), Rubinstein op.17 (G, c, F)
1854 ~ Molique op.42 (Bb)
1855 Raff op.77 (d), Spohr op.142 (Eb)
1856 Rubinstein op.47 (e, Bb, d), Spohr op.155 (Eb)
1857 Raff op.90 (A), Spohr op.157 (g)
1858
1859 Lalo op.19 (Eb), ~ Paine op.5 (D)
1860 Goldmark (D)
1861
1862 Bruckner (c), Dvořák no.1 op.2 (A)
1863
1864
1865 Tchaikovsky (Bb)
1866 Raff op.136 (e)
1867 ~ Castillon no.1 op.3 (a), Parry no.1 (g), Raff op.137 (a), op.138 (G)
1868 Parry no.2 (c)
1869
1870 ~ Dvořák no.2 (Bb), no.3 (D), no.4 (e)
1871 Rubinstein op.90 (g, e), Tchaikovsky no.1 op.11 (D)
1872
1873 **Brahms nos.1-2 op.51** (c, a), Dvořák no.5 op.9 (f), no.6 op.12 (a) **Verdi** (e)
1874 Dvořák no.7 op.16 (a), Fibich (A), Raff op.192 (c, D, C), Tchaikovsky no.2 op.22 (F)
1875 Rimsky-Korsakov (F)
1876 **Brahms no.3 op.67** (Bb), **Dvořák no.8 op.80** (E), **Smetana no.1** (e), Taneyev (d), Tchaikovsky no.3 op.30 (eb)
1877 **Dvořák no.9 op.34** (d)
1878 Chadwick no.1 (g), Fibich op.8 (G), Grieg op.27 (g)
1879 **Borodin no.1** (A), Chadwick no.2 (C), **Dvořák no.10 op.51** (Eb), Rimsky-Korsakov Quartet on Russian Themes
1880 ~ Dvořák Two Waltzes op.54, Parry

no.3 (G), Rubinstein op.106 (Ab, F), Taneyev (Eb)
1881 **Borodin no.2** (D), Busoni no.1 op.19 (c), **Dvořák no.11 op.61** (C)
1882 Glazunov no.1 op.1 (D)
1883 Foote no.1 op.4 (g), **Smetana no.2** (d), Taneyev (C, A)
1884 Glazunov no.2 op.10 (F), **Wolf** (d)
1885 Chadwick no.3 (D), Parker op.11 (F)
1886 Rimsky-Korsakov et al. 'Belyayev' (Bb), Wolf Intermezzo (Eb)
1887 **Dvořák Cypřiše**, Lekeu (d), Rimsky-Korsakov et al. 'Jour de fête' (D), **Wolf Italienische Serenade** (G)
1888 Glazunov no.3 op.26 (G), Nielsen no.1 op.13 (g)
1889 Busoni no.2 op.26 (d), **Franck** (D), Reger (d)
1890 d'Indy no.1 op.35 (D), Nielsen no.2 op.5 (f), Puccini *Crisantemi*, Taneyev no.1 op.4 (bb)
1891 Stanford no.1 op.44 (G), no.2 op.45 (a)
1892
1893 **Debussy** (g), **Dvořák no.12 op.96** (F), Ropartz no.1 (g)
1894 Glazunov no.4 op.64 (a)
1895 **Dvořák no.13 op.106** (G), **no.14 op.105** (Ab), Taneyev no.2 op.5 (C), ~ Zemlinsky no.1 op.4 (A)
1896 Chadwick no.4 (e), Ives no.1 (C), Suk no.1 op.11 (Bb), Taneyev no.3 op.7 (d)
1897 d'Indy no.2 op.45 (E), Rimsky-Korsakov (G), **Schoenberg** (D), Stanford no.3 op.64 (d)
1898 Chadwick no.5 (d), Glazunov no.5 op.70 (d), Nielsen no.3 op.14 (Eb), Rimsky-Korsakov et al. *Les vendredis* vol.1
1899 **Chausson op.35** (c), Novák no.1 op.22 (G), Rimsky-Korsakov et al. *Les vendredis* vol. 2, Saint-Saëns no.1 op.112 (e), Taneyev no.4 op.11 (a)
1900 **Reger op.54** (g, A)
1901
1902
1903 Pfitzner no.1 op.13 (D), **Ravel** (F), Taneyev no.5 op.13 (A)
1904 **Reger op.74** (d)
1905 Novák no.2 op.35 (D), **Schoenberg no.1 op.7** (d)
1906 Bridge no.1 (E), Nielsen no.4 op.44 (F), Taneyev no.6 op.19 (Bb)
1907 ~ Stanford no.4 op.99 (g), Webern (a)

235

1908 **Bartók no.1 op.7, Schoenberg no.2 op.10** (f#), Stanford no.5 op.104 (Bb)

1909 Kodály no.1 op.2, **Reger op.109** (Eb), **Sibelius op.56** (d), Vaughan Williams (g), **Webern Five Movements op.5**

1910 **Berg op.3,** Foote no.3 op.70 (D), Stanford no.6 op.122 (a)

1911 **Reger op.121** (f#), Ropartz no.2 (d), Suk no.2 op.31, Taneyev (c)

1912 Milhaud no.1 op.5, Wellesz no.1 op.14

1913 **Ives no.2,** Koechlin no.1 op.51, **Webern Six Bagatelles op.9**

1914 Ives Scherzo, **Stravinsky Three Pieces,** Zemlinsky no.2 op.15

1915 Bridge no.2 (g), Milhaud no.2 op.16, Villa-Lobos nos.1-2

1916 Cowell no.1, Delius, Koechlin no.2 op.57, Milhaud no.3 op.32, Villa-Lobos no.3, Wellesz no.2 op.20

1917 **Bartók no.2 op.17,** Honegger no.1, Szymanowski no.1 op.27 (C), Villa-Lobos no.4

1918 Bax no.1, Elgar op.83 (e), Kodály no.2 op.10, Martinů no.1, Milhaud no.4 op.46, Saint-Saëns no.2 op.153 (G), Wellesz no.3 op.25

1919 Cowell *Quartet Euphometric*, Hába no.1 op.4, Hindemith no.1 op.10 (f), Mason, Nielsen op.44 (F), ~ Stanford no.7 op.166 (c), no.8 op.167 (e), Weill (b)

1920 Casella Five Pieces op.34, Hába no.2 op.7, Malipiero no.1, Milhaud no.5 op.64 **Stravinsky Concertino,** ~ Wellesz no.4 op.28

1921 Glazunov no.6 op.106 (Bb), Hindemith no.2 op.16 (C), Koechlin no.3 op.72, Krenek no.1 op.6, no.2 op.8

1922 Hába no.3 op.12, no.4 op.14, Hindemith no.3 op.22, Milhaud no.6 op.77

1923 Hába no.5 op.15, Hindemith no.4 op.32, **Janáček no.1,** Krenek no.3 op.20, Malipiero no.2, Porter no.1, Weill op.8, ~ Zemlinsky no.3 op.19

1924 Bax no.2, Casella Concerto op.40, **Fauré op.121** (e), Krenek no.4 op.24, Ropartz no.3 (G), Seiber no.1

1925 Martinů no.2, Milhaud no.7 op.87, Pfitzner no.2 op.36 (c#), Porter no.2, Schmidt (A)

1926 **Berg Lyric Suite, Bridge no.3**

1927 **Bartók no.3, Schoenberg no.3 op.30,** Szymanowski no.2 op.56

1928 **Bartók no.4, Janáček no.2**

1929 Bush *Dialectic*, d'Indy no.3 op.96 (Db),

Martinů no.3, Schmidt (G)

1930 Blacher no.1 op.11, Glazunov no.7 op.107 (C), Harris no.1, Krenek no.5 op.65, Porter no.3, Prokofiev no.1 op.50 (b)

1931 Britten (D), **Crawford, Foulds no.9,** Malipiero no.3, Porter no.4, Villa-Lobos no.5

1932 Milhaud no.8 op.121, Roussel op.45 (D)

1933 Harris no.2, Maconchy no.1, Piston no.1, Ropartz no.4 (E), Rubbra no.1 op.35 (f), Schoenberg Concerto, Tournemire *Musique orante*

1934 **Bartók no.5,** Cowell no.2, Jolivet, Malipiero no.4

1935 Barber, Cowell no.3, Milhaud no.9 op.140, Piston no.2, Porter no.5, Seiber no.2, **Shostakovich no.1 op.49** (C), **Tippett no.1**

1936 Bax no.3, Cowell no.4, Honegger nos.2-3, **Krenek no.6 op.78,** Maconchy no.2, **Schoenberg no.4 op.37,** Sessions no.1, Zemlinsky no.4 op.25.

1937 **Bridge no.4,** Harris no.3, Martinů no.4, Porter no.6

1938 Eisler, Maconchy no.3, Martinů no.5, Novák no.3 op.66 (G), Villa-Lobos no.6, **Webern op.28**

1939 **Bartók no.6,** Rawsthorne no.1

1940 Blacher no.2 op.16, Milhaud no.10 op.218, Ropartz no.5 (D)

1941 **Britten no.1 op.25** (D), Holmboe op.26, Prokofiev no.2 op.50 (F), Villa-Lobos no.7

1942 Milhaud no.11 op.232, Pfitzner no.3 op.50 (c), **Tippett no.2**

1943 Hindemith no.5 (Eb), Maconchy no.4, Porter no.7, Wellesz no.5 op.60

1944 Blacher no.3 op.32, Krenek no.7 op.96, **Shostakovich no.2 op.68** (A), Vaughan Williams (a), Villa-Lobos no.8

1945 **Britten no.2 op.36** (C), Hindemith no.6, Milhaud no.12 op.252, Villa-Lobos no.9

1946 Martinů no.6, Milhaud no.13 op.268, Perle no.3, **Shostakovich no.3 op.73** (F), **Tippett no.3,** Villa-Lobos no.10, Wellesz no.6 op.64

1947 Fricker no.1, Henze no.1, Malipiero no.6, Martinů no.7, Piston no.3, Villa-Lobos no.11, Walton (a)

1948 Babbitt no.1, Maconchy no.5, Wellesz no.7 op.66

1949 **Boulez** *Livre,* Holmboe nos.1-3 opp.46-8, Milhaud nos.14-15 op.291, Schmitt op.112 (G), **Shostakovich no.4 op.83** (D)

1950 **Cage,** Hába no.6 op.70, Maconchy no.6, Malipiero no.5, no.7, Milhaud no.16 op.303, no.17 op.307, no.18 op.308, Porter no.8, Villa-Lobos no.12

1951 Blacher no.4 op.41, **Carter no.1,** Feldman *Structures,* Hába no.7 op.73, no.8 op.76, Piston no.4, ~ Ropartz no.6 (F), Rubbra no.2 op.73 (Eb), Seiber no.3, Sessions no.2, Villa-Lobos no.13

1952 Hába no.9 op.79, no.10 op.80, Henze no.2, Rochberg no.1, **Shostakovich no.5 op.92** (Bb), Simpson no.1

1953 Simpson no.2, Villa-Lobos no.14

1954 **Babbitt no.2,** Holmboe no.4 op.63, **Ligeti no.1,** Rawsthorne no.2, Simpson no.3, Villa-Lobos no.15

1955 **Gerhard no.1,** Holmboe no.5 op.66, Villa-Lobos no.16

1956 Berio, Cowell no.5, Feldman Three Pieces, Maconchy no.7, **Shostakovich no.6 op.101** (G)

1957 Goehr no.1 op.5, Hába no.11 op.87, Schuller no.1, Villa-Lobos no.17, Wellesz no.8 op.79

1958 Petrassi, Porter no.9

1959 **Carter no.2, Stravinsky Double Canon**

1960 Hába no.12 op.90, Penderecki no.1, **Perle no.5, Shostakovich no.7 op.108** (f#), **no.8 op.110** (c), Takemitsu *Landscape*

1961 **Davies, Gerhard no.2,** Hába no.13 op.92, Holmboe no.6 op.78, Pousseur *Ode,* Rochberg no.2, Wolff *Summer*

1962 Piston no.5, **Xenakis** *ST/4,* Wood no.1 op.1

1963 Hába no.14 op.94, Rubbra no.3 op.112

1964 Berio *Sincronie,* Hába no.15 op.95, Holmboe no.7 op.86, Lutosławski, Malipiero no.8, Rawsthorne no.3, **Shostakovich no.9 op.117** (Eb), **no.10 op.118** (Ab)

1965 Brown, Holmboe no.8 op.87

1966 Holmboe no.9 op.92, Maconchy no.8, Schuller no.2, Shnitke, **Shostakovich no.11 op.122** (f), Wellesz no.9 op.97

1967 Blacher no.5, Goehr no.2 op.23, Hába no.16 op.98, **Kagel,** Martin

1968 Boucourechliev *Archipel 2,* **Ferneyhough Sonatas, Ligeti no.2,** Penderecki no.2, **Shostakovich no.12 op.133** (Db), Wellesz Music op.103

1969 **Babbitt no.3,** Holmboe no.10 op.102, Maconchy no.9, **Perle no.6,** Wolpe

1970 **Babbitt no.4,** Crumb *Black Angels,* **Shostakovich no.13 op.138** (bb), Wood no.2 op.13

1971 Bussotti *Quartetto Gramsci, I semi di Gramsci,* **Carter no.3,** Milhaud *Hommage à IS* op.435, Wuorinen

1972 Gilbert, Holmboe no.11 op.111, Maconchy no.10, Rochberg no.3

1973 Holliger, Holmboe no.12 op.116, Muldowney no.1, **Perle no.7, Shostakovich no.14 op.142** (F#), Simpson no.4

1974 **Shostakovich no.15 op.144** (eb), Simpson no.5

1975 **Britten no.3 op.94,** Holmboe no.13 op.124, no.14 op.125, Simpson no.6, Wolff

1976 Dutilleux *Ainsi la nuit,* Fricker no.3, Goehr no.3 op.37, Henze no.3, no.4, Schafer no.2

1977 Harvey, Henze no.5, Holmboe no.15 op.135, Maconchy no.11, Rochberg no.4, Rubbra no.4 op.150, Simpson no.7

1978 Payne, Rochberg nos.5-6, Wood no.3 op.20

1979 Maconchy no.12, Simpson no.8, Smalley, Tippett no.4

1980 **Ferneyhough no.2, Nono** *Fragmente-Stille, an Diotima*

1981 Casken

1982 Muldowney no.2, Simpson no.9

1983 Dillon, Xenakis *Tetras,* Cage no.2

1984 Simpson no.10

Index

Bold figures indicate places where works are discussed in more detail.